THE DEVELOPMENTAL EDUCATION AND GUIDANCE OF TALENTED LEARNERS

Philip A. Perrone
University of Wisconsin
Madison, Wisconsin

Robert A. Male
Portland State University
Portland, Oregon

AN ASPEN PUBLICATION®
Aspen Systems Corporation
Rockville, Maryland
London
1981

Library of Congress Cataloging in Publication Data

Perrone, Philip A.
The developmental education and guidance of talented
learners.

Bibliography: p. 211.
Includes index.
1. Gifted children—Education—United States.
2. Talented students—United States.
3. Child development.
I. Male, Robert A.   II. Title.
LC3993.P36   371.95   81-3463
ISBN: 0-89443-359-8   AACR2

Library of Congress Catalog Card Number: 81-3463
ISBN: 0-89443-359-8

Printed in the United States of America

1 2 3 4 5

To my wife, *Lucille,* who adds a valued perspective to all that I do.

Philip A. Perrone

To my talented grandmother, *Angelina DeBiasse*, who taught me the important life values.

Robert A. Male

Table of Contents

Foreword ix

Preface xi

Acknowledgements xiii

SECTION I—ISSUES AND PROBLEMS RELATED TO THE
        UNIQUE DEVELOPMENTAL NEEDS OF PERSONS
        WITH TALENT POTENTIAL 1

Chapter 1—Talented and Potentially Talented Persons:
        An Operational Perspective 3

        Chris 3
        Pat 6
        A Framework for Learning and Behavior 8
        The Model as a Dynamic Concept 13
        An Operational Definition of Talent 17

Chapter 2—Talent and the Physical Environment 21

        Maslow Explained 22
        The Individual and the Environment 26

Chapter 3—Talent and the Psychosocial Environment 33

        Maslow's Needs and Terminal Values 33
        Maslow's Needs and Instrumental Values 34

Moving Beyond Coping 35
Achieving a Measure of Self-Direction 36
The Drive to Understand Nature 37
The Importance of a Broader Perspective 38
The Importance of Combined Effort 40
Developmental Consistencies 42
Talent Development in a Pluralistic Society 43
The Importance of a Broad Background 45
Implications 45

Chapter 4—Natural Manifestations of Talent Potential **49**

Symptoms of Talent Potential 50
A Chronology of Symptomatic Behaviors 55
Theories of Development 57

**SECTION II—THE FULFILLMENT OF DEVELOPMENTAL
          POTENTIAL IN TALENTED PERSONS** **63**

**Chapter 5—The Resolution of Problems and Attainment of
          Goals by Eminent Persons** **65**

Achievement Motivation 65
About the Vignettes 70
Art and Architecture 71
Literature 79
Music 88
Theoretical Science 94
Inventing 98
Letters and Philosophy 104
Politics 112
Business-Finance-Adventure 120
Summary 124

Chapter 6—Sequence of Development in Two Talented Individuals.. **129**

Case Study of Connie 129
Gifts-Grades 9-12 131
Case Study of John 135
Gifts-Grades 9-12 138
Summary 142

SECTION III—HOW TO PLAN AND IMPLEMENT PROGRAMS TO FOSTER DEVELOPMENT OF TALENT POTENTIAL 143

Chapter 7—Organizing Programs for the Talented 145

Where to Begin 145
Defining Program Goals 146
Recommended Phases of Program Development 147
Staff Involvement 155
Process of Identification 159
Selection Criteria 164
Individualized Assessment 165
Instructional Concerns for Developing Talent 166
Establishing Teacher Goals 168
Creating an Effective Teaching Style 169

Chapter 8—Model Education Programs 173

Conceptual Development and the Talented 173
Programming Issues 177
A Model Program for Conceptual Development 178

Chapter 9—Looking Ahead 203

Trends 203
Implications 204

SECTION IV—RESOURCES 209

Bibliography 211

Index 229

Foreword

Talented persons face both common and unique developmental tasks. Usually they are left to cope with these tasks on their own, while feeling the pressure to develop beyond the norm and contribute to society as well. The assistance needed by talented and potentially talented persons to realize their potential is supplied through the sincere interest and informed understanding of significant persons in their lives. Programs do not solve problems and facilitate development; people do.

The current "second coming" of interest in the development of talented persons is different from the interest shown in the 60s in that a much broader view of talent is recognized. Also, many persons now realize that affective and psychosocial development are every bit as important as intellectual development. The broadened focus is significant because it underscores that, in assisting talented and potentially talented persons, we must address issues related to physiology, psychology, and sociology as well as mentality. A talented person can now be viewed as an integrated whole with many facets, not as just a walking brain.

As fiscal, sociological, and environmental pressures to conserve continue to escalate, it will become increasingly more difficult for education to help all the "different" segments of our population to develop. Educators, parents, and concerned others will need to assume a position of enlightened commitment and leadership if talented and potentially talented persons are to receive assistance in meeting their needs. Often, something as simple as a change in attitude, the right question, or recognizing the value of a unique response may stimulate or allow talent to develop.

We believe we are on the brink of a social revolution that can only be averted if educational institutions assume leadership in fostering an evolution of attitudes, values, and opportunities leading to meaningful and satisfying human endeavors for nearly everyone. The institutions of family, work, religion, and government are barely able to sustain themselves, let alone strike out in new and meaningful directions. Unfortunately, our public education systems are experiencing "storm and stress" from within and without, forcing education into taking defensive positions.

Public education—the teachers and researchers alike—must focus on enhancing everyone's human potential. This takes resources that do not now currently exist. For example, public education will arrive only when elementary classrooms have a teacher-pupil ratio of no more than 1:12 and every teacher is intelligent, creative, and a responsive human being. Educators must direct their attention to increasing the responsiveness of other institutions to the emerging needs of an intelligent society which is experiencing social isolation, social and individual irrelevance, and even social alienation. It is time for education to lead, not passively follow. One positive outcome of teacher organizations may be that after attention shifts from serving teachers' basic security needs, teachers will begin looking beyond their immediate needs and translate the unmet needs of children into meaningful programs that can be implemented within the school and community.

Philip A. Perrone
Robert A. Male
September 1981

Preface

Our primary objective in writing this book has been to share our perspective regarding the unique developmental needs of talented and potentially talented children and adolescents. To accomplish this task, we had to integrate our counseling and our teaching experience and reexamine our case study analyses of talented students against knowledge gained from the writings and research of others. A major goal has been to formulate and present a concise and congruent framework of human development from which one can discern the unique characteristics of those with talent and talent potential. The framework is then used to explain the development and implementation of programs designed to meet the unique learning needs of these two general groups of students.

In discussing our personal perspective with one another, we have come to accept the fact that our perspectives are not static. Like others in this field, we are continually learning, and as a consequence our ideas and beliefs change. This book therefore represents a status report on our combined perspectives. We have devoted a great deal of study, research, and discussion to each of the concepts presented here. Writing this book underscored for us the wisdom of pooling individual resources when undertaking a complex and difficult task. The reader will note that throughout the book we have emphasized that children with talent and talent potential can be helped toward self-actualization without losing their ability to communicate and work effectively with others.

We believe that readers of this book are probably concerned enough about the development of human potential to want to do something to help. We approach these readers as concerned colleagues who are interested in integrating our concepts with their own ideas and applying them as directly as possible in their own situations. We believe that everyone, when operating from a position of concern and understanding, has personal resources that can be used to help talented and potentially talented youngsters make the most of their abilities.

Since the majority of our ideas are a synthesis of experience, research, and reading, it was difficult for us to cite all sources related to a particular idea, concern, or hypothesis. Recognizing that the concerned reader often wishes to consult original source material, we have included documentation that is intended to be both comprehensive and utilitarian. A list of resources to be consulted for further study can be found at the end of some chapters. In addition, an extensive annotated resource bibliography is provided in Chapter 10.

This volume is divided into four sections. Section One presents a detailed discussion of issues and problems related to the unique developmental needs of individuals with talent potential. This discussion takes the reader from theory to behavior.

Section Two focuses on the impact and resolution of developmental differences as experienced by talented individuals. In order to illustrate how talent potential was realized by people in highly diverse settings and at different points in history, we present vignettes of the lives of eminent persons plus two extensive case studies.

Section Three discusses the what, why, where, when, and how of planning and implementing programs to foster development in persons with talent potential. We suggest a step-by-step approach and analyze and explain each step.

Section Four presents a comprehensive listing of resources that readers can consult when planning and implementing specific activities or curricula for talented and creative students.

We hope that this book gives readers a starting point from which they can better understand, plan for, and meet the unique developmental needs of the talented and potentially talented. The concepts presented here are not put forth as "the gospel," to be swallowed whole and applied religiously. We hope that readers accept, reject, and build upon our ideas in their own efforts to help this special group of young people.

Acknowledgments

We are indebted to Lucille Perrone for editing and to Jan Lunda for typing the manuscript. We want to acknowledge the efforts of GIFTS staff members who, over the years, supplied materials and ideas. Since there are too many people to list and because we do not want to slight anyone, a blanket "thank you" is tendered.

Philip A. Perrone
Robert A. Male

Issues and Problems Related to the Unique Developmental Needs of Persons with Talent Potential

The four chapters of Section One are designed to provide the reader with a comprehensive framework from which our definitions of talent and talent potential are derived. Understanding our assumptive framework, presented in Chapter 1, will aid the reader in evaluating and eventually using the contents of this book.

In Chapter 2 we put talent development into an environmental perspective. We seek to answer the question: What is the relationship between those with talent potential and their physical environment? The discussion focuses on developmental differences between the nontalented and the potentially talented, and we examine how developmental inconsistencies affect the realization of potential. Using motivational theory we describe how the accelerated developmental patterns of the potentially talented foster behaviors that can set these youngsters apart from their peers.

The psychosocial development of potentially talented persons is discussed in Chapter 3. We take a look at the lives of eminent persons as a means to understanding the unique way in which talented persons develop values and goals consistent with society. Once again, we use motivational theory to explain the behavior of talented and potentially talented persons as they interact with their psychosocial environment.

In Chapter 4 we present a list of what we have termed "symptomatic behaviors" of persons with talent potential. The list is intended to give readers a sense of the complex network of developmental concerns they will encounter when attempting to identify and work with potentially talented youth. Each behavior is presented in conjunction with its implications for the development of talent potential. A discussion of developmental stage theory concludes this chapter. This discussion will give readers a framework for organizing all the concepts presented in this book prior to considering appropriate intervention strategies.

Chapter 1

Talented and Potentially Talented Persons: An Operational Perspective

CHRIS

From the very beginning Chris showed signs of being an exceptional child. Chris always learned new things faster and more conclusively than children of a similar age. Chris would spend hours exploring everything within sight and touch with a curiosity that seemed limitless.

As Chris grew, relations with people became increasingly important. Oh, getting along with mom and dad was always important, but relations changed somewhat when others came on the scene. Chris soon learned that there were a lot of people to learn from. Soon, not only mom and dad, but other children and relatives became objects of attention and sources of information.

Chris was always interested in touching, examining, questioning, and thinking about everything and everyone. It seemed that curiosity and a desire to understand guided all of Chris' actions. New objects were handled, looked at, and listened to. Mom and dad were touched, listened to, and watched intently (as were most other important people). It was as if Chris wanted to know and experience everything. Books and television were constant sources of interest and excitement.

All this interaction with physical, social, and intellectual environments led Chris to discover some very interesting things. Some things were okay to look at and listen to but should not be touched. (Chris once touched a hot iron and did not like it, but more often mom or dad hollered when certain things were touched and Chris did not like that either.) While most things were okay to look at and listen to, there were some taboos in these categories as well (like certain kinds of magazines and music). Chris also noticed that mom and dad liked the house quiet and that they read a lot of books and watched TV. Chris continued to look at things a lot, listen less, and touch things only a little. About this time Chris began school.

3

The teacher was very nice and seemed to reinforce a lot of what Chris had already learned about looking, listening, and touching. Seeing and listening were important, but only a little touching was allowed. Chris soon became very adept at reading and sight recognition and was rewarded for it; attentive and discriminating listening was rewarded, too; and while he was not so good at manipulating things and expressing feelings, this did not seem to matter much.

As time passed, Chris learned that different people expected and rewarded different behaviors and that home, school, and the neighborhood required different kinds of behaviors if a favorable response or a reward was to be forthcoming. This complexity led to some problems. Chris began to think that it was impossible to please everyone, let alone find personal enjoyment. At home and among family and friends, Chris was rewarded for certain behavior and for showing certain abilities. At school some of these same behaviors often got Chris into trouble, either with the teacher or with other students. So gradually Chris learned to be two people, one at home and another at school. Everything was fine . . . everyone was happy . . . Chris had learned how to succeed in two different social environments.

Then, just as Chris was really getting successful at being two different people, it happened. One day Chris' teacher sent home a letter that read: "It gives us great pleasure to announce that we believe Chris is *gifted.*" This was followed by a meeting at school. Chris' mom and dad, the teacher, counselor, and Chris were all there. After listening to everyone talk for a while and watching all the activity, Chris asked, "But what does it all mean for me?" Chris' mom said with pride, "It means you're *special.*" Chris had always believed that everyone was special, and so he did not understand all the fuss. Pursuing it further, Chris asked, "Then what does special mean?" "It means you are *different,*" answered the counselor. "Oh no!" thought Chris. "I've spent years learning how not to be different. If I am different, what will the other kids think of me? . . . What will my parents think of me? . . . What will my teacher and counselor think of me? . . . What should I do . . . now that I am different?"

Thomas Edison, William Faulkner, Henry Ford, Teddy Roosevelt, Marie Curie, Babe Ruth, Martin Luther King, Jr., Helen Keller, and Elvis Presley all achieved distinction by demonstrating their individual talents and worth. Obviously, many other talented people, past and present, could be added to this brief list. But what of the names to be added in the future? Is there any valid way to identify and subsequently nurture potentially talented individuals? Why are some individuals recognized as talented while others, possibly with similar abilities, are unable to achieve distinction? How do heredity, environment, learning, and behavior contribute to the development and manifestation of talent? This list of pressing questions goes on and on. Before we begin to answer these questions and many others, it is necessary to agree on the meaning of some commonly used terms and understand how "potential" fits within a context of human learning and development.

Our first task then is to provide an operational definition of talent. What constitutes talent and talent potential? In defining talent potential we explain how talent potential can be fostered and nurtured. Once these definitions are understood, we can proceed to our framework for understanding human learning and behavior. The framework should help readers understand what distinguishes the development of persons with talent potential; it will also provide a basis for planned interventions in the developmental process. Both the operational definitions and the framework will be described at some length because they form the foundation for better appreciating the ideas on assessment, programming, and evaluation presented later in this book.

It stands to reason that if educators, researchers, and parents are to effectively facilitate the development of talented and potentially talented young people, they must have an operational framework to guide their efforts. Since facts tend to be organized and used according to the observer's purposes and beliefs, the material presented in this book could be viewed from many different perspectives. While a number of these perspectives may be quite useful and acceptable, it is necessary that readers fully understand the authors' beliefs if the material is to be understood and appear consistent. A comprehensive understanding of our beliefs will also provide readers a basis for accepting, modifying, or rejecting these ideas.

Talent—What Makes Chris Different?

Over the years and across many different cultures, the talent label has been assigned to individuals for a wide range of accomplishments. Consider our earlier list of talented persons. Their contributions and the arenas in which they performed were all quite different from one another, yet they all achieved eminence on the basis of their somewhat unique capabilities. The manifestation of talent, and its acceptance or recognition as something of worth, is dependent upon the prevailing values, attitudes, and resources that surround a person at a given time. For example, would Babe Ruth's talent have been appreciated in Renaissance Europe? Why do so many adults who achieve eminence have backgrounds that would lead us to believe they were not regarded as talented children? We can only conclude that to a large extent talent appears to exist in the eyes of the beholders and may be of fleeting duration.

People will call another individual talented if that individual demonstrates some exceptional abilities or behaviors in an area the observer understands and values. Exceptionality can mean simply that the individual's performance is better (rated more highly according to some criteria) than that of peers or contemporaries. In this context comparative recognition is the process by which values are transmitted into action or labels. The work of some great painters was little understood in their own lifetimes, and it was not until later that people began to understand or appreciate their gifts and their art became valued. Albert

Einstein's theory of relativity, first sketched in 1905, was first recognized by the scientific community as having some value 20 years later. But even though Einstein's theories were the foundation for space flight technology, it was not until the era of manned space flights that others were able to finally test these theories. In essence, his theory of relativity was proven when the astronauts first circled the moon and reappeared after eight minutes. For years most people outside the scientific community could not fully appreciate the significance of Einstein's theory nor the extent of his genius.

So far, we have inferred that a talented individual is someone who demonstrates exceptional ability in an area that is understood and valued by others. While this criterion could explain why Chris was considered gifted, it is not a good operational definition. It is not enough to define talent solely in terms of manifesting valued behavior because such a definition does not allow for the identification of potentially talented or gifted persons. (At this point, we interject a note of caution. In this book we use many eminent people as examples. While these examples do aid in reader recognition, the reader should guard against equating talent with genius or eminence. Beware of drawing false conclusions or making false generalizations.)

PAT

Pat was born and raised in a place often referred to as "the wrong side of the tracks." Pat's mother and father were always fighting, drinking, and absent from home. Pat's earliest and strongest memories involve hunger, pain, and conflict. However, Pat learned quickly how to survive. After a few years he was able to shake off the effects of his family situation. He began to demonstrate an exceptional ability to assess people and situations and act in a manner that was beneficial not only to him, but to others as well. Pat's behavior was not surprising since he had always been able to think through and solve pressing problems, often using new approaches to come out on top. Pat was a quick, agile thinker who never forgot or ignored anything of importance in making a decision. Pat was also a loner; he relished independence and prided himself on being a match for almost any situation. All the tools for success were there. How and when these tools were used is the key to the direction Pat's life takes.

At home and in the streets Pat was always in control. No one ever got one up on him, at least from Pat's viewpoint. When Pat was young, others were able to beat him physically but never mentally. As time passed, few of his peers could handle him physically either.

Pat stopped going to school as soon as "the authorities" stopped insisting on his attendance. His teachers didn't mind; after all, Pat was incorrigible, insolent, bored, a troublemaker, moody, lazy, and any other negative adjective one cares to mention. It is interesting to note, however, that during his early school years some of Pat's teachers noticed a few redeeming qualities, such as "witty, quick, responsive—though not always appropriate, and exhibiting some leadership ability."

Once school was out of the way Pat was able to concentrate on more important matters. After a few years of trying out many ways to make a living, Pat finally found a job that provided everything: interest, challenge, security, and opportunity for advancement. He worked hard and began to get some recognition from others. Pat's coworkers listened to his ideas and respected his performance. He was promoted.

Buoyed by this new sense of security, belonging, and esteem Pat was able to pursue other activities that had never seemed important before. He went back to school at night and finally earned a high school diploma. New information and new experiences opened many avenues of personal expression, and before long Pat was being discussed as a rising new star in his company. In this instance, talent potential may have won out, in part at least.

Talent—Pat Was Always Different But Only Recently Considered Talented

It is easy to understand why persons like Pat are not considered talented in their early years: they do not demonstrate any exceptionality that is considered noteworthy or valuable by decision makers and persons who "label" children. Pat's story points up a problem that has plagued educators for a long time. How do we discover the potentially talented person? Obviously, it would be ideal if we could identify potentially talented individuals and nurture their gifts. In recent years the term *self-actualized* has been used to describe those persons who have realized their potential through use of their unique talents. We can only speculate what heights of accomplishment a person like Pat might have achieved had he been an early recipient of proper nurturance and guidance. Indeed, it is disturbing to consider the number of potentially talented people whose gifts are not realized or are impaired due to lack of recognition, proper guidance, stimulation, and support.

Since we now know a great deal about human physiology and have developed some understanding of how a person's mind and body function together to produce observable behavior, we can use this knowledge to infer some of the things we cannot readily see. Our framework of human learning and behavior must be sufficiently comprehensive to include the physiological and psychological elements necessary for understanding the unique thinking and learning processes of exceptional persons. Once the important elements of talent are understood, these elements can serve as the basis for generating an operational definition of talent that allows us to identify potentially talented persons as well.

Therefore, we first present a framework that explains and describes the elements and activities involved in most human learning and behavior. Subsequently we will use this general framework to develop our operational definition of talent and explain the developmental needs and nuances of talented and potentially talented individuals.

A FRAMEWORK FOR LEARNING AND BEHAVIOR

Figure 1-1 is a graphic representation of the authors' framework for understanding learning and behavior. Two prime considerations governed the development of this framework. First, it had to be inclusive enough to account for the reality it attempts to portray. Second, it had to be integrated enough to be understood and applied.

Following Figure 1-1 is a list of the elements that comprise the framework, along with their definitions and necessary explanation. These elements and their supporting terminology will be referred to throughout the remainder of this book. After the elements are presented, the framework is explained in a manner intended to further clarify the relationship of the various parts, their interaction, and the dynamic nature of learning and behavior.

The Individual is a separate, self-contained entity whose inner world consists of two main elements—the physiological self and the psychological self. The individual exists in and interrelates with the three primary environments that make up the outer world.

The Outer World is everything that exists independent of the individual. It consists of three primary environments—physical, social, and intellectual. Physical, social, and intellectual environments are considered by the authors to include the major sources of data and stimuli coming from the outer world. These three categories are most useful in discussing how the environment affects the physiological and psychological activities and development of the individual.

> *The Physical Environment* is nature exclusive of people. It is the world of day and night, temperature, air, water, plants, animals, and soil. This environment is often studied by scientists attempting to understand the laws of nature. More fundamentally, it is the environment with which humans must successfully relate in order to survive and grow.
>
> *The Social Environment* consists of all other people who cohabit an individual's physical environment or influence the individual in any way. People with whom the individual has a high degree of contact or those who greatly influence the individual are often labeled *significant others*. The social environment is the primary means by which a person becomes encultured and develops a value system.

Figure 1-1 Framework for Understanding Learning and Behavior

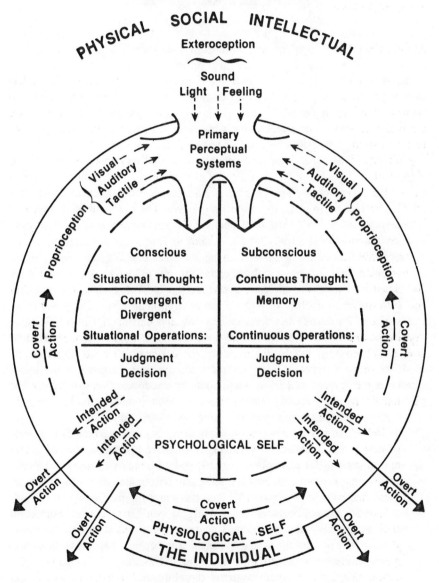

OUTER WORLD

PRIMARY ENVIRONMENTS:

PHYSICAL   SOCIAL   INTELLECTUAL

Exteroception

Sound
Light ¦ Feeling

Primary
Perceptual
Systems

Visual
Auditory
Tactile

Visual
Auditory
Tactile

Proprioception

Proprioception

Conscious

Subconscious

Situational Thought:

Convergent
Divergent

Continuous Thought:

Memory

Situational Operations:

Judgment
Decision

Continuous Operations:

Judgment
Decision

Covert
Action

Covert
Action

Intended
Action

Intended
Action

Intended
Action

PSYCHOLOGICAL SELF

Overt
Action

Overt
Action

Overt
Action

Overt
Action

Covert
Action

PHYSIOLOGICAL SELF

THE INDIVIDUAL

OUTER WORLD

The Intellectual Environment is the world of knowledge, thoughts, ideas, and concepts that originate and exist outside the individual. The intellectual environment ranges from concrete to abstract and is normally communicated to the individual via abstract symbols and behavioral forms such as words, gestures, numbers, art, music, and dance.

The Physiological Self is all human structure and activity that is physical in nature, from nerve impulses and the operation of glands to the more obvious movements of muscles. The physiological self enables an individual to see, feel, hear, think, and move about. It involves the entire physical being and genetic endowment including appearance, response, and behavior capabilities. The physiological self is the machinery within which the psychological self exists. An individual experiences and controls physiological existence through psychological activity. The physiological self has two important sets of systems in this framework—behavior systems and primary perceptual systems.

Behavior Systems are the nerves, muscles, and other bodily tissues that function to perform all the activities prescribed by the individual's psychological self. All overt and covert behavior is thus a product of psychological and physiological activity. The *conscious* and *subconscious* elements of the individual's psychological self initiate, monitor, evaluate, and control physiological and psychological activities; the physiological self carries them out. *Overt behavior* includes everything an individual does that is either observable by another or impacts the environment in some way—in other words, all external manifestations of life and existence. *Covert behavior* includes everything an individual does that is not ordinarily observable by others—in other words all internal manifestations of life and existence.

Primary Perceptual Systems describe the physical structures and apparatus that gather data from, and about, the outer and inner worlds of the individual and transmit this data to the psychological self. The primary perceptual systems are *visual, auditory,* and *tactile,* since these systems are the ones that individuals use most often in learning and behavior. A perceptual system includes the sense organs that are responsible for the detection of stimuli (for example, the eyes), and all bodily structures and mechanisms that support and facilitate their activity (such as the head, muscles, neck, nerves, and skeleton). All data that enter the psychological self are accessed via the operation of perceptual systems. Two types of information are "picked up" and transmitted—exteroceptive and proprioceptive. *Exteroceptive data* are those that originate from outside the individual. *Proprioceptive data* originate from within the individual.

The primary perceptual systems therefore function to receive light, sound, and feeling from exteroceptive stimuli. As suggested by the framework, these systems deliver data to both the conscious and subconscious and are subject to control by both. Also note that covert actions (such as imagery or other thought and emotional and autonomic activity) are considered and treated by these systems as proprioceptive stimuli.

The Psychological Self is the sum total of an individual's experience. The psychological self has two elements—conscious and subconscious activity. Together these two elements monitor and direct all physiological activity and experience. The psychological self is the construct that serves as the point of reference for everything a person does. It is the sum total of the awareness, understanding, beliefs, abilities, and concepts that a person experiences relative to the outer world and self. It is the individual's perception and memory, and as such it is phenomenological in character. The psychological self represents reality for the individual. Without it there is no personal experience of one's existence.

Conscious Activities are what constitute awareness. Conceptually, this element of the psychological self is often referred to as consciousness or the conscious mind. Conscious activities are situationally specific. There are two types of thcught (convergent and divergent) and two types of operations (judgment and decision) that constitute conscious activity. These activities of the conscious psychological self serve to make it a processing stage for perceptual and recall data, the seat of "directed" thought and subsequent action.

Conscious Thought is psychological activity experienced and directed as part and parcel of the individual's awareness. It is the manipulation of perceptual and recalled data and is normally purposeful. In our framework two types of thought are represented—convergent and divergent. *Convergent thinking* is conscious psychological activity that is directed toward the development of conventional, logical, or deductive conclusions. Emphasis is placed on the correctness and appropriateness of the process; it is usually guided by past experience and the expectation that others would approve of the methods used and the conclusions drawn. Convergent thinking is deductive, exclusivistic, and systematic thought directed toward the production of correct answers or behaviors.

Divergent Thinking is conscious psychological activity directed toward the development of both a variety and large quantity of relevant hypotheses. Emphasis is placed on the goodness or potential worth of the process. Divergent thought is undertaken after convergent thinking has exhausted itself as a means of problem resolution. Convergent thought ordinarily precedes and lays the foundation for divergent thinking. Divergent thinking is usually inductive, inclusivistic, and nonsystematic thought directed toward the generation of many possible questions or behaviors.

Conscious Operations differ from conscious thought (which is the act of thinking) in that operations represent the purposes and goals of thought. There are two conscious operations represented in the framework—judgment and decision. An individual may use one or both types of thought as part of judgment and decision processes. *Judgment* refers to the process of forming an opinion or evaluation by discerning and comparing. Judgment also refers to the opinion so formed. It is the conscious operation involving the discrimination and comparison of perceptual and recall data, leading to the formulation of values and relations.

Decision is the determination arrived at after judgment; it precedes the initiation of activities or behavior intended to carry out judgment. The decision operation therefore includes the initiation of appropriate action (overt or covert) in response to the decision made. In the framework the initiation of response is represented by arrows labeled *intended action*. The arrows represent instructions from the conscious psychological self to the physiological self. These instructions can include anything from continued thought (which is covert behavior) to gross motor activity (involving movement or overt behavior).

Subconscious Activities refers to all psychological activity that occurs out of the individual's awareness. Not enough is known about this element of the psychological self to speculate significantly on the types of thought utilized, so we limit our presentation to one area—memory. Note that thought and operations are described as *continuous*. It is generally accepted that the subconscious is always functioning. This continuous operation is important, particularly in light of the fact that the subconscious directs all autonomic body functions. If subconscious operations were not continuous, the individual might "forget" necessary activities such as breathing or pumping blood.

The conscious and subconscious are connected via the physiological self, and they share responsibility for and codirect the activities of the individual's physiological self. The encoding or transfer of information from awareness to memory is carried out by the conscious and subconscious working together. For example, a visual image is received by visual perceptual systems and is transferred from consciousness to the subconscious via covert proprioceptive activity. Recall, which involves a transfer of information from memory to awareness, is initiated by the subconscious and accessed into consciousness by the perceptual systems. Exteroceptive and proprioceptive stimuli may be accessed by the perceptual systems into either the conscious or subconscious. Information so received is, of course, then subject to future transfer.

Subconscious Thought is, in our framework, limited to memory. *Memory* represents the sum total of stored experience. It is believed that data are stored in two ways: (1) images that represent the experience in its original sensory form, and (2) words or symbols that represent concepts, some of which are a direct analogue to sensory experiences. Memory as subconscious thought provides data necessary for the function of the subconscious and conscious operations. Memory, as conceptualized here, uses data acquired from three sources—direct perception, transfer from consciousness, and genetic inheritance.

Subconscious Operations are parallel in function to conscious operations, except that they are continuous instead of situational. Through these operations the subconscious judges and directs physiological behavior. The activities can be either covert or overt and provide for all autonomic, reflex, and habitual physiological behavior, including supplying the consciousness with stored data.

THE MODEL AS A DYNAMIC CONCEPT

Now that the parts of the framework have been presented and defined in a static way, we would like to demonstrate how the framework "functions" by applying it to a living person. In order to accomplish this we need the reader's cooperation. We would like you to take a few moments to examine how the framework relates to your own learning and behavior.

To begin, imagine that you have just awakened from a nap. Since the act of awakening involves the activation of your consciousness after a period of inactivity, one of two things probably happened to bring it about. Either your subconscious decided that you had slept long enough and stimulated conscious activity, or some sort of exteroceptive stimulus (for example, a loud noise or physical discomfort) triggered activity. Remember, your perceptual systems are under the control of both consciousness and subconsciousness, so they function even while you are asleep.

Your first conscious activities probably focused on the identification, classification, and disposition of the stimuli that awakened you. For example, let us assume that an external noise was responsible. Your experience of the sound was transmitted into consciousness by the auditory perceptual system. Upon arrival, the sound was evaluated for location, strength, and a host of other properties. This process of identifying and classifying the sound required that the subconscious be notified to search your memory and provide consciousness with appropriate examples of similar sounds you had experienced previously. The comparison process continued, and involved exchange between the conscious and subconscious in the form of covert activity, until a satisfactory level of recognition was reached. These procedures are so rapid they appear to be automatic and are only barely noticed.

Understanding or recognition means that you know the source of the sound; this probably includes information about its location, strength, and significance. Understanding of this sort was brought about through convergent thinking applied in the operation of judgment. Based on the opinion reached about the sound, you make a decision concerning subsequent action—for instance, you decide to turn off the alarm clock.

The subconscious could also be responsible for your conscious arousal. Can you remember an occasion when you woke with a start after having shut off the alarm some time before? You may have thought something like, "I wonder how long I dozed. Now I'll probably be late for work!" Or have you ever almost fallen asleep while driving and been nudged back to awareness by some unknown stimulus? In these two situations it was probably your subconscious looking out for you—in the first instance attempting to keep you from being late and in the second trying to keep you alive. The subconscious can provide these services since its operation is continuous and since it contains your stored experiences, beliefs, knowledge, values, plans, and expectations.

Now that you are awake, conscious activity is self-initiated. You decide what to think about, how to think about it, and what your purposes are. You also can consciously decide when it is again time to turn yourself off. Keep in mind, however, that your actions result from both conscious and subconscious operations. Your activities (such as thinking, sitting still, moving, looking, or talking) are brought about by judgments and decisions in both the conscious and subconscious. Therefore, your conscious intent may be affected; the resulting covert or overt actions may not be exactly what you consciously intended, due to the influence of the subconscious.

For example, suppose while reading this text you consciously try to concentrate and read for maximum understanding. Your conscious thought processes are probably very convergent. The operations of judgment and decision are comparing any new data with stored concepts and evaluating their worth, sending new material for storage, and directing further activity such as reading and thought. Now suppose while this is going on, your subconscious operations are evaluating conscious activities and judge these activities to be dull, unimpressive, and boring. The decisions made in the subconscious may then cause your perceptual systems to seek out other more interesting sources of stimuli. If you are easily distracted while trying to concentrate, this may be what is happening. Another possibility is that your subconscious is sending out signals designed to turn off your conscious activity. Before you know it, you have dropped off to sleep again.

The impact of the subconscious on perceptual and behavioral systems is especially noticeable in terms of habit acquisition. You learn some things so well they become automatic. This is true of everyone, and often not by choice or intent. Looking back to what happened to Chris, one can see that Chris developed habitual patterns as a result of the use of certain perceptual systems; gradually he learned to use the visual system the most and the tactile system the least. This means that when not consciously directing perceptual system use, Chris habitually slipped into the visual mode, perhaps even when this was not the most appropriate selection.

Consider cigarette smoking. It is a difficult habit to break. You may consciously understand the dangers of smoking and may want to stop, but until your conscious operations exert more influence than your subconscious on your physiology, you will continue smoking. Undoubtedly you can think of other examples where the subconscious influences and diverts conscious intent, especially where strong habits, beliefs, values, and other stored memories come into play.

However, conscious activities need not always be at the mercy of subconscious operations. Persons can learn to exert conscious control over most aspects of their physiological activities, even autonomic functioning. The growth of biofeedback programs and materials testifies to the fact that such control is attainable and apparently desirable. Although such topics as biofeedback are beyond the scope of this text, suffice to say that in some individuals conscious activities can and do exert maximal situational control of physiological operations; habits can be, and sometimes are, negated and changed.

Let's focus on conscious thought processes for a moment. We have stated that convergent thinking is the type of thought used most often by individuals in their everyday lives. This is due to the fact that most human activity is goal directed. Any behavior, covert or overt, is usually carried out with the intent of meeting a need or achieving a goal. Convergent thought and behavior is normally the most efficient means of reaching an appropriate conclusion. Figure 1-2 presents a simplified diagram of a convergent thought sequence.

Stimuli are accessed into consciousness. These stimuli can be either exteroceptive or proprioceptive. The stimuli are judged; usually this requires obtaining data from subconscious storage. The original stimulus is attended to by the perceptual systems or recycled in conscious thought while data are transferred from memory to consciousness. All of these activities required decisions and subsequent covert and perhaps overt action. The individual sifts the facts as perceived and makes a decision. This initiates appropriate action. The individual has thus made use of a convergent thought sequence to pull together all relevant data and make a decision. Suppose the subsequent decision is deemed inappropriate or insufficient due to some adverse environmental action or due to some further judgment within the individual. The individual can then recycle the entire process or change the process in some way. Most changes that involve going beyond or altering common existing methods of operation require divergent thought.

Figure 1-2 A Convergent Thought Sequence

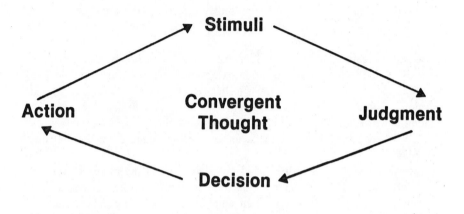

Simply stated, divergent thought provides for a suspension of the rules that govern convergently controlled operations so that more and different information can be included. Figure 1-3 graphically represents this process.

Figure 1-3 A Divergent Thought Sequence

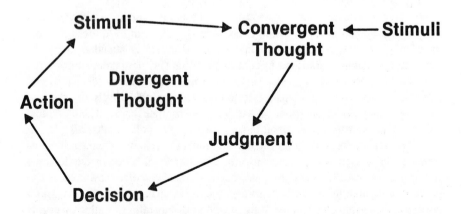

Apparently, divergent thinking suspends operations long enough to include additional data and even alter the rules governing what constitutes worth and value, thus changing the resultant judgment. The operations of judgment and decision are effective only while performed convergently, so divergent thought intercedes to manipulate the quantity, quality, and value of the data judged.

To illustrate this process, consider Figure 1-3 again. When you first looked at this diagram and read the explanatory text, you were trying to understand an abstract phenomenon. You were engaged in a convergent process—acquiring data, recalling stored data, comparing, integrating, and forming an opinion. Suppose that at the end of this process you were not satisfied with your understanding or appreciation of the concept as presented. You may have proceeded to reinstitute convergent operations once again, or you may have stopped to think about the process in a different way. For example, you may have thought about many things that you previously considered unrelated, or perhaps you tried to think of instances where divergent thinking played a part in some product or behavior. If this describes what happened to you, you were engaging in divergent thought. Divergent thinking is an important part of creative production and is absolutely necessary for the production of anything original.

AN OPERATIONAL DEFINITION OF TALENT

Now that we have discussed a means of analyzing and explaining learning and behavior, we can present our operational definition of talent. The definition uses elements of the framework considered important to the production of effective behavior. Since we cannot see what actually occurs within individuals, we must infer these events from their behaviors.

Talented individuals are those who evidence:

1. More effective behavior than their contemporaries.
2. Effective behavior results from:
   a. more efficient use of perceptual systems.
   b. more efficient use of conscious thought.
   c. more efficient transfer of data between conscious and subconscious.
   d. more extensive amounts and diversity of stored information.
   e. more efficient use of conscious and subconscious operations.
   f. more efficient use of behavior delivery systems.
   g. combinations of the above.

In this definition the term *effective* means that the individual is producing or is capable of producing a desired behavior. The emphasis here is placed on the actual production or the power to produce a desired result. It implies the fulfillment of a purpose or intent, especially as viewed after the event. This part of the definition allows for product evaluation. The question is whether the individual can and does succeed at endeavors better than peers. (Observers must be careful to understand the objectives of the person under observation and not attempt to interpret that person's behavior solely on the basis of the observer's personal value system.)

The second part of the definition provides for process evaluation and relates directly to the framework for human learning and behavior. The second part also enables this definition to be used to discover potentially talented individuals. Effective behavior is broken into six component parts, with each part contributing to the behavioral product. The term *efficient* is used here since we are discussing what is actually operative and producing a result; it implies application with a minimum of effort or waste.

We believe that the six points in this definition can be used to identify talented and potentially talented individuals because if individuals do better than their contemporaries in:

1. using their primary perceptual systems, they access more and richer exteroceptive and proprioceptive information into their conscious and subconscious. This means they have more information to use operationally.
2. using convergent and divergent thought when optimally appropriate, they are able to resolve problems and complete psychological operations more quickly and more successfully.
3. transferring data between the conscious and subconscious, they will have more accessible data quicker, and without loss due to transfer.
4. having a higher data storage capacity in more forms, they will have more data available for application in more situations.
5. coordinating the output of the conscious and subconscious (so that both contribute beneficially to goal attainment with little crossing/negation of intent), they will perform intended activities better.
6. having better delivery systems (including structural differences), they have an obvious edge when it comes time for performance.

Consider the case of an outstanding ballerina. To become outstanding she had to use her perceptual systems to access information through all of the primary sensory modalities. Sight was necessary to effectively observe others and self and to appreciate proper movement, poise, and grace. Hearing was necessary for incorporating music and rhythm. Feeling was essential in achieving proper body position and movement. Both exteroceptive and proprioceptive sources of information were necessary to give her sufficient information to proceed. Convergent thought enabled her to learn the accepted way, and divergent thought allowed her to expand.

When she is dancing, she performs complex movements matched with sound in time and space. For this to happen, information is continually being shuffled back and forth from conscious to subconscious, with enough speed so as not to limit her other abilities. She remembers every movement, every sound, each pause, each place; she can perform all the intended activities without distraction or inhibition. She is strong, lithe, and statuesque; her body is matched perfectly to the task at hand. She is very talented, a fact that no one can dispute.

In Russia, the selection of students for intensive ballet training involves an extensive physiological examination and some psychological evaluation. Evaluators first must decide if a candidate has the tools to perform in an exceptional manner. Then instructors spend many hours working with individuals to develop most of the elements in our definition. This explains why over the years many of the world's most renowned ballet dancers have been Russian. (Of course, many are called, but relatively few succeed. The issue of individual choice and the question of what happens to the failures are two other important considerations.)

We now have an operational definition of talent and a model of human behavior to use as a guide in exploring and explaining the needs and developmental nuances of talented people. This is exactly what we will do in the next three chapters. We will look at the three primary environments in turn, and we will discuss the implications that each has for the growth and development of talented individuals.

If you wish to pursue in more detail some of the concepts presented in this chapter, the following reading list may provide some guidance.

Suggested Readings

Brown, B.B. *Stress and the art of biofeedback*. New York: Bantam Books, Inc., 1977.

Combs, A., & Snygg, D. *Individual behavior* (rev. ed.). New York: Harper and Row, 1959.

Ellis, H.C. *Fundamentals of human learning, memory and cognition* (2nd ed.). Dubuque, Iowa: William C. Brown Co., 1978.

Gibson, J.J. *The senses considered as perceptual systems*. Boston: Houghton Mifflin, 1966.

Horowtiz, M.J. *Image formation and cognition* (2nd ed.). New York: Appleton-Century-Crofts, 1978.

Mahoney, J.J. *Cognition and behavior modification*. Cambridge, Mass.: Ballinger, 1974.

Massaro, D.W. *Experimental psychology and information processing*. Chicago: Rand McNally, 1975.

Messick, S., et al. *Individuality in learning*. San Francisco: Jossey-Bass, Inc., 1976.

Neisser, U. *Cognition and reality: Principals and implications of cognitive psychology*. San Francisco: W. H. Freeman & Co., 1976.

Paivio, A. Dual coding: Theoretical issues and empirical evidence. In J. M. Scandura and C. J. Brainerd (Eds.), *Structured/process models of complex human behavior*. Leiden, The Netherlands: Nordhoff, 1978.

Richardson, A. *Mental imagery*. London: Routledge and Kegan Paul, 1969.

Chapter 2

Talent and the Physical Environment

Ever since the first signs of self-awareness flickered in the minds of our distant ancestors, the human (or pre-human) mind has pondered on its relationship with the world outside. We can only guess that early humans, say a million or so years ago, were conscious of themselves as an integral part of the environment in which they lived: they were hunters and gatherers and they survived only if they respected the world in which they lived. And yet they may have already begun the age-old human practice of attempting to secure more favorable treatment for themselves by appealing in diverse ways to the greater natural forces that rule the world. (Leaky & Lewin, 1977).

Human development and behavior can be viewed from the perspective that suggests that each person exists as a biological unit in a physical universe, governed by certain inexorable rules. An individual may choose to, or for some reason be forced to, withdraw from the social or intellectual environments. However, the physical environment is a constant, everpresent part of every person's existence. The interrelationship that exists between the individual and the physical environment has a significant impact on subsequent behavior and development.

This chapter focuses on the unique ways in which talented people interrelate with the physical environment and how this relationship influences their overall development. But first we present a perspective on human development that will help organize our discussion.

There are numerous theories to explain human growth and development. The merits and limitations of each theory have received the attention of countless writers and researchers. We have based our discussion of psycho-physiological development on one such theory. We will not argue that it is the best theory or that it is without faults. However, Maslow's (1971) theory of human motivation covers the physical, social, and psychological aspects of coping and offers a

21

self-directed or self-actualization dimension. The theory is useful in explaining the development of many people who seemingly realize their talent potential.

Before we begin our discussion, it seems worth noting that human potential is best considered in relative rather than fixed terms. Life is a dynamic process, and one's potential changes as one lives. It is a mistake to think of potential as a static, predictable level of attainment that one can be programmed to achieve but cannot exceed. Potential has a horizontal as well as a vertical dimension, and it requires enrichment as well as acceleration.

Consider the case of a boy who while young wants to become a professional basketball player. However, he is the shortest player on the team. He works hard and perfects his abilities, but his height is considered to be such a barrier to achieving his goal that he is generally considered by others to have little potential. Suppose he then experiences a prolonged period of latent growth and attains a height of six feet seven inches before he stops growing. Suddenly his potential is much improved, and all of those enrichment activities he did prior to his growth spurt pay large dividends in terms of achieving his potential.

MASLOW EXPLAINED

In Maslow's (1971) need theory one can discover all the ingredients necessary to explain the striving for both mastery and self-competence. Maslow discusses a hierarchy of human needs that differentiates between physiological and psychological needs, between deficiency needs and self-realization needs, and between conscious and unconscious drives as a basis for behavior. In brief, Maslow suggests a five-level hierarchy of needs. The lower-level needs are physiological in nature. As lower-order needs become routinely satisfied, they give way to the higher-level psychological needs. As with most stage theories, the hierarchical ordering of the needs is considered to be somewhat invariant. That is, persons may progress to the next higher level of need only after satisfying the need below. The need hierarchy as presented is considered to apply to humans everywhere.

The five levels of needs, as represented in Figure 2-1, are: (1) physiological needs, (2) security needs, (3) needs for love and belongingness, (4) needs for esteem, and (5) self-actualization needs. The two lower-level needs are said to motivate and direct human behavior toward survival and the elimination of privation. A hungry person seeking food is an example of someone attempting to satisfy a deficiency need. A person so motivated is attempting to cope with the demands of staying alive. At the next two levels, the need for love and for esteem, while deprivation needs, are seen as motivating behavior in accord with the goal of achieving self-realization. When a person is motivated toward actualization, she or he is striving for self-improvement and growth. Striving

Figure 2-1 Maslow's Need Hierarchy

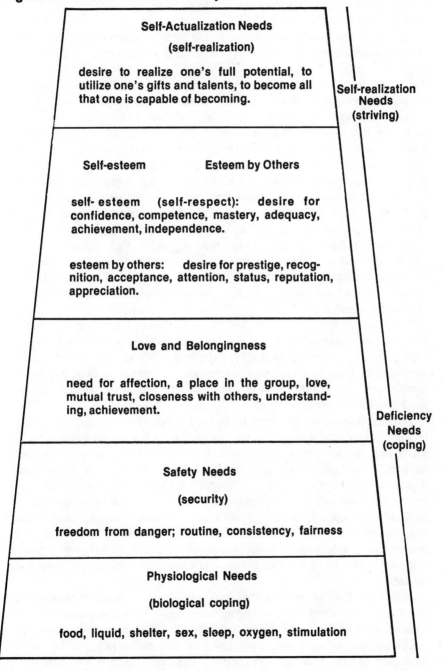

Self-Actualization Needs

(self-realization)

desire to realize one's full potential, to utilize one's gifts and talents, to become all that one is capable of becoming.

Self-realization
Needs
(striving)

Self-esteem   Esteem by Others

self- esteem (self-respect): desire for confidence, competence, mastery, adequacy, achievement, independence.

esteem by others: desire for prestige, recognition, acceptance, attention, status, reputation, appreciation.

Love and Belongingness

need for affection, a place in the group, love, mutual trust, closeness with others, understanding, achievement.

Deficiency
Needs
(coping)

Safety Needs

(security)

freedom from danger; routine, consistency, fairness

Physiological Needs

(biological coping)

food, liquid, shelter, sex, sleep, oxygen, stimulation

toward self-actualization is quite different from being drawn toward equilibrium, as is the case at the four lower levels.

All needs are seen as originating in the form of unconscious motivators, possibly inner drives, that control the individual's behavior until the need is routinely satisfied. Routine satisfaction raises the need to a conscious state; at that point individuals recognize the need and thus can direct their behavior toward satisfying the need or delaying immediate satisfaction. For example, persons who regularly have enough to eat will sometimes consciously skip a meal or postpone eating. They may choose not to eat because of dieting, preoccupation with some task, or a variety of other reasons. The key issue is that they are choosing to satisfy a higher-level need and are able to postpone satisfying a lower-level need because they know that they can always eat if they want to. Persons who have learned they cannot depend on the availability of food usually find it difficult to consciously decide not to eat when they are hungry. In fact, they may spend much of their time thinking about and seeking food. The less frequently persons can regularly satisfy their hunger, the more unconscious and consuming becomes the motivation to satisfy this need. Individuals are driven by or act upon more than one need at a time, depending on the situation and their inner state; the lower-level need is dominant if there is conflict between needs.

Physiological needs are those that humans have as a direct result of their biological existence. These needs can thus be described in terms of biological coping. Everyone needs food, liquid, oxygen, and rest in order to survive; and to almost as great an extent everyone needs stimulation, shelter, and sexual gratification. The fulfillment of physiological needs is fundamental to the survival of all living organisms.

The next level in the hierarchy is the need for psycho-physiological security or safety. This need is most readily satisfied by a consistent, nonthreatening social environment that establishes and maintains realistic parameters or limits for human maintenance and growth. Predictability and orderliness, combined with flexibility, characterize an environment in which the individual can safely test and receive useful, growth-enhancing feedback. In this environment the individual can expect to receive support without being suffocated. The individual can test and find limits without risking more than momentary failure or slight punishment. A safe, orderly, flexible environment facilitates self-awareness and helps the individual move toward consciously controlling and directing the need for security.

At the next level in the hierarchy we find the need to belong, to be accepted, and to be loved. Obviously, belonging takes many forms due to the nature of social maturation and the complexity of social roles. Belonging must be routinely satisfied in the family, among peers, and eventually within new "social" structures such as school and the work setting. The person who is not accepted as a group member, and thus either needs to conform to or fight the social environment, is one who is being group controlled or group rejected. Being accepted by others consistently or routinely leads the individual to recognize an inner need to belong; this in turn releases the unconscious drive or motivation toward self-acceptance and self-esteem, the next ranking needs.

Maslow says that the need for self-esteem and esteem by others occurs only when the individual is physically and psychologically secure and believes he or she is accepted by others. The need for esteem may be met through both personal and social achievements. Conscious awareness of this need, following routine satisfaction, readies the individual to operate in a self-actualized or consciously self-directed manner.

It is important to keep in mind that the four lower-order needs are described by Maslow as deprivation or survival needs. That is, if the individual is unable to routinely satisfy and recognize these needs, his or her behavior is affected by unconscious motives or drives for homeostasis (equilibrium). Behavior motivated toward coping is not consciously directed or controlled by the individual. In order to take risks, to generate new ideas, to unselfishly give oneself to others, or to be self-directed in Maslow's terms, the individual must have conscious control of all the lower-order survival needs; this occurs only through routine satisfaction of these needs. Hypothetically, the individual cannot achieve or maintain self-actualization or self-competency without a supportive and stimulating environment.

The highest-level need is for self-actualization. Note that this level is seldom achieved, and if it is reached it is not maintained for long periods of time. An individual must overcome many obstacles and meet many needs before achieving full potential and being able to maintain that state.

How is it then that some persons do achieve the lofty heights of self-actualization? In this and subsequent chapters we will attempt to answer this question, discussing and integrating concepts and data from our framework for learning and behavior, from Maslow's hierarchy of needs, and from the biographies of eminent people. To take just one example, George Washington Carver was able to overcome the deprivations he suffered as a young boy, and later he seemed to forsake acclaim, recognition, and social contact. Nevertheless, he achieved the level of creative and original functioning attributed to the self-actualized individual. Perhaps his early childhood experiences in coping with his physical and social environment enabled him to maintain the level of confidence and self-esteem needed to move beyond coping. Perhaps the strain of having to survive independently, as early as age five, allowed him to satisfy the need to belong almost as soon as others demonstrated their belief in him at the age of 30.

If one compares Maslow's hierarchy of needs (Figure 2-1) with the framework of learning and behavior (Figure 1-1), it becomes apparent that the physical environment relates most directly to the two lowest levels of needs. An individual's physiological and safety needs are most often met through interaction with the physical environment. Similarly, the needs at the higher levels of Maslow's hierarchy are most often achieved through interaction with various social and intellectual environments.

THE INDIVIDUAL AND THE ENVIRONMENT

We have stated that an individual's learning and behavior result from interaction between the individual and the environment. This interaction is a dynamic process characterized by a continual flow of information, with associated changes in the environment and the individual. While some factors of an individual's existence are defined almost solely by heredity (such as eye and skin color), others (for example, height, weight, and intelligence) are a product of the interaction between some genetic predisposition and physiological and social nourishment from the environment. Still other aspects of human development (such as personality characteristics) are considered to be shaped more by the individual and the environment than by heredity. The individual can thus be depicted as an organism capable of very complex thought and behavior as well as being a proactive contributor, observer, and evaluator of events. In order to observe, evaluate, and contribute to events, the individual must first achieve awareness and understanding and be able to process diverse stimuli.

Perception, the key to this process, is the detection, differentiation, and transmission of exteroceptive and proprioceptive stimuli for use in the individual's psychological and physiological operations. By detection we mean that stimuli have "made contact with" the components of the perceptual systems responsible for picking up such activities. Differentiation involves the searching of the available data for details that provide direction for conscious and subconscious activity and subsequent behavior. Differentiation necessarily follows detection as the data are transmitted into the psychological self where the higher-level activities of judgment and decision making occur.

How a person experiences an event has a great deal to do with the information obtained and its corresponding meaning. Each perceptual system must orient itself in appropriate ways in order to perform its task. Effective orientation suggests that all perceptual systems are to some degree dependent on the general orienting system of the body. Body, head, hand, and eye movements are all part of the perceptual systems they serve. Adjustments constitute attention and contribute to the individual's ability to explore available stimuli.

Ordinarily there are more exteroceptive and proprioceptive stimuli available than the individual can accommodate. This being the case, subconscious operations selectively determine what will be attended to and direct perceptual orientation systems accordingly. Conscious operations can often override the subconscious and direct attention elsewhere. Awareness is the key. If an individual is consciously aware or decides to consciously seek out certain stimuli, then he or she can exert control over the subconscious. Normally, however, attention is directed subconsciously and is therefore subject to habitual patterns of activity. Thus, the functions of both the perceptual systems and the behavior delivery systems are influenced by conscious and subconscious psychological activity; this can account for the differential use of the various perceptual systems.

The work of Bandler and Grinder (1976) suggests that as individuals mature, one of their perceptual systems may become dominant in terms of both quality and quantity of use. This dominance could occur for a number of reasons. For example, suppose some individuals grew up in environments that promoted the use of one system more than the others. As these individuals began to use that system more, they would be reinforced for doing so by elements within the environment and probably from within themselves as well.

Simply stated, people do not experience the world in its entirety. Everyone is dependent upon the operation of their perceptual and behavior systems to experience and interact with the environment. These systems are in turn dependent upon the operation of the individual's conscious and subconscious. The implications are clear. A potentially talented individual is able to relate more effectively with the environment than others who are less capable.

In Chapter 1 we described the differential performance capabilities of potentially talented persons. We present this list again for emphasis and further discussion. Potentially talented individuals do better than their contemporaries in:

1. using their primary perceptual systems; they access more and richer exteroceptive and proprioceptive information into their conscious and subconscious. Therefore, they have more information to evaluate and use operationally.
2. using convergent and divergent thought when optimally appropriate; they are able to resolve problems and complete psychological operations more quickly and more successfully.
3. transferring data between the conscious and subconscious; they have more data that is readily accessible without loss due to transfer.
4. having a higher data storage capacity in more forms. They have more data available for application in more situations.
5. organizing the output of the conscious and subconscious in such a way that both contribute beneficially to goal attainment with little crossing/ negation of intent. They therefore perform intended activities more efficiently.
6. having better delivery systems (including structural differences). Thus they have an obvious edge when it comes to performance.

Let us examine these capabilities and discuss some possible implications for the way a potentially talented person would interrelate with the physical environment. It appears that these six capabilities are all interdependent and that a person blessed with all of them would have little difficulty moving to the upper levels in Maslow's hierarchy. However, the very nature of their interdependence often becomes a source for problems.

When a person's capacities do not develop in a uniform, coordinated manner, the individual may be at odds with self and with the environment. For example, consider a person whose perceptual systems function very efficiently and therefore can access a high quantity of data. If the individual's value systems and memory are not sufficiently developed to provide direction and control over what is perceived, the individual could very well suffer from information overload. Similar types of dysfunction could occur due to the individual's inability to either selectively attend to or organize the flood of available data. Conflicting information might thus be stored, jeopardizing the usefulness of the information recalled at the moment of action.

For the sake of clarity and thoroughness we will now illustrate some of the problems that might result from mismatching capability and efficiency across the six dimensions. We will present each possible simple combination of one through six and briefly discuss the implications of each. Please keep in mind that these combinations are hypothetical and rarely if ever exist in isolation as they are represented here.

1–2: High access efficiency combined with relatively inefficient conscious thought. When a person accesses a lot of information, more than conscious thought processes can efficiently handle, there is potential for mass confusion. There are many stimuli available for divergent thought, but efficient divergent thinking requires a foundation of convergent thought and organization. If either convergent or divergent thinking functions inefficiently when attempting to handle a mass of input, or if either type of thought is used inappropriately, the results could prove highly dysfunctional. Can you remember a time when you were confronted with too much information? Now suppose you were accessing twice as much. How would you have felt? This type of mismatch has ramifications in terms of Maslow's hierarchy; one's impaired ability to evaluate physical stimuli could influence sleep and even one's perception of external danger. Without appropriate direction or focus, the perceptual systems gather data indiscriminately. All data then become distracting.

Obviously the opposite condition is also possible, where the person's capacity for thought outstrips the capacity of the perceptual systems to supply data. In this instance, the individual may spend much time and effort seeking stimulation. For example, it is physiological fact that humans can think much faster than they or other people can talk. The average person can think at a rate of about 400 words per minute, while speakers can usually talk at only about 200 words per minute. This implies that, on the average, half of a listener's time is spent thinking of other things. Now consider a potentially talented person who can think at a rate of 800 words per minute. When listening to another person talk, this individual needs to only use one quarter of his or her capacity. Is it any wonder that talented people get bored and seek stimulation from other sources?

1–3: Access capability high and encoding and recall efficiency relatively low. In this instance, the individual can experience and organize lots of data but has trouble getting the information into and out of memory. What does one do—access less information, or spend a lot of time trying to get all the data into memory without loss or alteration? If one accesses less data or only certain types of data, what are the implications for meeting physiological and safety needs?

1–4: Access capacity high and storage capacity low. This combination leaves the individual very dependent upon exteroceptive stimuli. When the data available for use come primarily from external sources and the person cannot recall comparable information from memory, most action will be initiated, governed, and evaluated by external sources. This happens in young children before their compiled memories begin to supply adequate amounts of information to counter, balance, and compare with new experiences. Only after the inner world becomes a rich source of stimuli, can the person begin to develop an internal locus of control.

1–5: Access capability high and organization of conscious and subconscious activities low. Whenever there are lots of data for conscious and subconscious operations, but little efficiency and coordination of effort, the results can be quite frustrating. With large amounts of data entering both the conscious and subconscious, and each having a different "idea" as to the proper course of action, the resultant behavior may reflect a cancellation of intent. Have you ever consciously decided to do something a certain way and then discovered as you attempted the task that something was holding you back or making you perform differently than you had intended? The inability to perform as intended may have reflected a lack of coordinated effort between the conscious and subconscious. At times like these, the more information a person has available, the more frustrating it is to be unable to follow through with appropriate action. This type of conflict can effectively decrease a person's ability to satisfy a need or may even create a need for order or predictability. In this kind of situation, people often become dependent on experts who tell them "what is best for them."

1–6: Access capability high and behavior delivery capacity low. Here high acquisition efficiency makes the individual aware of many events occurring in the environment, but he or she lacks the physical tools to relate back to the environment at the same level of efficiency. Have you ever had a wealth of information to give but felt frustrated because verbalizing seemed too slow a response method, and writing seemed even slower? Many potentially talented individuals continually experience this kind of frustration, particularly when fine motor skills needed for writing are still hampered by immaturity.

2–3: Thought efficiency high and transfer efficiency low. Here the individual is an efficient, productive thinker but is often hampered because of an inability to effectively transfer information for storage or recall it from memory. Often the person knows that the information is stored but simply cannot get it out when needed. For example, have you ever watched a movie and saw a star whose name you should remember, but for some reason the name escapes you? Later on, usually long after you've stopped caring, the name may pop into consciousness. In terms of need fulfillment, many a good opportunity is missed because a person does not recognize the worth of stored data in time, only adding to the frustration of someone whose thought processes were capable of taking advantage of the situation.

2–4: Highly efficient conscious thought and inefficient memory. Memory is where a person's representations of self and the outer world are stored. When an individual's capacity for conscious thought outstrips the supply of stored information about self and the environment, the individual is often induced to act on the basis of insufficient historical or stored data. This often results in naïve behavior—naïve at least from the individual's perspective, since the impact of one's behavior is evaluated consciously during and after the act. To others, the behavior may appear impulsive or ill conceived, only adding to the individual's conscious frustration.

2–5: Efficient thought and inefficient operations. When a person can think about something efficiently but cannot make judgments and decisions efficiently, the result is often inactivity and passive resignation. Withdrawal and a lack of self-motivated activity is counterproductive to the satisfaction of needs.

2–6: Efficient thought and inefficient delivery. The potentially talented individual may exhibit a high degree of physical restlessness when physical motor ability lags behind the conscious desire to concentrate and achieve mastery. The result is increased anxiety which further reduces the individual's behavioral effectiveness.

3–4: Efficient transfer of data and inefficient storage, and vice versa. These two functions are so closely related it is probably safe to suggest that in terms of conscious operations one is of little value without the other. It is possible to store data in many forms (visual, auditory, tactile), and often a person may be adept at storing certain types of data but not other types. For example, a person may be efficient at storing data in only one perceptual form. When searching memory for representations of the experience, only this one form will be completely recovered: the other data are lost. The person may be aware that some meaning is missing and may experience confusion, frustration, and lack of self-confidence.

3–5: Transfer efficiency of information between conscious and subconscious high and transfer efficiency between conscious and subconscious operations low. These two operations are also very closely interrelated, especially when considering motivation. Without the efficient transfer of information between the conscious and subconscious, each will act in ignorance of the other until one learns his/her behavior is inappropriate. This evaluation often occurs too late; the individual has already acted inappropriately and has suffered subsequent consternation and frustration. In situations like these, the person often reverts to habitual behavior; the subconscious takes over because there is safety in consistency and routine. Frequently, this combination may be used to explain why some people order the same food and buy the same style clothes over and over again, even though they say they would like to change.

3–6: Transfer efficiency low and behavior delivery efficiency high. Here we have a person whose physical ability is limited because she or he is unable to transfer skill and knowledge efficiently between the conscious and subconscious. As a result, this individual may be forced to depend on the control of only one or the other in times of stress or when quick action is necessary. People operating under this restriction often find it difficult to integrate new physical skills into existing patterns, and may require much repetition to succeed at such an attempt. In this instance the individual is not hampered by "physical" limitations, but by a less efficient knowledge transfer system.

4–5: Imbalance between memory and organized behavior control. Both these components must function efficiently if the individual is to become effectively self-directed. Whenever one component impedes the efficiency of the other, the individual becomes less effective in satisfying needs. A diverse storehouse of experience is necessary to form the foundation for the values and operational tenets that control conscious and subconscious activities. Conversely, all the stored knowledge in the world is useless if it cannot be applied efficiently.

4–6: Highly efficient memory and less efficient behavior systems. With this combination, the individual is prone to rely on habitual or known activities and is often reluctant to attempt anything new. Security rests in the realm of the known, and innovation involves taking a risk because behavior systems cannot be counted on to deliver the goods.

5–6: Coordinated intent and efficient systems. Suppose both of these components are efficient. Sometimes the potentially talented person is then in a position where there is little opportunity to test personal limits. The physical or social environment may not allow a young person to attempt activities reserved for "older" people. Although these sanctions are often evoked for the young persons's own protection, the fact is that potentially talented young people are often ready to perform certain tasks well before their contemporaries. If they are stifled or do not have the opportunity to test their limits, they will experience the frustration that results from the suppression of natural growth tendencies. Sometimes when they are allowed to act, there is the frustration of receiving no direction or feedback. One cannot achieve self-realization without being allowed to test one's limits. Thus, even the totally efficient potentially talented person is not without problems.

Saying that persons are potentially talented is similar to saying that they have the ability to be different. Interaction with the physical environment can either minimize or accentuate these differences. The physical environment, if we can refer to it as an entity, tends to require that everyone make the same accommodations. That is, everyone basically must meet similar physiological and psychological requirements in relating to the physical world. Ordinarily, one would think that highly capable people would have a decided advantage in coping and in mastering the upper levels in Maslow's hierarchy. Such an assumption leads many people to believe that talented people do not need any special help, that "they can make it on their own." In this chapter we have attempted to demonstrate that in many instances having a better than "normal" capability is not always beneficial when it comes to learning about and interacting with the physical environment while meeting one's needs.

In the following pages we will elaborate on how the social and intellectual environments also pose special problems and opportunities for talented and potentially talented persons. For example, we have just noted how many people believe that talented and potentially talented individuals can make it on their own. The implication is that talented persons can succeed as long as they don't expect to be treated any differently and don't behave differently. According to George Moore (1964): "If we are to have genius we must put up with the inconvenience of genius, a thing the world will never do; it wants geniuses but would like them just like other people." The implications of prevailing social attitudes will be discussed in more detail in the next two chapters.

REFERENCES

Bandler, R., & Grinder, J. *The structure of magic II*. Palo Alto, Ca.: Science and Behavior Books, Inc., 1976.

Leaky, R., & Lewin, R. *Origins*. New York: E.P. Dutton, 1977, pp. 9–10.

Maslow, A. H. *Motivation and personality*. New York: Viking Press, 1971.

Moore, G. *The new dictionary of thoughts*. Garden City, N.Y.: Hanover House, 1964, p. 230.

Chapter 3

Talent and the Psychosocial Environment

MASLOW'S NEEDS AND TERMINAL VALUES

The socialization process can be said to have accomplished its fundamental objective when an individual has acquired or subscribes to a socially acceptable set of values. These values in effect become parameters within which behavior should occur. The person who has recently done the most research and writing regarding the acquisition of social values is Milton Rokeach (1973). His writings and research identify two basic sets of values, which when adopted by an individual, serve to direct behavior. One set is comprised of "terminal" or life goal values. Terminal values are those that represent an individual's long-range or ultimate goals. These values can be categorized to correspond with Maslow's hierarchy of human needs as illustrated below.

Maslow's Needs	*Terminal Values*
Psychological security	A comfortable life, family security, national security.
Affiliation	Pleasure, salvation, true friendship.
Esteem	A sense of accomplishment, self-respect, social recognition.
Self-actualization	An exciting life, a world at peace, a world of beauty, equality, freedom, happiness, inner harmony, mature love, wisdom.

The majority of Rokeach's terminal values seem to correspond with Maslow's self-actualization level of human needs. One could also equate these goals with the so-called "sacred" or religious values. Assuming that the above is somewhat accurate, it can be seen that people are motivated to live their lives in order to achieve security, affiliation, and recognition. If it is true that higher-level needs emerge as lower-order needs are satisfied, it can be hypothesized that higher-level terminal values may emerge when lower-order needs are routinely met. Rokeach (1973) has found that generally adolescents consider a "world at peace" and "freedom" as the highest value and "salvation" as the least important value. From the age of 20 through 70, Americans value a "world at peace" and "family security" most and "social recognition," "pleasure," and "an exciting life" least. Therefore, it seems that as people age there is a noticeable shift away from actualizing to the lower-order needs. These data definitely refute the assumption that people mature into a self-actualized state.

No research has focused on which terminal values are least important and more important to talented persons and adolescents with talent potential. However, based on case studies of adolescents with talent potential and on the biographies of talented persons in several fields, there may be two major differences between their values and the values held by people in general. First, the terminal values of talented persons remain more consistent from adolescence through adulthood. This may occur because talented people frequently are motivated by higher-level needs earlier in life, or they are better able to override or hold in abeyance the lower-order survival needs when developing their area of expertise.

Second, we would hypothesize that the most prized values among the talented would be "an exciting life," "a sense of accomplishment," and "obtaining wisdom." The least prized values would likely include "a comfortable life," "family security," and "national security." If these hypotheses were borne out, adolescents with talent potential would be guided by values somewhat compatible with the values of their nontalented peers, but talented adults would not find their values similar to the values of other nontalented adults. Adolescents with talent potential would benefit from learning that their terminal values may increasingly be at odds with values of those around them. The importance of self-understanding, social awareness, and self-directedness becomes readily apparent if talented adults are going to emerge and survive in an adult society with different values.

MASLOW'S NEEDS AND INSTRUMENTAL VALUES

The second set of values delineated by Rokeach are labeled instrumental values. These are the values that guide the way we behave in our daily lives. One would expect consistency between an individual's instrumental and terminal values. That is, one would expect that the means by which we do things would be consistent with the end or goal we have in mind.

Let us examine the instrumental values as they relate to Maslow's need hierarchy.

Maslow's Needs	*Instrumental Values*
Psychological security	Clean, obedient, polite, self-controlled.
Affiliation	Cheerful, forgiving, helpful, honest, loving.
Esteem	Ambitious, capable, logical, responsible.
Self-actualization	Broad-minded, courageous, imaginative, independent, intellectual.

How do the results of Rokeach's survey of Americans' instrumental values match up with the values we would expect talented adults and youngsters with talent potential to embrace? From Rokeach's research we find that the majority of American adolescents and adults from age 20 through 70 put the least value on being "imaginative" and "logical" and the greatest value on "honesty" and "loving." Our studies would suggest that adolescents with talent potential and talented adults place the greatest value on being "imaginative," "logical," and "independent" and place the least value on "politeness" and "self-control." Thus from an early age, talented and potentially talented youngsters may experience a conflict between the values that guide their daily behavior and the values that guide the thoughts and behavior of others—a conflict that may last throughout their lives.

MOVING BEYOND COPING

In addition to considering the importance that individual and social group values have in the fulfillment of human potential, we should also consider the relative importance of nature versus nurture. Thomas Edison, George Washington Carver, Albert Einstein, and Damon Runyon achieved eminence in spite of spending the first 20 to 30 years of their lives in discouraging, even hostile, environments. On the other hand, John F. Kennedy, Franklin D. Roosevelt, Margaret Mead, and Robert Oppenheimer all grew up in family environments that provided considerable psychological support. Additionally, both Kennedy and Roosevelt had considerable financial and political support in their quest to become president of the United States. The formative years of Presidents Truman and Eisenhower and of Alexander Graham Bell were marked by neither privilege nor privation. Even though these three achieved eminence, we cannot say for sure whether any of them came close to realizing their potential.

Persons with talent potential who eventually do achieve some form of eminence can be said to have been born with and/or developed more ability than required to effectively cope with environmental demands. Environments that are more demanding or less supportive require an extra measure of human ability or effort to meet the physical and psychological needs for survival, belonging, and self-esteem. In these nonsupportive environments, the individual who is able to move beyond merely coping will more likely evidence behavior that is considered indicative of talent. The more favorable or supportive the environment, the less ability or effort is needed to move beyond coping. Thus, socially and psychologically advantaged children are more likely to act "talented" and are more likely to realize their potential than the socially or psychologically disadvantaged.

ACHIEVING A MEASURE OF SELF-DIRECTION

A second aspect in the development of talent potential will be the major focus of this chapter. It becomes apparent in studying the lives of eminent persons and in our work with the more creative children and adolescents in the Guidance Institute for Talented Students (GIFTS) that an "internal locus of control," which we usually describe as direction, is necessary to the realization of talent potential. Without it, the individual can and does perform well in prescribed situations, but cannot go beyond the prescribed. Individuals without an internal locus of control are almost totally dependent on others to provide both the stimulus to act and the criteria to evaluate their performance. Robert Taft can be seen as an excellent example of a high achiever who lacked an internal locus of control.

The fulfillment of talent potential requires that individuals achieve a measure of independence as early as possible in their development. The sooner individuals develop the tools or skills they need to reach beyond the immediate environment (through walking and reading, for example), the sooner they begin to strive for independence and for mastery. The more secure individuals feel, the more risks they will take and the more limits they will test.

An example of this phenomenon occurred on a large scale on college campuses during the Vietnam War. The colleges attended by middle and upper-middle class students were the scene of considerable conflict and turmoil. However, there was hardly any noticeable disturbance at technical schools and junior college campuses or at those state colleges that were attended largely by students from the lower-middle and upper-lower socioeconomic classes. It is generally recognized that children raised in so-called "liberal" homes challenge their parents' values more than children raised in more "traditional" homes. Some interesting confrontations occur when parents who have encouraged their children to think for themselves later ask why their children challenge parental values and patterns of behavior.

The movie *Guess Who's Coming to Dinner* provides another graphic example. The story line is simple. Well-educated, liberal-thinking parents have raised an independent, conscientious daughter who brings home a young black man she likes. The movie centers on how the parents' consternation over their daughter's behavior leads them to reexamine their own values. They finally recognize that their "liberalism" had hidden limits which did not exist for their daughter. In essence, by creating an environment that fosters self-direction, parents (and society, for that matter) lose some control over an individual's behavior.

Persons who have the abundance of energy, drive, and ability needed to cope with the demands of everyday living are the ones who are most likely to challenge and test physical, social, and intellectual limits. On the other hand, parents (and, on a broader scale, the society or culture) are concerned with achieving a certain degree of stability and predictability, while allowing for acceptable levels of improvement and change. Self-directed individuals with talent potential who challenge the status quo may therefore be seen as extremists. (Keep in mind that we are discussing individuals whose abilities allow them to generate their own challenges to society.) They will not appear much different from people who strike out and challenge society as a result of being suppressed.

THE DRIVE TO UNDERSTAND NATURE

In addition to moving beyond coping and achieving a measure of self-direction, nearly all eminent persons have another common denominator: a drive or desire to understand "nature." Some pursue this quest on an abstract scale as did Newton and Einstein; others, like Bell and Edison, work on a more applied or specific scale. Still others, like Whitman and Hemingway, strive to understand and explain human nature in literary form. Those self-directed persons who can readily cope with their environmental demands and still have unspent energy and ability seem to continually ask why and how? As knowledge accumulates, there is more knowledge to master and the questions become more complex. In one sense then, yesterday's genius may seem less special when measured by today's standards, and today's genius will be someone who is truly exceptional.

The foregoing has been an attempt to provide a background for understanding what is unique in the social development of children and adolescents with talent potential. We have suggested that one dimension of talent potential finds its source in the ability and energy the individual has left over after coping with typical demands made by the social and physical environments. We have further suggested that the behavior of those with talent potential may be both unpredictable and occasionally perceived as socially undesirable. It is equally important to note that self-directed persons who are able to go beyond coping will need to access a great amount of knowledge and develop higher-level skills if they are to move beyond existing knowledge or better understand nature.

THE IMPORTANCE OF A BROADER PERSPECTIVE

We cannot use Maslow's theories alone to explain or help us understand a Thomas Edison, a George Washington Carver, or a Damon Runyon. These three suffered physical neglect and severe deprivation throughout their formative years. They grew up without family or friends. They were self-educated. They had a disdain for wealth, and Carver also seemed to scorn recognition. From infancy on, all three seemed inner-directed, almost driven to know and to understand. Based on what we have said about Maslow's theories, one might think that all three may have attained even greater heights had they been raised in a more supportive environment. However, while a rosier childhood and adolescence may have resulted in their being happier, more well-rounded individuals, it is unlikely that they would have been more driven or more committed if operating from higher-level needs. We will have to look for other ways to explain how individuals from such unsupporting home environments were able to willfully override their lower-level needs and follow their quest for knowledge. Possibly through deprivation they achieved direction or a focus early in their lives, and discovered at the same time a vehicle for pursuing their quest.

Both Bell and Edison spent years trying to improve telegraphy. In fact, unknown to one another, both were caught up in trying to send more than one message at a time over a single wire. Bell had a rich background in speech and hearing, while Edison had years of experience as a telegrapher. Both men continued to be aware of broader questions even as they dedicated years to studying a single problem. Both made their major breakthroughs by what some describe as serendipity, but they created the atmosphere in which these chance occurrences could happen and they were able to recognize their significance.

Thus, while a focus or goal is important, a broader perspective is also necessary. Edison, who easily becomes a favorite example, is said to have read the entire contents of the Detroit library between the ages of 13 and 15 while riding the train to his home each day. During these three years he earned his keep by selling papers and food on the morning and evening train. (He also had a lab in the baggage car until it blew up, but that's another story.)

A person engages in several processes while striving for self-competence. These processes are described briefly below. Where Maslow's need hierarchy provides an explanation of *what motivates* individuals to become self-competent, these seven processes describe *how persons may achieve* self-competence. We believe that a self-competent person is one who successfully satisfies survival needs and masters the following learning elements.

Learning Elements As a Key to Mastery and Self-Competence

Assimilating requires data intake through auditory, visual, and tactile modes with minimal distortions. The channels must be open and operational. Data are then evaluated (accurate feedback is necessary if distortion is to be kept minimal), utilized, and stored for future use.

Demonstrating effective and accurate understanding of one's emotions and needs requires that parents and teachers be more cognizant of a youngster's unconscious motivations, as the child probably will not be aware of his or her own needs, and thus behavior may not be purposeful.

Reporting means providing congruent nonverbal communication of emotions, needs, self-concept, and perceptions of the environment to both oneself and to others. It includes identifying the physical, psychological, and social aspects of self; recognizing the commonalities and uniqueness of self and others; understanding how past experiences affect perception and behaviors; and knowing how to maintain and change self and the environment. It would facilitate development to teach motivation theory to children so they could understand the processes that control their development and more readily apply this knowledge to themselves, rather than being dependent on change or life experiences to belatedly establish a theory of self-development.

Valuing involves prioritizing experiences and aspirations in a way that is personally meaningful and socially responsible. One could think of this as acquiring a philosophy of life and living. Philosophical understanding should be offered in concert with value clarification programs.

Decision making is using one's value system to identify and organize all personal and environmental data that might be relevant to a decision and anticipating the consequences of decisions.

Acting intelligently, whether following or leading, is represented by the individual who is responsible for and monitors his or her own behavior. It involves considering alternatives while pursuing a course of action; in this way the individual can continually move toward a goal or end while maintaining flexibility in the means or path to that end. It may be necessary to modify personal value systems when there is difficulty in deciding or coping. It may also be necessary to develop new goals or aspirations as previously established goals are realized; this may also require review of one's values and life philosophy.

Legacy involves creating by example and deeds an environment that will help others develop faster, broader, and more comprehensively.

Most humans enrich others primarily by example. Only a few achieve the eminence of a Carver, Einstein, Longfellow, Christ, or Curie. It seems the foundation of development is provided by nurturant parents and teachers who support, stimulate, set limits, adjust, and let go. These are the necessary social and psychological conditions. Developing individuals also need external models whom they can emulate and an internalized philosophy or value system that can provide direction from within. The models or heroes provide a temporary goal and behavioral structure that helps young people direct their abilities until they are ready and able to direct themselves from within.

Ensuring that children are adequately fed, clothed, sheltered, and free from physical threat is a social responsibility that extends beyond the resources of the school. Children who are functioning at the physiological need level cannot generally be expected to demonstrate more than coping behaviors. Hot lunch programs provide only one small answer to this very large social problem. (Nevertheless, it is important to remember that some of the most remarkable persons of recent times—like George Washington Carver, Thomas Edison, and Albert Einstein—did not have their physiological needs routinely satisfied. Still their need to know produced a greater drive than their need for food and shelter. While these three are exceptions, they are mentioned again here to remind us not to overgeneralize. Theoretical explanations are a poor substitute for the firsthand knowledge that comes from taking the time and effort to know an individual.)

At the preschool and elementary school level, the greatest challenge to both parents and teachers is to provide potentially talented children with broader parameters for learning than the age or age-grade norm historically suggests. At the same time, teachers and parents must recognize the importance of setting individual physiological and psychological limits appropriate to each child. The child must be allowed to test these limits if she or he is to achieve a foundation for self-direction and social responsibility.

The notion of social responsibility deserves further comment. During the Nuremberg Trials and during other military trials following the Vietnam War, it was concluded that an individual must answer to a higher moral order that supersedes the existing social order. How is this related to the development of talent? Many eminent persons spend a lifetime trying to unravel this moral or natural order. Without developing this chapter into a philosophical treatise, it is necessary to remember that there are regional, urban-rural, and a number of other bases for differentially defining "social responsibility." The constant threat to the development of talent potential is that social responsibility will become equated with social conformity. How can anyone decide how far or in what manner a person can deviate from the norm and still be socially responsible?

THE IMPORTANCE OF COMBINED EFFORT

In 1981 pollution, energy problems, population explosion, and economic and political problems all threaten human existence. At the same time we see on the horizon the promise of doubling or tripling one's life span, maximizing human potential, and generally elevating human existence to a level only dreamed of a generation ago. The threats and the promises are immense, and it will take self-directed, talented individuals *working together* to cope with these problems and realize the promises. Only by pooling individual talents will many problems be solved.

Today it is unusual to find a "genius" working in absolute isolation, except perhaps in the arts. Cooperation and communication are commonplace among talented persons who focus on social and environmental problems. This is evidenced by the growth of research centers and "think tanks." Even in science, the efforts of the individual achiever have been superseded by team effort. Vast sums of money—beyond the reach of a single individual—are required to provide materials, equipment, and the technicians needed to achieve today's scientific breakthroughs.

In the past geniuses have gone their own way, keeping their own counsel. In this new era, communicative, organizational, and administrative skills are as critical to conducting physical and social inquiry as the more traditionally accepted skills in mathematics, logic, and reasoning. How will today's talented self-directed persons acquire the values and skills that enable them to work cooperatively and productively with one another?

Returning to the child, what are some of the social pressures experienced by those with talent potential? Consider some of the difficulties that arise for children when:

- intellectual understanding and problem solving skills are far more developed than their social and physical skills, creating a sort of internal imbalance.
- reasoning skills are far in advance of age-grade norms, and scholastic accomplishments constitute a threat to peers and possibly to siblings.
- accomplishments are rewarded by teachers and demanded by parents, possibly resulting in a loss of self-direction and a decrease in the personal joy of learning.
- knowledge exceeds wisdom because children usually cannot or have not tested or applied what they have learned. They've had no opportunity to integrate and evaluate stored information; they can only accumulate, regurgitate, and act in accordance with a comparatively underdeveloped personal value system.
- accomplishments breed more *externally* imposed "challenges," and additional material must be learned in the name of acceleration.
- achievements are frequently "rewarded" by independent or isolated study.
- teachers resent their domination of classroom discussions and the extra attention they demand.
- having received intensive attention at home, they experience a drastic decrease in attention in the classroom, resulting in their feeling neglected or rejected.

We can see then that eventually both the general culture and the unique situation or circumstances that surround the child help shape, direct, or focus that child's talent potential.

DEVELOPMENTAL CONSISTENCIES

Simonton's (1975) historical analyses of eminent persons from 500 B.C. through 1900 A.D. suggest that certain cultural and national patterns and trends are related to attaining eminence in various fields. Using the statistical procedures of path analysis and factor analysis, Simonton identified two major types of eminent creative individuals: (1) the discursive type, including those in fields such as science, philosophy, literature, and music; and (2) the presentational type, including those in the fields of painting, sculpture, and architecture.

Simonton found certain developmental consistencies among most of history's original creators. Eminent philosophers and artists were found to have grown up and have been most productive in social systems that were relatively stable and accommodated many different points of view. There usually was no powerful role model for those achieving high levels of eminence, although lesser thinkers and musicians apparently produced better if they had worked with mentors. Formal education was related to creative eminence to a point; however, higher levels of education seemed to stifle creativity. Political and social leaders were found to be versatile, dabbling in several disciplines while excelling in no particular area. Amount of education was found to be unrelated to attaining leadership positions.

There was one other noteworthy finding: sensitivity, integration, and creation are essential elements in achieving eminence or mastery in the arts. Philosophy, literature, and the arts flourish where diversity of thought exists, although those who excel in these areas require a relatively stable government for maximum accomplishments.

In examining Nobel prize winners and nominees, we have found that since 1900, eminent scientists have become less creative *as individuals* and less independent in their scientific pursuits. This change is explained in part because the achievement of "scientific breakthroughs" requires that scientists first master all the "known" knowledge before moving beyond to the "unknown." In addition to assimilating vast amounts of scientific knowledge, they must be able to manage sophisticated laboratories and must also supervise technical staffs.

An examination of Nobel prize winners clearly demonstrates that eminence in areas such as music, philosophy, poetry, and prose are international in scope, while the Soviet Union and the United States have become increasingly dominant in physics and physiology or medicine. Chemistry has seemingly captured the attention of scientists in Europe and the United States. Although historical analyses indicate that creative and scientific achievement are not limited by geographical or geopolitical boundaries, a review of the Nobel prizes awarded in science suggests that the concentration of a country's resources can affect individual accomplishments.

It seems apparent that better instructional methods must be discovered and implemented in order to shorten the period required to learn and accumulate the knowledge needed for scientific productivity. Unless there is some change in this area, scientists will spend their lives accumulating knowledge with little time left for being productive. Scientific practitioners (engineers and physicians, for example) would benefit as much as theoretical scientists from a system that allows for increased learning efficiency. Edison is quoted as saying that discovery is ninety-nine percent perspiration and one percent inspiration. If this was true in the early 1900s, one can only hypothesize that the contribution made by inspiration has shrunk even further by the 1980s.

Where do we find those with the potential to become eminent scientists, artists, and leaders? Do we continue to hope that a few of these people will naturally emerge or can society create an environment in which thousands of potentially "eminent" persons will eventually become productive? Of course, there is reason to believe that eminence is valued only if it remains a rare commodity. Interestingly, as the world's population has doubled and doubled again, and as the number of literate persons has multiplied, there has been no corresponding increase in the number of eminent persons as measured by the number *nominated* for Nobel prizes. The number of nominees has remained consistent, even though the number of persons and organizations making nominations has increased greatly in recent years.

Not all children who learn faster or are more creative than their peers will achieve the kind of eminence recognized by some international standard such as the Nobel prize. What about those young people who are exceptional but not marked for eminence? As society becomes more intricate and interdependent, and as social and environmental problems and solutions take on life or death consequences, our survival as a species may depend on large numbers of creative persons pooling their talents. Moreover, as changes in social organizations and institutions come thick and fast, even coping with change will require a higher level of individual, intellectual, and interpersonal skill.

TALENT DEVELOPMENT IN A PLURALISTIC SOCIETY

The United States, and other pluralistic societies with one dominant subculture, present a variety of challenges in defining and nurturing the talented among all its subcultures. Before focusing on talent potential as manifested within the specific subcultures, let's look at academic achievement orientation among different subcultures in the United States. Banks, McQuater, and Hubbard (1978) have critiqued and summarized the research on divergent patterns of achievement in whites and blacks. Although similar analyses have not been conducted among Mexican-American, Puerto Rican, and American Indian populations, the conclusions seem applicable for all children who are not middle-class whites.

These investigators found that the relationship between interest in the learning task and achievement orientation in blacks has not been the subject of much research. Citing a number of motivational studies, they conclude that high interest increases effort. Educators and curriculum builders are reminded that children whose early developmental experiences occur within a distinct subculture are likely to develop some interest patterns that differ from those seen in children raised in the dominant subculture.

An additional finding has major implications for educators. In controlled experiments, approval of black experimenters (teachers) more favorably affected performance of black pupils than did approval of white experimenters (teachers). The results of another study by Banks, Stitle, Curtis, and McQuater (1977) suggest that when a black child's initial interest toward a task is positive, the support or attention of a white teacher lowers the child's interest in achievement. Conversely, black students receiving support from black teachers were found to maintain their level of interest in achievement. It can be inferred that children from the black subculture, and probably from other minority subcultures, have learned to doubt the sincerity of white persons if they are supportive. Meanwhile, they expect hostility or apathy from white teachers and this may even serve to motivate the nonwhite child to achieve. In effect, the black child learns in spite of or to spite the white teacher. This finding has far-reaching implications for school staffing. However, what children learn is often not what the teacher intended or the curriculum was designed to teach.

At GIFTS we have begun to confront the issues involved in understanding multicultural talent, and we would like to share some of what we have learned. Our primary objective is to help students maintain or acquire a realistic belief in their ability to control their achievement behavior and develop the skills needed to successfully pursue their educational and occupational goals. Research has demonstrated that children from "minority" cultures judge their ability and effort as less important than luck when explaining their scholastic success (Frieze, et al., 1975). Females are generally more likely than males to attribute failure to a lack of ability and attribute their success to luck (Nicholls, 1975). These two findings suggest that minority students, females in particular, may perform below their potential in the classroom because they believe scholastic success is beyond their control, regardless of how much effort they put forth. On the other hand, achieving white males are more likely to attribute scholastic success to their own ability and hard work and are therefore more likely to be motivated to continue trying harder.

THE IMPORTANCE OF A BROAD BACKGROUND

The dominant cultural values and the more specific ethnic and community values create parameters within which children develop their potential. While luck and the existence of specific resources do play a large part in achieving eminence, a child's quest to know and understand and the drive toward mastery can be instilled or blunted by the family, teachers, peers, and members of the community. Education is not concerned with changing genetic functioning (although advances in applied pharmacology suggest brain functioning can be altered). Rather, it is the function of education to provide students with knowledge, facilitate student self-understanding and direction, foster social understanding, unlock human potential, and motivate achievement.

Children with talent potential should have an opportunity to develop across the arts, the sciences, and literature. Premature concentration in one area may prevent individuals from developing the broad base of experience they need prior to intelligently focusing their potential. For example, the potentially talented young person who is prematurely focused by others would ultimately be handicapped in career decision making.

A well planned, comprehensive exposure across the arts, sciences, and humanities increases the likelihood that those with talent potential may discover the focus that best fits their cognitive style. They may be able to capitalize on their self-directed orientation to more effectively participate in planning the area they will pursue in greater depth.

Anne Roe (1931) concluded from her study of eminent physical and social scientists that everyone she studied seemed motivated to excel due to some negative aspect in their family lives. In effect, it appeared that achievement was a compensatory behavior. She asked if there isn't a better way to achieve excellence than to be driven or pushed to excel.

We believe there is a better way—through self-direction. This in turn implies being knowledgeable and having the social and psychological freedom to act in a manner that is personally satisfying and socially meaningful.

IMPLICATIONS

In conclusion, the information presented in this chapter has several major implications for the socializing of talented and potentially talented individuals.

1. Talented and potentially talented individuals do not always behave in predictable, socially acceptable ways. This can be due to many factors, including their being better able to deal with their physical, social, and intellectual environments than their contemporaries. This surplus ability

enables and often encourages these individuals to strive for higher-level goals than might be ordinarily expected.

2. Talented and potentially talented individuals can expect to have different values than their contemporaries. Throughout their lives their instrumental and terminal values probably will be different from those of their peers.

3. Growing up in advantageous environments will help all individuals realize their potential and should allow talented and potentially talented persons to achieve even more. The less personal energy needed to meet lower-level needs, the more energy can be applied to the fulfillment of potential.

4. Talented and potentially talented persons need an internal locus of control if they are to achieve their potential. They must be "free" enough from external constraints and pressures to develop original, new, or expanded products. To go beyond prescribed limits, individuals must perceive they have achieved personal mastery. However, a sense of personal mastery and independence may lead to negative social responses by others.

5. Talented or potentially talented persons may have a strong need to understand nature. This quest can become a problem, since they are often not concerned with fitting in or being accepted by others. If there is little or no flexibility in parents' and educators' attitudes and behaviors, this also may encourage the gifted to resist being enculturated or socialized.

6. As the levels of human knowledge increase, there are greater amounts and levels of knowledge that must be mastered before those with potential can achieve noteworthy accomplishments. We need new methods for earlier identification of talent potential and for nurturing development of talent.

7. Communication and combined effort among talented individuals will probably be necessary if significant social and scientific advancements are to continue. Cooperation may prove problematic since talented individuals have normally prospered by "going their own way." Social responsibility, social skills, and appreciation of others should become important components in educating the talented and potentially talented.

8. Talented and potentially talented persons who are outside the cultural or ethnic mainstream experience special obstacles in their development due to lack of understanding, support, and stimulation. This area deserves special attention in order to avoid wasting valuable human resources.

9. Most children require a broad range of experiences in order to properly focus their potential. If others insist on premature concentration in one area of endeavor, this may hinder a potentially talented person from full realization of personal capabilities.

REFERENCES

Banks, W. C., et al. Perceived objectivity and the effect of evaluative reinforcement upon compliance and self-evaluation of blacks. *Journal of Experimental Social Psychology*, 1977, *13*, 452–462.

Banks, W. C., McQuater, G. V., & Hubbard, J. L. Toward a reconceptualization of the social-cognitive bases of achievement orientations in blacks. *Review of Educational Research*, 1978, *43*(3), 381–397.

Frieze, I., et al. Attributing the causes of success and failure: Internal and external behaviors to achievement in women. *Paper at Conference on New Directions for Research on Women*, 1975, Madison, Wisconsin.

Nicholls, J. G. Casual attributions and other achievement-related cognitions: Effects of task outcome, attainment values and sex. *Journal of Personality*, 1975, *31*, 379–389.

Roe, A. *The making of a scientist*. New York: Dodd & Mead, 1931.

Rokeach, M. *The nature of human values*. New York: Free Press, 1973.

Simonton, D. K. Interdisciplinary creativity over historical time: A correlational analysis of general fluctuations. *Social Behavior and Personality*, 1975, *3* (2).

Chapter 4

Natural Manifestations of Talent Potential

In this chapter we identify some major intellectual and personality dimensions of children and adolescents with talent potential. We attempt to accomplish this by presenting symptomatic behaviors with brief descriptions of some accompanying psychological effects.

The term *symptom* is used in this chapter as it is defined in *Webster's New Collegiate Dictionary:* "2a: something that indicates the existence of something else" (1973, p. 1181). In this chapter we have attempted to illustrate how some behaviors can be indicative of talent potential in accord with the definitions of talent presented in previous chapters.

There are several dangers in developing a list of behaviors that characterize persons with talent potential. First, any of the listed behaviors, by itself, can be descriptive of almost any person at one time or another. Moreover, it is not possible to communicate the emotional intensity that accompanies the behavior or the extent to which the behavior dominates the individual's being. Second, symptoms can be deceiving, since symptomatic behavior can be learned. For example, shortly after "Sputnik" schools were filled with "bored" children because boredom was then considered a major symptom of giftedness. Many children had quickly caught on to the value of acting bored whenever they did not want to do something. Third, symptomatic lists cannot be inclusive. Therefore, each list is at best a representative sample of possible behaviors that are symptomatic of talent potential. This caution is particularly relevant when seeking to identify talented youngsters in multicultural communities.

After reading these cautions it may seem better to avoid such lists altogether. Unfortunately, when discussing talent potential it is necessary to rely on bits and pieces of symptomatic behavior because the individual's talent has not yet been crystallized into easily recognizable behaviors. In order to avoid adding just another list of behaviors, or symptoms, to the literature, and to provide some necessary clarification, we have discussed the etiology of many listed behaviors. This list of symptoms will serve readers best if it broadens their understanding of talent potential and if they can relate these symptoms to one or more of the six characteristics that define talent, as discussed previously.

SYMPTOMS OF TALENT POTENTIAL

The following 27 points describe individuals with talent potential.

1. Intellectually curious; inquisitive; questioning.
2. Intellectually assertive; raises underlying questions as original "surface level" questions are answered.
3. Intellectually restless; not satisfied with present or current understanding; seeks to make finer discriminations and broader, more encompassing generalizations.
4. Physically restless; fine motor coordination and attention span often lag behind conceptualization level. Impatience and frustration result when the individual cannot get all faculties to appropriately attend to the task at hand.
5. Frustration and impatience with written forms of expression. This often occurs when a lack of fine motor skills prevents a child from writing as clearly or as rapidly as she or he can think or verbalize. Children with talent potential are often oriented to auditory and visual memorization and forsake notetaking because it interferes with the efficiency of their learning process. This can ultimately have serious consequences in college or professional school.
6. Usually comfortable working alone if the environment has been stimulating and supportive. The individual can be aloof from the immediate surroundings and particularly likes to observe or study insects, animals, plants, and the forces of nature, including the sea and wind.
7. Dominates peers intellectually; seeks to establish a mentor relationship with younger children; frustrated when others do not comprehend as readily or as conclusively.
8. May experience informational overload in that there is no regulatory system (values or opportunity to test validity of input) to stem informational flow or help synthesize and integrate input with existing information. Storage of conflicting and overlapping information may impede efficiency of recall and subsequent behavior.
9. Learning is frequently indiscriminate or unfocused. Frequently, the initial source or sources of stored information must be recalled prior to behaving, making recall cumbersome and difficult.
10. The individual and others may confuse the storing of considerable amounts of information (memory) with wisdom or having tested the value

of the stored information. Equating knowing a great deal with knowing how to act wisely places the individual in a precarious position. What would be considered trial behavior for others is judged as finalized behavior, and many gifted individuals suffer from being judged on the basis of one-trial learning. This phenomenon helps explain why children with talent potential are sometimes reluctant to take risks.

11. There is a tendency to be attracted to authoritarian persons. In the early stages of learning, the expertise or authority of the information source gives the information credibility in the learner's mind, especially when no internal evaluation criteria have been developed and the value of the input cannot be tested (applied) to establish its validity. In this circumstance, absolutes are more comforting or attractive than relative or comparative thoughts and ideas.

12. Effective use of mental imagery (equated with right hemispheric functioning) and the use of more than one sensory access system may cause individuals to develop a quality, quantity, and complexity of knowledge that tends to confuse and overwhelm them. In this situation it is helpful if gifted individuals can discuss the significance of what they know with another person and receive feedback.

13. Processing of linear information (equated with left hemispheric functioning) at a rate more rapid than the rate at which information is being presented detracts from the individual's attentiveness. This distraction may manifest itself as boredom, restlessness, and even disrespect or impoliteness. Frequently, the resulting behavior is interpreted to mean the child already knows the area being taught. However, evidence suggests that talented adolescents frequently lack certain fundamental knowledge and skills. Therefore, it is important to understand how to synchronize the rate of presentation with the rate of acquisition. It is also necessary to continually assess whether a child understands the information being presented as well as the information that preceded it.

14. Indiscriminate feedback (for example, almost always receiving a "good" or "excellent" evaluation no matter what the behavior) precludes learning to effectively differentiate among levels of performance. A lack of opportunities to test limits also interferes with establishing discriminatory learning goals. In essence, learning becomes an ambiguous experience, almost a frightening experience, due to the lack of meaningful limits and feedback. For a child who may be uncertain of his or her identity and direction, terms like self-actualization and self-realization are threatening. "Being all that one is capable of being" reads well but can cause panic in a child who lacks built-in direction finders. Children with talent potential run the risk of becoming indiscriminate information seekers, believing that more is better; they strive for A's with no emphasis on mastery or self-direction.

15. Unable to test limits, receiving indiscriminate feedback, and receiving direction primarily from outside sources, the potentially talented youngster is precluded from making the personal investment required to become intensely involved in learning.

16. Being conditioned to believe that everything *can* be learned may become equated with believing that everything *must* be learned. The individual may later equate choosing between courses of action, usually the result of time restraints, as evidence of personal failure. These individuals often view themselves as being able to do everything well; poor performance in any area may result in their being labeled as failures by themselves and others.

17. Often these individuals receive intense emotional support from members of their family. A teacher's inability to provide the same level of emotional attention may be interpreted by the pupil as rejection. This in turn may lead the child to resort to a variety of attention-seeking or withdrawal behaviors. Attention-seeking behaviors may turn off or aggravate the teacher, who in turn will often label the child hyperactive. Such a label reduces any dissonance the teacher experiences regarding his or her inability or unwillingness to do more for the child. This problem is often exacerbated by a lack of communication between parents and teachers.

18. Intellectual development or rate of information acquisition (as hypothetically measured by an intelligence test) is frequently equated with level of conceptual development. Conceptual development depends on the attainment level and integration of an individual's social, physical, and intellectual modes. Unless the social, physical, and intellectual aspects are accelerated uniformly (at least a 50–60 percent overlap), the individual is likely to experience internal imbalance or dissonance. Unfortunately the intelligence test (IQ) is used by both parents and the school, often in a power play, to say whether the child is special. This limits the meaning of talent potential and severely limits the kind of unique learning experiences the child will be provided.

19. Terman's studies (1959) of 50 years ago, and subsequent follow-up studies, promote the conclusion that talented children, who we view differently than those with talent potential, are healthy, happy, and socially well adjusted. This has encouraged the pervasive stereotype that those with talent potential are accelerated in all aspects of their development and can take care of themselves. Quite the contrary. While some children with talent potential seem to progress in an accelerated manner along physical, social, and intellectual dimensions of development, rarely are all three aspects accelerated simultaneously. Many children we see in GIFTS manifest accelerated development in only one dimension, usually the intellectual. Only a few evidence accelerated development in both

intellectual and social areas. If identification occurs for the first time as late as ninth grade, we find the students are either well rounded and not particularly exceptional in anything, or are very exceptional in the intellectual dimension.

20. High-achieving children, particularly those who are well behaved, may be the recipient of so much praise and reward that they do not acquire the capacity for either self-motivation or self-reward. In essence, the individual becomes controlled by others, usually well-intended people, who frequently fail to recognize the significance of self-control and self-reward.

21. Reasoning, logic, and memorization may be valued to the exclusion of emotional development or the understanding of feelings. In fact, feelings and emotions are frequently suppressed in the mistaken belief they interfere with learning and productivity. This imbalance often creates the stereotypical "egghead" or "computer personality," sometimes to the exclusion of creative and energetic thought. The resulting imbalance often heightens feelings of being different or odd. It is not unusual for children with talent potential to begin masking their potential in fourth grade and sometimes earlier. Interviews with young children have led us to hypothesize that toward the end of third grade, the need to find approval and acceptance among peers rivals and begins to exceed the need to satisfy parents and teachers. By fourth grade, peer approval and the values and attitudes of peers become very significant guides to behavior. Children who realize their talent potential must come to terms with adult and peer influence and control in order to achieve self-direction.

22. Abstract or book learning is valued over learning from or trusting direct experience. Only what is taught and graded by others is perceived as having worth or importance, blunting the opportunity to learn from experiences outside the classroom.

23. An orientation develops in which competition and accumulation of information are regarded more highly than mastery. Failure anywhere along the line in any endeavor is likely to produce a negative self-concept and lowered expectations and aspirations. An orientation that values personal mastery would likely increase the individual's motivation to acquire additional knowledge or skills when frustrated and would encourage the individual to use a more divergent approach to solving a task or problem. A divergent orientation is often poorly received in an achievement-oriented society.

24. Accelerated conceptual development increases the likelihood that the individual will become aware of death or finiteness earlier than peers. This heightened "future" awareness gives gifted individuals a time perspective that is qualitatively different from that of their more "present-ori-

ented'' peers. If the child also has a vivid memory of past events and a keen sense of history, it can be expected that all the child's thinking and behavior will be influenced by this simultaneous awareness of three time dimensions. Those individuals with accelerated development, those who understand finiteness and value the past, must necessarily process information through a more elaborate system than individuals who process each input primarily in terms of its immediate context. This being the case, responses or behavior may seem odd or out of place, requiring the individual with talent potential to painstakingly explain what initially seemed relevant and attractive. The child does not have to endure many of these explanatory experiences before voluntarily limiting the number of spontaneous public responses. Unfortunately, in having to mask one's public behavior, considerable creative and productive energy is lost.

25. Conceptual, social, or intellectual differences with one's peers may lead to isolation. This often prevents the individual from having someone with whom she or he can discuss feelings of being different or of being dominated and wanting independence. Many precocious children experience long periods of depression brought about in part by their social isolation from peers.

26. Accelerated conceptual development can result in early decisions regarding accelerated grade placement, independent study, or intensive lessons in the arts. These decisions are usually made by adults with the best interests of the child in mind. It should be recognized, however, that the child does not usually participate in the decision, and maybe does not even understand why the decision was made. Most of the decisions made regarding the child's education reflect the values of parents and teachers without fully appreciating the child's views. Many children and adolescents have expressed their dislike for continually being faced with acceleration in a particular subject area as a ''reward'' for their prior success or achievements. Often children will consciously or unconsciously reduce their level of performance in order to avoid being programmed for further accelerated study. Such defensive, self-protecting behavior can become self-defeating if it is not recognized and treated early. Both the child and others may have to compromise.

27. School becomes an end in itself rather than a means of achieving personal and career goals. Grades can become a measure of self-worth. The likelihood of creating a perpetual student, one for whom others are responsible for organizing the input and evaluating the performance, becomes a distinct possibility.

This list could, of course, be extended. We encourage readers to draw upon their own experiences and include other symptomatic behaviors and motives that characterize children with talent potential.

While our list presents some of the major intellectual and personality characteristics of young people with talent potential, a list format at best presents behaviors in sketched, segmented pieces. We would like to put some of these pieces into a chronological framework to give the reader a context for understanding and assisting children and adolescents with talent potential.

A CHRONOLOGY OF SYMPTOMATIC BEHAVIORS

The accelerated intellectual development of potentially talented children allows them to conceptualize the world differently than agemates. For example, while most first graders are learning to read, write, and print, those with talent potential may be creating and writing stories and using resources like the dictionary. While other first graders are learning the number system and learning to add, gifted children may be developing math games. And while others are playing the usual playground games, talented children may be devising new games and adding new wrinkles to old games.

In the early grades, it is likely that potentially talented children will get along well with teachers and peers because their accelerated development requires relatively little special attention or extra instructional resources. Their development will, however, suffer if they receive no special attention or instruction. In many instances, these pupils will be widely accepted because they enhance the enjoyment of school for other pupils and teachers.

As these potentially talented children progress through the grades, their accelerated development is likely to foster behavior that increasingly sets them apart from their peers. And as a result, they begin to require resources that extend beyond the classroom. They need to draw upon a larger universe of ideas and people in order to feed their developing emotional and intellectual appetites.

As the developmental gap between them and their peers widens, some will begin to make greater demands on the teacher's time. Some pupils with talent potential may thus be viewed by others as selfish or demanding. If these demands occur at a time when agemates are still relatively deferent and obedient, the gifted children may be viewed negatively by teachers, peers, and parents.

Second graders who enjoy chess, crossword puzzles, and other relatively complex games will grow impatient with agemates who are unable to play these games. When the gifted child expresses this impatience, other children may be further alienated because those with talent potential often have not developed the social skills necessary for expressing their disapproval in an acceptable manner.

If the pupil's accelerated development is not to be frustrated or thwarted, it is important that students be allowed to learn and to behave in ways appropriate to their developmental stage. For example, a gifted fourth-grade student may need to apply knowledge that other fourth graders do not yet comprehend.

An even more difficult problem relates to accelerated affective or emotional development. Since a large portion of affective and social development is dependent on peer and teacher acceptance and recognition, many potentially talented students are likely to be frustrated or prevented from continuing at an accelerated rate of development because they do not receive the acceptance and recognition they crave.

Development is even more complex in the middle grades. At this point students with talent potential are moving toward independence in a manner that is more characteristic of teenagers. These independence-seeking behaviors may prove odious to adults, and are often sufficiently misguided to offend peers as well. Like teenagers seeking independence, talented children need peer support, but agemates are developmentally unable to provide it.

At the high school level, talent potential may become crystallized and focused as individuals have worked through their separation from adults, established a sense of identity, and developed personal value structures. Meanwhile, agemates are working on separation problems. The gifted are again out of step. Their behavior is now likely to be approved by adults but *disapproved* by peers. If they maintain adult approval, they may have problems with peers. If peer approval is valued, trouble may arise with adults.

Potentially talented students should achieve psychological autonomy in advance of agemates. With the development of an internal frame of reference, they will want to chart a more personalized course, one that teachers may have trouble accepting. Self-directed students need less *external* direction and stimulation and more opportunities to pursue their personal goals.

It is important to distinguish between stimulation and motivation. Stimulation can be defined as that which is provided externally by others. Motivation, on the other hand, is intrinsic or controlled by the individual. Motivation is the calling of one's self to action. It should be apparent that there is the possibility, even the probability, of conflict occurring between a motivated student and the demands of educators and parents who assume students have to be stimulated and rewarded.

Knowledge, developing an internal frame of reference, and being motivated are essential ingredients of creativity. Failure to recognize and nurture the accelerated developmental needs of talented and potentially talented pupils will probably result in a waste of creative potential so desperately needed to meet the challenges of human existence.

In order to understand and plan interventions based on a person's level of accelerated development, we have found it beneficial to subscribe to the concepts underlying developmental stage theory. Stage theory maintains that entry into a different stage of development precipitates changes in information processing, methods of relating to the environment, and criteria for evaluating one's behavior. Movement from one developmental level into a higher stage necessitates more complex functioning and a more sophisticated understanding of self in relation to society. Providing a stimulating, psychologically supportive environment, in conjunction with a healthy physical environment, will in turn foster higher levels of development. As persons with talent potential mature, their behavior becomes increasingly effective and efficient; this sets them apart from their agemates. Even when considering acceleration, it is important to note that the method of instruction should be qualitatively different because the individual will be operating at a higher motivational and conceptual level than previously.

THEORIES OF DEVELOPMENT

A primary goal of all social institutions, and education in particular, is to help individuals acquire coping skills needed to function in society as it is and adaptability skills needed to function in a changing society. When we refer to a person's developmental functioning, several psychosocial dimensions are involved. We have chosen to examine a few. We will explore their relationship to one another and their relationship to the goals of education. Specifically we are examining the relationships among:

- Loevinger's (1976) Theory of Ego Development
- Maslow's (1975) Theory of Human Motivation (Need Hierarchy)
- Land's (1972) Stages of Growth Processes Based on Systems Theory
- Kohlberg's (1969) Moral Stages (Motivation for Learning)
- Samples' (1976) Hierarchical Description of the Metaphoric Mind
- Bloom's (1975) Taxomony of Cognitive and Affective Educational Objectives

We have arranged the fundamental components of each writer's work on the accompanying chart (Figure 4-1) with an eye to achieving "horizontal" congruence. That is, when reading the chart from left to right, we have placed compatible dimensions from the various contributors on the horizontal, separated by a broken or solid line. We have arranged the various psychosocial dimensions beginning with ego development (Loevinger) on the left, moving to motivation (Maslow, Kohlberg), then to growth processes (Land), and to conceptual development (Samples), and ending with educational objectives (Bloom et al., 1974) on the extreme right.

We think several things become apparent when studying the chart. The bold horizontal lines should draw your attention to stages where significant developmental changes must occur if growth is to take place. We hypothesize that before crossing the lowest solid line and moving into the next highest stage, individuals who accomplish cognitive and affective educational objectives

Figure 4-1 Stage Theories of Development

LOEVINGER'S THEORY OF EGO DEVELOPMENT	MASLOW'S THEORY OF HUMAN MOTIVATION	LAND GROWTH PROCESSES	KOHLBERG'S MORAL STAGES/ MOTIVATION FOR LEARNING
INTEGRATED Understanding of life's complexities	SELF-ACTUALIZATION Being all that one can be. Essential to have freedom to explore, to speak, to search & to know.	IV. TRANSFORMATION-SELF-ACTUALIZATION Destroy in order to create (Positive Disintegration). Giving up what is comfortable & rewarding in order to create a new "gestalt."	SELF-ACTUALIZATION Universal ethics—justic, equality, dignity as individuals.
AUTONOMOUS Acknowledge and cope with inner conflict about responsibilities and needs. Beginnings of striving for self-fullfillment.	SELF-RESPECT/ESTEEM Based upon actual achievement & recognition from others.	III. MUTUALITY Accomodating differences in the environment which are not subject to influence & expanding the environment making of *Hybrids*.	ESTEEM Examined individual rights prevail.
CONSCIENTIOUS Adult conscience. Long term goals evaluated by personal values. Ruler of own destiny. Time perspective.			Oriented toward authority, duty.
CONFORMIST Welfare identified with group. Obeys rules, disapproval feared. Perceives others in stereotypes. Behavior externally evaluated.	LOVE, AFFECTION, BELONGINGNESS NEEDS Looking to others for satisfaction both to give & receive. Being accepted for what one is & what one does.	II. POWER Through processes of influence & being influenced inevitably "using up the environment" which can be integrated through the power process. Making modifications in form but not basic functions.	Conformity for social approval.
SELF-PROTECTIVE Anticipation of reward Recognition of rules, manipulative use of rules.			PSYCHOLOGICAL SECURITY Essentially satisfying one's own needs.
IMPULSIVE Present oriented; Aggressive seeking of immediate gratification.

PRESOCIAL Differentiation of self from others. | SAFETY (Security Needs) A safe, orderly, predictable world.

Physiological needs are not met routinely (food, shelter) | I. DISSONANCE REDUCTION Connection between disorder & order through *Dominance* & absorption. If successful, a pattern of order—An identity is Discovered. Patterned Identity produces Likenesses & connects to Likenesses. Enlarge an idea or change in scale.

Competitive. | PHYSICAL Physical consequences determine goodness & badness. |

(Read Figure across two pages.)

SAMPLES METAPHORIC MIND	BLOOM'S TAXONOMY OF EDUCATION OBJECTS	AFFECTIVE
INVENTIVE MODE The mind uses existing knowledge to create objects & processes that have never existed. There is a total synergic combination of external and/or internal qualities with no link to precedence. *All metaphoric & rational modes may contribute.*	COGNITIVE 6.00 Evaluative 6.10 In terms of internal evidence 6.20 In terms of external criteria.	Self-Actualization 5.0 Characteristic Behavior 5.1 Internal consistency at particular moment 5.2 Universal view, philosophy of life.
INTEGRATIVE MODE Personal analogy, becoming something. Total immersion, e.g., becoming a fall-feeling, sensing the way a ball rolls, bounces, etc.	5.00 Synthesis 5.10 Produce unique communication 5.20 Produce a plan 5.30 Derive set of abstract relations	*Social Recognition & Self-Esteem* 4.0 Organization 4.1 Comparing 4.2 Ordering
	2.30 Extrapolate 3.00 Application (use) 4.00 Analysis 4.10 Elements in communication 4.20 Relationships 4.30 Organizational principle	*Self-Acceptance* 3.0 Valuing 3.1 Acception 3.2 Preferring 3.3 Committing
COMPARATIVE MODE Direct analogy such as "a city is like a heart, one pulse beat in the morning when corpuscles (traffic) flow out."	2.00 Comprehension 2.10 Preserving original communication 2.20 Interrupt, explain or summarize	*Accepted by Others* 2.0 Responding 2.2 Willingness 2.3 Satisfaction from responding
SYMBOLIC MODE: Substitution of symbols for natural realities, e.g., I-90 for a four-lane road running from Chicago to Minneapolis.	1.11 K terminology (symbols with concrete referents) 1.12 Specific facts 1.20 K ways to organize, study, judge & criticize 1.21 K conventional ways 1.22 K trends & sequences 1.23 K classification & categories 1.24 K criteria for testing facts, opinions, conduct 1.25 K inquiry methodology 1.30 K Universal 1.31 Principles & Generalizations 1.32 Theories & Structures	*Affective Domain:* *Security* 1.0 Receiving 1.1 Awareness 1.2 Willingness to receive 1.3 Selective attention
	1.00 Knowledge 1.10 Specific bits of information	

(Bloom) must also attain the concrete level of ego development (Loevinger), master the symbolic mode (Samples), be psychologically secure, trusting, and autonomous (Maslow, Kohlberg), and be ready to move beyond the growth processes involving dominance and absorption (Land). New needs and new growth processes should emerge and should be satisfied along with corresponding changes in cognitive development. These changes in turn require that attention be paid to helping the individual achieve higher educational objectives in a balanced or congruent manner.

We would like to put forth two additional hypotheses. One, that considerable growth potential exists in the higher levels of the metaphoric mind described by Samples. Such growth requires a learning environment that reflects the motivational atmosphere (self-respect, self-actualization, generativity) described by Maslow and Kohlberg. The growth processes would be mutuality and transformation (Land), which parallel achieving the highest educational objectives outlined by Bloom.

Second, transition points represented by bold lines should become focal points for psychosocial education within the educational system. For example, movement beyond the lowest levels of ego development (impulsive and self-protective levels) into the next higher level of ego development (conformist level) requires considerable personal confidence (risk taking). Before becoming more in tune with the society (conformist level), the individual may again need assistance in breaking somewhat free from society's conventions (conscientious level) in order to understand and deal with the contradictions of life. Moving into the highest level of ego development requires another significant transition, in which one learns to trust self, deal effectively with the stresses associated with a heightened awareness of self, and recognize a person's responsibility to self and others within a social context fraught with contradictions.

The list of developmental characteristics and concerns, the chronology of symptomatic behavior, and the brief discussion of stage theory as presented in this chapter are intended to provoke further thought and increase the reader's understanding of potentially talented individuals. No attempt has been made to discuss remedies or intervention strategies. This topic is the major focus of Section II of this book.

REFERENCES

Bloom, B. S. *Taxonomy of educational objectives—Handbook II: Affective domain* (rev. ed.). New York: David McKay Co., 1974.

Bloom, B. S. (Ed.). *Taxonomy of educational objectives—Handbook I: Cognitive domain* (rev. ed.). New York: David McKay Co., 1975.

Kohlberg, L. Stage and sequence: The cognitive-developmental approach to socialization. In D. A. Goslin (Ed.), *Handbook of socialization theory and research*. Chicago: Rand McNally, 1969.

Land, G. T. *Grow or die*. New York: Random House, 1972.

Loevinger, J. *Ego development*. San Francisco: Jossey-Bass, 1976.

Maslow, A. H. *Motivation and personality*. New York: Harper and Row, 1975.

Samples, B. *The metaphoric mind*. Reading, Mass.: Addison-Wesley Publishing Co., 1976.

Terman, L., & Oden, M. Genetic studies of genius. Vol. 5, The gifted group at mid life. Stanford, California: Stanford University Press, 1959.

Webster's new collegiate dictionary. Springfield, Mass.: G. & C. Merriam Co., 1973, p. 1181.

The Fulfillment of Developmental Potential in Talented Persons

In Chapter 5 we draw upon the biographies and autobiographies of eminent people to show how certain individuals have managed to achieve at least a measure of their potential despite or because of situations and circumstances that colored their developmental years.

Most of these people reached the zenith of their accomplishments in the first half of the twentieth century. Most were loners who persevered against great odds. The frontiers they were exploring, however, were primitive compared to the frontiers that confront us today. Nevertheless, we believe there is much to learn from these historical examples, even though it may be necessary to make some adaptations relevant to our own times.

In Chapter 6 we present 20 years in the lives of two individuals identified in ninth grade as superior students. The purpose here is to focus on how more contemporary, and less noteworthy, talented individuals live their lives and meet their unique needs. In Section Three we will draw upon the examples suggested by both the eminent and the high achievers in suggesting and outlining intervention strategies.

Chapter 5

The Resolution of Problems and Attainment of Goals by Eminent Persons

Chapters 2 and 3 explained human motivation in terms of Maslow's hierarchy of needs. This chapter includes a brief discussion of McClelland's research in the area of need achievement to supply a more specific focus on school-related motivation. Mastery, attribution, and serendipity are cited as factors essential to the realization of talent potential. We quote the words and cite the works of many eminent persons in order to provide a personal and comprehensive description of mastery and the results of motivation. We discuss attribution theory because we hypothesize that assuming ownership or responsibility for one's accomplishments and failures is an essential component in becoming self-motivated and self-directed. Finally, we take up the notion of serendipity. In explaining motivation and behavior, psychologists and sociologists may give the impression that all behavior is explainable and predictable. We shall see, however, that serendipity and chance are important factors in realizing one's potential and achieving eminence.

ACHIEVEMENT MOTIVATION

The human need to achieve, or for our purposes, the need to realize one's talent potential has been studied extensively by McClelland et al. (1953, 1978). McClelland maintains that a person is motivated to achieve in a particular situation when a discrepancy exists between his or her performance level and the expected level of performance. An individual's expectations are derived from previous experience and from personal beliefs. In a sense, individuals measure their performance against a set of personal standards they have acquired. In McClelland's operational definition, behavior is self-initiated either to avoid failure or to achieve success.

Persons also strive to improve their performance because of external rewards and to avoid punishment. It would be more appropriate to describe this latter behavior as being externally stimulated rather than motivated.

Atkinson and his fellow researchers (1957, 1966) have pursued a line of research that may have more significance for educators who design curriculum for potentially talented children and adolescents. They believe that the motive to succeed and the motive to avoid failure are equally powerful. Persons driven by a motive to succeed are likely to take risks when they perceive there is a reasonable chance of succeeding. Persons motivated by a fear of failure are unlikely to take risks; they prefer tasks in which they are either certain to succeed or are expected to fail.

Why would people motivated by fear of failure engage in a task that will almost certainly end in failure? The following example is offered as an explanation. Several years ago one of the authors designed a counseling program at the University of Wisconsin for second-year liberal arts undergraduates who were on final probation. Individuals on final probation had achieved less than a C average the two semesters of their freshmen year. Students were selected for the special counseling program if, based on their high school rank and College Board scores, they were predicted to have been able to achieve at least a C average in college.

These students were flunking out for a number of highly idiosyncratic reasons. Nevertheless, their self-defeating behavior could be generally attributed to their conscious choice of unrealistic career goals and their pursuit of university course work that was beyond their immediate capabilities. One student had flunked the same four-credit physics course the first two semesters and had registered for it again, even though it wasn't required, because his father had said anyone who couldn't pass college physics didn't deserve a college degree. The boy was convinced that he could not earn a college degree (on his father's terms), yet he insisted on taking a physics course he could not pass. He was literally programmed for failure. It took a great amount of support and confrontation to get him to redefine his goals in terms that were personally meaningful and achievable.

We also discovered that 54 or 55 of the 60 liberal arts students with whom we were working had identified their majors as either prelaw or premedicine. In actuality, the university did not have an undergraduate major in either field, nor was there a specified undergraduate program suggested by either the Law School or the School of Medicine. But even though these students had cumulative grade point averages ranging between 0.85 and 1.65 (on a 4.00 scale) for their first two semesters, and were unlikely to achieve a grade point that would give them access to either law or medicine, they insisted on holding to these career goals.

In our work with these individuals we tried to get them to establish lower, more realistic career goals; this meant they would have to accept responsibility (risk) for not achieving these more realistic goals. During the course of our interviews most of the students acknowledged that it was more acceptable to them and others if they failed in a "premed" or "prelaw" program because everyone knows how difficult these programs are. By setting achievable goals, and possibly not succeeding, *they* had to risk public and personal failure. Career counseling involved helping these students consider a succession of occupations, from the most academically demanding to those that were less demanding and were personally attainable. Every student who could abandon the "impossible dream" and accept the risk involved in setting attainable goals made it through a third semester of final probation, where less than a C or a 2.00 would have meant dismissal from the university. Moreover, every student who established attainable career goals graduated from the university, even though many changed the specific career goal in their junior or senior year. In subsequent follow-up studies, it was learned that two students had been admitted to law school—no longer an unattainable goal.

In our work with high-achieving secondary school students, we hear a constant complaint from teachers that these students will not enroll in a course if they are not sure of getting an A. Why should high-achieving students avoid taking an advanced calculus course or a course in literary criticism? Why should they fail to enroll in a university-level course that the school had made available? Why won't these high-achieving students take risks? It is our hypothesis that these students do not accept responsibility for their accomplishments or their achievements. In effect they attribute their success to luck or to other persons. They are not guided by feelings of mastery.

In our 20-year follow-up studies of high-achieving Wisconsin high school graduates, we find the vast majority graduated from college. Only after college graduation do they seriously begin to question their values and goals. We find these individuals are programmed, almost from birth, to think in terms of a college education. They are likely to pursue college majors that correspond closely to their best subjects in high school. If they continue to excel in these same areas in college, they try to turn these academic specialties into an occupation. At best, this is a narrow perspective for career planning.

Before describing how the concept of mastery or needing to know played a significant part in the attainment of eminent Americans, let's look briefly at Weiner's (1972) discussion of attribution based on Heider's work. In the second part of this book we detail intervention strategies where the basic objective is to help students attribute their success and failure to their own efforts and ability (or to luck and the failure of others when appropriate).

Heider's theory is based on the assumption that people want to understand the underlying cause of events in order to gain control over their world. The poetry of Robert Frost and the comments of Albert Einstein and others in this chapter suggest that these eminent creators and innovators are motivated mostly by a wish to understand the underlying cause of events; control is irrelevant to them. Possibly in postulating his theory Heider was thinking more in terms of the applied scientists. However, even inventors like Edison and Bell appear more taken with the challenge of conquering a technical problem than with the resulting product.

In his discussion of attribution Weiner describes four ways to explain achievement outcomes: effort, ability, luck, and task difficulty. Effort and ability are "owned" by the person, while luck and task difficulty are not. Weiner considers task difficulty and ability as relatively stable, whereas effort and luck are considered unstable. Since both task difficulty and one's own ability are colored by one's perceptions, it is conceivable that to the extent that perceptions can be modified, ability and task difficulty are subject to change. The self-concept studies would support this contention.

Within the perspective of attribution theory, the educational objective would be to help the individual acknowledge that his or her accomplishments are the product of personal effort and ability, rather than the result of luck and the ease of the task. Obviously luck can play a part, and if this idea is to have merit the tasks must be difficult enough for the individual to experience a real sense of mastery.

In our interviews with potentially talented elementary and secondary school students, we discovered a basic difference in attribution between females and males. Males are more apt to attribute their accomplishments to their own efforts and ability; females often cite luck, the fact that teachers like them, or the fact that the assignment was easy and everyone did well. At the secondary level we also discovered a "fear of success" syndrome existing among several females but not among males.

In our interviews and small group discussions with these students, it became apparent that some high school females felt that if they achieved high grades it would reflect negatively on their femininity. They feared high grades would cause them some social isolation and would pressure them to pursue a career *instead* of marriage and family. These feelings and attitudes were being expressed in "enlightened" educational communities in the 1980s. Parents, teachers, and peers—as well as media—have maintained or reinforced highly traditional, and we would add outmoded and unproductive sexual attitudes, values, beliefs, and stereotypes.

We have helped some school systems institute a rather simple technique for helping elementary school females attribute more of their achievements to their own efforts and ability. Teachers have been instructed to elaborate slightly on the typical written and oral comments they make regarding a female pupil's performance. Instead of simply writing "good," "excellent," or pasting a gold star at the top of a paper, teachers now say, "You did _____" or "The work you did is _____." This emphasizes that the work is a product of the child's own effort and ability. It should never be taken for granted that children with talent potential, particularly females, attribute their successful performance to their own efforts.

It bears repeating that excessive and indiscriminate rewards and praise from others, particularly if the individual's effort is ignored, makes it less likely that students will own their behavior and attribute their success to their own efforts and ability.

The research of Covington and Omelich (1979), Nicholls (1976), and Sohn (1977) suggests that individuals who attribute their success to their own ability are most likely to sustain achievement behavior. The biographies of eminent persons bear this out. Consider the years of sustained effort required by Edison and Bell to achieve significant scientific breakthroughs, and the years that Robert Frost struggled to perfect his style and achieve any recognition. Robert Frost earned less than $200 from his poetry during the first twenty years of his writing career. He must have had tremendous belief in his ability as well as a fixation on one task or mode of expression in order to sustain his effort for so long in the face of total societal disregard.

In a most comprehensive and stimulating article, Nicholls (1976) reminds us that the concepts of ability and task difficulty necessarily invite social comparison. Individuals conceptualize their own ability by making comparisons with their peers. Any elementary school teacher knows that every first grader recognizes the significance of being a member of a particular reading group, despite attempts by teachers to disguise these groups with cute names. Nicholls is concerned that when achievement and ability are based solely on social comparisons (which often results when distributing grades according to the normal curve), then invariably individuals with positive self-concepts achieve these concepts only at the expense of others. He suggests that this results in lower motivation, and hence still poorer achievement, by those with less ability. Furthermore, nearly everyone's self-concept becomes vulnerable as individuals move into more competitive situations. This dynamic operates not only in American education but in society in general.

What does Nicholls suggest? First, he recognizes that competition and survival or achievement of the fittest will persist because our society is structured after a pyramid with just so many spaces at the top. He argues that not all human endeavors nor all of education need be predicated on what an individual produces in comparison to others. He supports Kruglanski's (1975) contention that more emphasis should be placed on whether the individual enjoys or is satisfied with the activity or learning process.

Whether people enjoy the process is a most telling consideration. In our interviews with high-achieving students we have found that they frequently dislike doing assignments and perceive a good grade not as recognition for what was produced but rather as payment for having endured such a painful or dull experience. Good grades may in fact lead good students to resent formal learning, while poor grades combined with a dislike of the learning task may lead poor achievers to abhor formal learning.

One twelve-year-old boy we know labors silently and alone over school assignments that usually require highly specific learning behaviors. This is in contrast to the behavior he evidences when playing "Dungeons and Dragons," a game that is the current rage. In connection with this game he works for hours on tasks that could be described as mathematical and logical. He and his friend develop schemes to challenge one another. Learning the rules is a matter of reading and applying what is read. Highly energetic junior high school boys are comparatively quiet as they plot and draw and then meet to test their skills on one another. They revel in the battle or the process of the game, and winning is treated as an afterthought. The game requires that players develop a somewhat antiquated vocabulary. It also leads to a reading of medieval history and a heightened interest in probability. When learning or mastery can be fun as well as meaningful, motivation takes care of itself.

Will individuals persevere at tasks when their performance doesn't measure up to others? Individuals labor at great length to improve while recognizing that others, perhaps everyone they know, play or score better. Consider for a moment the handicap system in golf. This system firmly establishes not only a comparative performance standard but also a personal standard against which an individual competes or strives to improve. Everyone would like to shoot par or better, but failure to do so has not caused millions of people to quit playing golf. People keep striving, although half the time, by definition, they do not shoot their handicap.

Possibly if schools more openly accepted individual differences, and in addition to group standards (on a scale of 100 percent or par) provided individual performance standards (one's handicap), mastery would be within the reach of all students. This would address the question of motivation as well as classroom management concerns.

ABOUT THE VIGNETTES

We would like to conclude the introduction to this chapter by noting how various persons who achieved eminence during the early part of the twentieth century have defined mastery or what spurred them on. Few of these individuals suffered as a result of comparing their ability to peers. In fact, several grew up either isolated from age peers or indifferent to the accomplishments of others in school. This indifference may be the result of their having attended one-room schools where students ranged in age from six to twenty. In effect, instruction was individualized for each pupil.

Eminent persons have been selected to help explain how the quest for mastery motivates people to know and to produce. The direction this quest takes—whether it be science, literature, finance, education, art, or politics—seems to be largely dependent upon the times and circumstances in which the individual exists. By quoting from the biographies and autobiographies of these people, we hope to give the reader a perspective regarding what drives eminent Americans in eight broad areas of endeavor: art and architecture, literature, music, scientific theory, scientific inventions/development, letters and philosophy, politics/government, and business/finance.

A helpful preface to this chapter is provided in a book edited by Summerfield and Thatcher (1964), *The Creative Mind and Method*. In the introduction Bryson is quoted as saying

> Each of the arts is a way of communicating meanings which are uniquely suited to the particular form of expression the artist has chosen. . . . Creativity comes from discipline—from knowing the structure of one's existence—and mastering the form of expression. Knowing itself has become increasingly complex because so much has been brought forward to be recognized (p. 7).

Bryson has the following to say regarding creation.

> The greater the emphasis on producing quickly, on measuring to an external standard, the less likelihood of creativeness emerging. Creativeness must rise from within the individual—based on knowledge and skill in communicating. Historical understanding and vision is required. Contemporary man, living in and for the present, is in a situation which works against creation (p. 7).

ART AND ARCHITECTURE

In Summerfield and Thatcher's book (1964), artist Ben Shahn has the following to say regarding painting:

> Art, eventually, is a series of experiences upon a certain individual, given a certain amount of talent and ability. The output will be the result of all those experiences. It is dangerous for a young painter or sculptor to go through academic training first and then to start painting in their twenties. Personal critical faculties, facility of one's hand and ability of the eye to perceive should be developed in unison. Education

pursued in this manner should allow for freedom of expression and more importantly the integration which marks creative artists.

I discover as I paint—otherwise I would lose interest if I had a complete image and were only applying the colors as it were. I am not always ready or able to paint the vague sketches I work from. I keep my sketches because years later I find I may be ready to complete the work because I have acquired more life experience and skill.

As my memory builds I begin to rely less on photographs—at first I needed them. Young painters must go through a period of imitation. It takes a long time to express your personality. The greatest difficulty is producing what you think others will like—it is inconsistent for a creative artist to think about what others will like (Chapter 5).

It was necessary to search beyond the United States for biographical works on artists and sculptors. We have decided to discuss two popular European artists, Rodin and Picasso.

Auguste Rodin

In a biography of this eminent French sculptor by Champigneulle (1967), some of the following notations seem pertinent. Auguste did rather poorly in school. At age nine he was sent to his uncle's boarding school which was run like a detention home. He was a loner, and his teachers agreed that he was retarded. The only thing that appealed to him was drawing. After four years he was sent home from this school unable to read or write. Auguste's father was unsure how his illiterate son would earn a living. Auguste proved exceedingly stubborn, however, and insisted on pursuing art. Out of desperation his father enrolled him in art school where he performed fairly well until he chanced upon modeling class.

Rodin describes what occurred. "I began shaping parts of the body—then an entire figure. I grasped the whole thing in a flash, and I did so with as much facility as I do today. I was in transports" (p. 14). He made up his mind from that day to be a sculptor. He had a teacher-mentor who encouraged him. However, three times he was denied entry into the École des Beaux-Arts. Finally he quit trying to gain admission. Rejection spurred him on. He spent the next twenty years barely surviving, yet constantly producing. He lived for his work, not just for recognition, although by his own standards he wanted to achieve a level of mastery comparable to the great Italian sculptors.

For Rodin, it was imperative to work from living, moving, human models. His creative process included capturing motion and life in his mind's eye and translating these perceptions through his hands to his sketches and sculpture. The model provided but one element as he integrated several viewpoints in his work. His preliminary effort was to create movement. Movement and modeling were considered by Rodin to be the lifeblood of any great work.

Rodin's biographer hypothesizes that it was fortunate Rodin was not accepted into formal academic training at the Beaux-Arts, since his maturation as a sculptor would have been delayed or even denied. Rodin's works inspired controversy throughout his career. His methods and unconventional interpretations were not "up to the standards" of the time, yet his work has long been recognized as having exceptional merit.

Pablo Picasso

Penrose (1962) describes Picasso as a product of his community as well as his family. The biographer summarizes his work in this way:

> revealing the immense variety with which Picasso is able to display the drama between two opposite poles, comedy or gaiety and tragedy or suffering. Instead of becoming more refined as he aged and progressed, he managed to become more skillful in presenting the unselfconsciousness and originality of his first major work at age nine (p. 16).

Picasso could draw long before he could speak. It appears he had a photographic memory for detail and color. He grew up in a community where there was a fear of completing a task. People felt completion brought with it an unbearable finality resembling death. This feeling was symbolized by the city's cathedral which remained in an unfinished state for generations.

Picasso hated school, math in particular. Even rudimentary reading and writing gave him trouble. As an adult he admitted that he could not remember the sequence of the alphabet, but this did not bother him. Except for art, all his learning was left to chance. By age 12 he could paint better than his father, who taught art. The son's talent apparently caused the father to quit painting at this time. Picasso worked very rapidly. Given a month to complete the drawings required for admission to art school, he did so in one day. His work was held in such high esteem by the examiners that he began his formal training at the most advanced levels. Throughout his training he had a disregard for standard human proportions, although he could draw the human body very exactly if required to do so. As his reputation and economic security grew, he experimented more and more, finally incorporating his unique perspective that merged life and still form.

One cannot help but wonder what would happen to a Rodin or a Picasso in contemporary American schools and society. As young men both were poor, almost illiterate, stubborn and determined, wanting to pursue art in rather singular fashion, with a total disregard for social conventions.

It was interesting to discover that architects like to write about themselves and are willing to comment on almost all aspects of society, particularly education.

Frank Lloyd Wright

This eminent architect writes that his mother was a teacher, much taken with Froebel's system of teaching children to understand the system of design and elementary geometry behind all forms (Wright, 1943). His mother taught him through use of various art forms and by providing materials he could manipulate and learn from. She felt he was predestined to build beautiful buildings.

When Frank was 11, due to his health problems, the family moved from New England to Madison, Wisconsin. Summers were spent hardening him up on his uncle's farm, though he continually tried to run away. From September through May he lived near the University of Wisconsin campus on Lake Mendota. After a couple of summers he began to enjoy the farm and nature.

At age 16 he began studying engineering at the University of Wisconsin. He felt his university education was too abstract, too remote to be meaningful. The level of instruction seemed no different than high school. A few months before graduation he quit school and went to work for a series of Chicago architects, eventually taking a job with Louis Sullivan.

His thoughts regarding his own architectural style may be summed up as follows:

> . . . in building a house I designed it around a human being. All my houses scaled to my height of 5' 8½'' and if I were taller it's likely my houses would be scaled differently. A house should fit into the landscape—it should not be a barrier of walls—but exist in harmony. The outside is a result of what happens inside (p. 141).

Regarding solving problems he writes, "It has been proved by my own experience that every problem carries within itself its own solution, a solution to be reached only by the intense inner concentration of a severe devotion to truth" (p. 380).

Wright's architectural training consisted of apprenticing himself into various firms in Chicago where he could learn what he felt was needed. In his later years he became the center of political controversy in the Madison area, and one of his grander designs, for a civic center, was never developed. The architect's social-political nonconformity was met by sufficiently strong community opposition to stifle the development of his ideas locally. Fortunately, Wright's works were not held in low repute everywhere.

Louis H. Sullivan

In his autobiography (1924), Sullivan claims that from infancy his greatest fascination was watching things get done. He was always wandering off asking why, and he was singularly determined in his quest to know the answer. His first letter home from his teacher described him as dull and inattentive and claimed that he wouldn't study. He had been attending a one-room school; it was discovered later that he had been learning the lessons of those ahead of him because he already knew his own lessons. Between the ages of five and ten Louis lived in the country with his grandparents. There he was left to do pretty much as he pleased. He strongly disliked the physical and intellectual confines of school, and when he was seven he stopped going in order to seek out craftsmen who would show him their skills. Once after a month-long truancy was discovered, his parents decided to take him back to Boston with them.

At 12 Louis found himself interested in buildings. By that time his family had moved to Chicago because of his mother's poor health. By happenstance he learned that an "architect" drew plans for these buildings and that the architect was the boss of everybody. After learning that architects made buildings out of plans in their heads, he decided that architecture was for him. Given this goal he became an excellent student almost overnight. In school he discovered the word that guided his work from then on, the word "self-expression."

Louis demonstrated the power of his will and mind in his preparation for the entrance examinations at the Beaux-Arts in France. Six weeks before that exam he discovered he had to learn conversational French, advanced mathematics, and logic. He had some previous training in French, but he had to learn advanced math from scratch. In the examination he proved that he had learned to think in French and had mastered mathematics during this six-week period of study with a tutor. Sullivan attributed his performance to his will to succeed and his ability to concentrate. The Beaux-Arts examiners felt he was a diamond in the rough and even encouraged him to consider pursuing mathematics. Sullivan concludes his autobiography by stating, ". . . the initial instinct of the child is the basis of all fruitful ideas, and the growth in power of such ideas is in itself a work of instinct. It has been convincingly shown that instinct is primary and intellect secondary in all the great works of man" (p. 330).

Sullivan's ideas on creativity also seem instructive. In another book (Sullivan, 1947) he writes "a person cannot strive for originality. Proper training, and freedom to act with spontaneity, will lead to individuality of expression. Only the learned can be creative. The young can be simplistic and even unusual but the process is not creative even if the product is judged to be so" (p. 218).

Sullivan also has some very specific ideas about what a person should learn from his or her education (1947, p. 222).

- the history of the struggle for freedom
- understanding the great drama, the broad sweep of life in which he is a unit, an actor
- optimism from the study of history
- pride of one's human capability
- that a mind empty of ideals is an empty mind
- lovingly shown the beauty of nature
- an open heart and mind to the inspiration of nature
- taught the full span of life and life's purpose
- develop the art of expression
- taught reality combined with high ideals.

The relationships that connect instinct and intellect, knowledge and nature weave themselves throughout the writing and comments of artists and scientists, inventors and politicians. We will see that most of these eminent persons deplore the neglect of instinct and the lack of emphasis on learning from nature.

Eliel Saarinen

"Reasoning is a two-edged sword. The sharper man's intellectual reasoning becomes, the less sharp is his intuitive and instinctive sensitiveness bound to grow. The more man reasons, the less chance have his senses to conduct his actions" (Saarinen, 1948, p. 24). Saarinen provides useful definitions for several pertinent terms: "Intuition is the establishment of immediate contact with primary facts and truths. Instinct is recording life's vibrations and transmuting vibrations into corresponding form. Imagination produces mental ideas and pictures that have no relationship to previous concept, knowledge or experience" (p. 25). The province of reasoning includes: truth, logic, function, color, decoration, space, theory, and tradition. The province of instinctive sensing includes: beauty, taste, and imagination (p. 193). He summarily describes architecture as "the art-form of correlation par excellence."

Buckminster Fuller

Fuller is credited by many as introducing the term and concept of synergy. He indicates that he was ". . . seeking in the whole of experience and knowledge, rather than in specialized isolations, for a comprehensive mathematical scheme of patterning" (Fuller, 1963, p. 21). Fuller believes that nature wrote all the rules on structure and that we seek to discover them, not invent them.

He believes that one of the most important contributions that science can make to society is in developing the ability to consider all of nature as measurable and rational and of immediate practical significance. A danger he sees is that the scientist, and rational man, have become specialists in the isolation of phenomena, discovering simple component-behavior phases.

What Fuller sees as needed are people and approaches that integrate the better-defined pieces into a meaningful, yet more complex whole. He feels we are apparently more skilled in deducing than inducing or integrating. He writes that the more detailed and specific our knowledge becomes, the more complex the task of achieving or perceiving an integrated whole. There is an underlying warning that the very knowledge that is created becomes a barrier to further creativity. In essence, it becomes increasingly difficult to both know and create, because there is so much to know.

Richard Neutra

Neutra (1962) has a telling description of a physiological abnormality to which he attributes his success as an architect. He built the "disability" into an asset.

> My eyes were unequal and didn't work together. My right eye was shortsighted and my left eye normal. Most of the time I worked with one eye, either the right one for minute sharp detail or the left one for overall composition, my mind similarly also swung back and forth— oscillated, so to speak, between an attempt at total comprehension, an integrated over-all view, and the minute perfectionism of nearsightedness. I kept using each eye, one imaginatively and wholesale for over-all form, the other more observationally, for fine, neat detail (p. 73).

This brief self-description certainly tells us something about hemispheric functioning at a very overt and useful level. One can only wonder whether some children with particular learning disabilities would be better served by helping them develop their uniqueness rather than making them "normal."

Walter Gropius

Of all the architects, Gropius has some of the most pointed thoughts on the subject of education. In the prefatory section of his book (1955) he writes, ". . . words, and particularly, theories not tested by experience can be much more harmful than deeds" (p. xviii). His comments on democracy, the principles of which educators must communicate to the young, suggest some of the dilemmas these educators face.

Democracy is based on the interplay of two contrasting manifestations. Diversity of minds, resulting from intensive, individual performance; also a common denominator of regional expression, springing from the cumulative experience of successive generations who gradually weed out the merely arbitrary from the essential and typical (p. xix).

Good architecture, he writes,

. . . should be a projection of life itself and that implies an intimate knowledge of biological, social, technical and artistic problems. To make a unity out of all these requires a strong character. Education must produce people able to view an entity rather than let themselves get absorbed too early into the narrow channels of specialization. Needed are less experts and more visionarys [sic] (p. 4).

Is talent distributed to just a favored few? Gropius believes every healthy human being is capable of conceiving form. The problem seems to be finding the key to release it.

Regarding creativity Gropius writes,

It is true the creative spark always originates within the individual, but by working with others toward a common aim, individuals will achieve greater heights of achievement through the stimulation and challenging critiques of others—rather than live in an ivory tower (p. 86).

Common Threads

A final note regarding architects, architecture, and the times. As this was being written, one of the architects we had interviewed called to pursue an idea regarding his own formative years and his architecture style as compared with current values and corresponding architectural tastes. He commented that being born in 1931, he was a Depression Baby. While his family never really wanted for the necessities, everything they had was functional, whether it was food, clothing, or work. What brought this to mind was that over the weekend he had purchased the currently "in" boots for his two sons. This set him thinking about Levi jeans, Nike running shoes, lettered T-shirts, junk food establishments, and so forth. He began to relate these signs of the times to the capriciousness of architectural styles produced by younger architects. He didn't evaluate this as either good or bad; he only cited it as a major contributor to personal and social values, an influence that eventually found its way into design.

LITERATURE

Because we have relied on biographies and autobiographies for insights into creativity, productivity, and eminence, we see few women cited in this chapter. This does not mean that the creative and productive processes are masculine based. It simply means that, historically, opportunities were more likely to be made available for males, and the literary products of females were judged more harshly if recognized at all. The few women who do appear in the biographical literature demonstrate that quality is recognized by society regardless of sex. There are no existing data to suggest that certain fields are more suitable to men because there is something unique in their mental processes, feelings, or attitudes.

Literature covers a broad sweep of works and styles. Only a small sample of writers have been selected for study, but what they write is powerful and telling, particularly their quotations regarding their own lives and motivations.

Walt Whitman

Whitman's biographer describes him as ". . . emphatically a thinking man, a delver in thought. His effort was to reach conclusions through reflection and observation, and then to give them written expression as he was not an orator or a speaker" (Donaldson, 1896, p. 7). "Impressions were made quickly in his mind, but his speech and ideas came slowly. He seemed as if mentally groping" (p. 8). Whitman had little formal education but held a variety of jobs including clerk in a law office, printer's assistant, schoolteacher, printer, writer, editor, government worker, and eventually poet, author, and publisher. Whitman considered his writing as messages to the world and published many of his works at his own expense. He described his method of writing as, "I just let her come, until the fountain is dry" (p. 125).

Whitman liked being alone so he could have mental dialogues with himself. He read very little and did not travel much, only to New Orleans and Denver for short periods. He could not explain his own gift. He expressed his philosophy thus:

> The world is an oyster any man of courage can open, as it is made for all. It's a free bottle. The best equipped and bravest will lead. Tomorrow is just before you. So go in, my lad. Science, art, knowledge, are all aids to the fighter; so utilize all—brain, body, nature and her resources. They are yours; they are any man's or woman's who will use them (p. 128).

It is little wonder that Whitman has been called the poet of democracy. He wrote to stimulate ambition, arouse a sense of inquiry, and encourage action. His primary goal was to aid man in relying upon self.

Like so many of his contemporaries, Whitman alternated between living in the city where understanding and coping with people was a constant challenge, and living in the country where there was an opportunity to enjoy and wonder at nature. It is tempting to hypothesize that urban living demanded logical, rational thinking and behavior, whereas country living stimulated the poet's need to wonder, to delve, to question, and to develop an appreciation for the interdependence that underlies divergent thought processes.

Robert Frost

Frost spent his boyhood in open spaces (Mertins, 1965). Early on he tried to measure up to his father, who was a Harvard graduate. Both parents were teachers, although Frost seldom went to school. In fact, he hated school and it appears that teachers were just as pleased when he didn't come. He first experienced success in raising a vegetable garden at age 10, so he decided to become a farmer. At this same point his father died. The family, now destitute, went to New England to live with his grandparents. At age 13 Robert entered high school, where he was exposed to the McGuffey readers and several poems and short stories by great authors. He never finished any book he read, although he enjoyed reading. From his teachers and his mother he received an excellent education in grammar, analysis, and sentence structure. He entered Dartmouth and left within a few weeks. With his grandfather's financial support he eeked out an existence on a broken-down farm. It was there that he began to write poetry seriously, an effort that earned him only $200 in each of the first twenty years of his writing.

Frost's eventual success can be attributed to his having captured certain youthful feelings when he first drafted his poems. In later years he reworked these early pieces into poems marked by a smoother, more flowing, more attractive style. It took Frost years to develop his own style. He labored over his poems, as words didn't flow easily for him. Even after receiving critical recognition in England, he received no income from his writing. He seems to have been self-directed and sustained by his own writing. He apparently had very little need for recognition, and his family was always supportive even though nurturing Frost's talent meant considerable sacrifices. One wonders whether literary potential can survive today without being subsidized by an appreciative community or a wealthy family.

Tennessee Williams

Tennessee Williams had an unsettled childhood, but with the help of his grandfather he was able to attend school and eventually attended the University of Missouri in 1931. He received prizes for his prose and poetry, but began drinking a great deal to compensate for his shyness. For two years he spent his days working in a warehouse and his nights writing, leading finally to a mental breakdown. In 1936, after spending a year recuperating in Memphis with his grandfather, he went to Washington University in St. Louis. There he received a prize for a one-act play he had written. He bounced around until 1942 when *The Glass Menagerie* was written for MGM. Williams received further recognition in 1945 when the play was performed on Broadway.

Williams' biographer writes (Falk, 1961):

> Williams has created from theory or prejudice a number of type characters whom he uses again and again. In a sense he has to double back on his life and experiences because he doesn't grow possibly due to the almost neurotic basis for his writing. Writing is seen for Williams as an escape from the world in which he lived as a child and a cathartic for his psychological difficulties (p. 27).

In Williams' words, "Every artist has a basic premise pervading his whole life, and that premise can provide the impulse to everything he creates. For me the dominating premise has been the need for understanding and tenderness and fortitude among individuals trapped by circumstances" (p. 163). Later Williams admitted he began writing more for the money, and that he sought out experiences as material for his writing. His biographer suggests that the main characters in Williams' plays repeatedly ask: Where did I come from? Why am I here? Where am I going? It is as if the playwright hoped to find the answer through his plays. His favorite theme seems to be the idea of sex as the symbol of freedom, sex as the only valid manifestation of, the only synonym for, love (p. 167).

It seems easy to understand that Williams writes out of his own insecurities and inhibitions, his own bitterness and distrust. It is not possible to even hypothesize why he put pen to paper and stayed with writing in the first place. He began writing at 13 and continued writing despite being called a "sissy" by his father and his peers. Writing proved to be his tool of expression and he chanced upon it early. Writing is the salvation of the poor; it seems that art, music, politics, and even the sciences require the availability of sufficient resources or opportunities to learn even the basics. A writer's material demands are small.

This does not mean to imply that only the poor write or achieve eminence as writers. Certainly Hemingway, Buck, and O'Neill are noticeable exceptions.

Arthur Miller

Miller was an undistinguished student who enjoyed sports. He moved from Manhattan to rural Long Island after his father's business slackened in 1928. After high school Miller took a series of odd jobs and then worked as a shipping clerk for several months. Finding that his existence was eroding into "automated oblivion" and wanting to make something of his life, he began reading to better understand what was happening to him. He was particularly impressed by Dostoevsky's *Brothers Karamazov*, more by the drama than the meaning it had for him. He ended up reading more in one year than he had read in his entire life and began to think of writing as a way to express himself. He wrote what he termed a "pleading" letter to the University of Michigan where he was accepted on probation.

For a course assignment he decided to write a one-act play. He never had seen a one-act play and didn't even know how long one ran. He had only a week in which to write it because his studies and his two part-time jobs occupied all his time until spring break. After the week's end he had written a three-act play, and so he submitted it and was awarded a prize. He later won other awards and recognition for his college writing.

Miller graduated in 1938 without promise of a job. He began his career by writing for four months on a WPA project, then worked as a steamfitter and truck driver in the Brooklyn Navy Yard. He wrote some radio scripts, earning $300 the first year and $1,200 the second year. According to Miller's biographer (Nelson, 1970), his style was "to link familial conflicts to broader problems beyond but impinging upon the family" (p. 29). Miller described his own shortcomings as a writer in this way: "I had picked themes at random, which is to say that I had no awareness of any inner continuity running from one of these plays to the next, and I did not perceive myself in what I had written . . . I was writing about what lay outside me" (p. 44).

In Nelson's biography of Miller we find a most detailed account of Miller's writing style. It is worth reviewing because it provides so much detail regarding both creation and production.

> I begin with an event, an individual, or even a few words of dialogue which may suddenly grab and hold my interest. An incident related to me during a casual conversation, someone does something which catches my fancy, or a sudden image that explodes in my mind from nowhere.

Starting with something concrete, then I test and develop its dramatic context in my mind. If it shows promise of evolving into something meaningful I begin writing. I fill notebooks with anything I can associate with the topic (free association). At this stage everything is fragmented. Next I try typing scenes from the fragments. I do this weeks at a time, usually with nothing tangible in writing but I do develop a mental framework. If nothing emerges I may set it aside or abandon it (p. 98).

Miller continually writes out his ideas in order to communicate with himself. If the framework he develops holds together, then he begins developing particular characters or events. At this point he stops writing and begins visualizing, projecting mental images of characters and events.

His notebooks now display long and detailed passages of dialogue, action, and situation. He works and reshapes until "thinking is left behind and everything is in the present tense and a play emerges which has resemblances but little else to the mass of notes left behind" (p. 98). Now he must blend character, theme, and action into a structural unity. Sometimes he cannot bring it together, and months of work are physically destroyed. He doesn't retain the written product of his self-acknowledged failures.

Death of a Salesman emerged and was developed when he was in the midst of another play which he readily abandoned because the images for *Salesman* came through so strongly. It seems Miller has developed a process by which he can synthesize external events into his inner world. The criteria he uses for determining the value of what he is attempting to put together seem to rest on his ability to put everything into the present tense and actually visualize what previously had only been written thoughts and ideas. He describes writing for the stage as both difficult and demanding, with no assurance of how critics and audiences will respond.

William Faulkner

Faulkner's family described him as having all his grandfather's appetite for adventure but none of his talent for constructive achievement (Blotner, 1974). Faulkner learned to read on his own and roamed around the countryside with his two brothers until he was eight and had to begin school. As a boy he spent a great deal of time reading books in his parents' and grandfather's library. At first he behaved "perfectly" in school, although he was described as more an observer than a participant. In the meantime, his practical jokes and scientific experiments increased at home, serving to irritate and endanger the family.

At age 11 he lost interest in school, developing a particularly strong dislike for history. He began to skip school and hang out at the livery stable. By sixth grade all he cared about was drawing. He seldom paid attention in class and in a few years quit school. His family noted also that he was showing a strong disinclination toward work of any kind. He got along by telling stories. At age 13 he began writing stories and bits of poetry, and by age 14 he didn't want to do anything but read and write poetry. An older friend who had been away to college began to drill him in punctuation and grammar, and also criticized his work, thus becoming a combination tutor and mentor.

At 18 Faulkner was a heavy drinker and took to writing poetry in imitation of Swinburne. After nearly 20 years of writing, with many of these years devoted to trying to succeed as a poet, he admitted that he couldn't write poetry because it took him too long to say things. Most of his years from late adolescence past age 30 were spent as postmaster in the college town of his birth, a job he managed to bungle completely. He continued to write when the spirit moved him and when there weren't any friends to join him in drinking, golf, or tennis. The years of rejection and his marginal life didn't deter him from writing. He had difficulty developing his own style and finding the best form to express himself, even after chancing upon storytelling as his most suitable form of expression.

Faulkner was continually torn between trying to write so he would be published, trying to capture the best of other writers' styles, and trying to discover himself. After marrying his childhood sweetheart and gaining some recognition and financial security, he was able to write in a manner that pleased him and was well received by others.

Pearl S. Buck

Buck's biographer (Harris, 1969) describes her as continually asking "why" throughout her childhood. Sometimes her mother begged her and even bribed her not to ask a question for at least 15 minutes. From her inquisitiveness and the unique circumstances of her childhood we can see how she "developed" the requisites for becoming such a successful writer.

Pearl's father was a missionary in China. She spent her childhood in China and received a high degree of personal attention from her mother. Pearl's first language was Chinese and she even thought as an oriental. At age four she realized she was different from the children with whom she was growing up.

She was very concerned with death as a child, largely because her brother died of diphtheria when Pearl was seven. She had had diphtheria but lived. She describes her early life as occurring in the dim world of in-between.

> Somehow I have always been an object, rather than a person. As a
> child, I was white with yellow hair and blue eyes in a country where

everyone knew the proper color of eyes and hair was black and skin was brown. I can remember my Chinese friends bringing their friends to look at me because I was different. By the time I came to America I was different again (p. 81).

She wrote her first books for money and learned "I cannot do that and do well. I must write with no thought of whether the book will sell. I write because I have something to say" (p. 84).

As a child she was close to no one, even though her relationship with her mother seemed close, almost stifling. She had no one in whom to confide when young so she started writing. Her book *The Child Who Never Grew* describes her experiences with her own retarded child. *The Good Earth,* which earned her over $1 million, describes China through the eyes of an American. Her life was marked with no feeling of permanence or roots; she always felt restless. Winning the 1938 Nobel Prize for literature renewed her waning confidence.

Ernest Hemingway

Baker (1969) describes Hemingway as immensely ambitious, competitive, almost driven by an urge to excel, to be admired for his physical, emotional, and intellectual superiority. Hemingway was also beset by a mass of contradictions. He was both shy and a braggart, sentimental and a bully, a warm friend and brutal enemy, loyal to friends yet would fight off anyone trying to possess him. He was an omnivorous reader, a naturalist, a skilled observer, and superstitious.

Hemingway was a robust child who reacted strongly to any limits that were placed on him. By age two he could correctly identify 73 different birds. His physical appearance and conduct led people to think he was five. In his early years he lived in Chicago and spent summers in the country. He felt comfortable in both environments, but seemed to prefer the country. Even at five years old Hemingway liked to tell stories. He had a rich imagination and was fascinated by the study of history. He was a good student throughout school and at 15 had his first story published in the school paper. In school he wrote a story a week, using Ring Lardner for a model. Every summer, beginning at age 14, he was given complete freedom to roam the country with his friends.

When he graduated from high school he didn't want to go to college, which disappointed his physician father. In 1917 it was either go to war or get a job. Hemingway decided to work at the *Kansas City Star* for six months, and then became an ambulance driver for the Red Cross. He was the first American wounded in Italy, a feat for which he received considerable attention when he came home.

Hemingway returned from Italy with no particular plans for the future. While he was convalescing he began to write magazine articles. He discovered he could turn his experiences into rich, attractive stories. His subsequent career and universal recognition do not require elaboration.

Lillian Hellman

This author and playwright describes herself (Hellman, 1969) as having been raised in a family that demonstrated little emotion or caring. She describes herself as a lonely child who turned to books and fantasy. Writing was about the only avenue available to a woman who wanted to achieve independence and didn't want to be in a position of having to relate with other persons. She has always been driven by her restlessness, by her search for meaning outside of people, and by herself. Her acquaintances in New York and her association with publishing houses gave her the opportunity to try herself as a writer. The title of her autobiography, *An Unfinished Woman,* suggests she is still looking to move beyond where she is as a person.

Eugene O'Neill

O'Neill is described by his biographer (Clark, 1929) as, "fundamentally a passionate observer of humanity, a man to whom life is a tragic and beautiful adventure; a theatrical craftsman of compelling power; an artist in intent even in his failures; an uncompromising idealist" (p. 7).

After knocking around through his early twenties and two prolonged illnesses (the second, at age 23, put him in a sanatorium for six months where he started to think things over), O'Neill wrote, "It was during this enforced period of reflection that the urge to write first came over me. At 24 I began my first play after learning that I wasn't the actor my father was but that I still wanted a place in the theater" (p. 8).

O'Neill cannot explain why the urge to write came over him, why he had the desire to express what he knew and felt about life in the form of drama. In acting with his father, he realized there was no satisfaction for him in saying the words of another person. After the breakdown in his health he tried to maintain a balance between physical activity and writing.

O'Neill's plays grew out of his experiences. He had a fairly deep fund of human experiences to draw upon. He demonstrated a good understanding of the theatre and a sensitive and powerful imagination. He was also well read. This is how he describes his approach to writing:

> I intend to make whatever I can make my own, to write about anything under the sun in any manner that fits or can be invented to fit the subject. And I shall never be influenced by any consideration but one: Is it the truth as I know it—or, better still, feel it? If so, shoot, and

let the splinters fly where ever they may. If not, not. This sounds brave and bold—but it isn't. It simply means that I want to do what gives me pleasure and worth in my own eyes, and don't care to do what doesn't. . . . It is just life that interests me as a thing in itself. The why and wherefore I haven't attempted to touch on yet (p. 195).

Moss Hart

In his words (Hart, 1959), "My goad was poverty and my goal was Broadway and the theatre" (p. 7). He had no close friends as a child or adolescent; he felt nothing for his parents, and had every reason to believe they had no feelings for him. While peddling papers and doing anything else he could to help the family acquire the necessities of life, his errands took him through Broadway. The excitement and activity he saw there appealed to him. Since the age of seven his aunt had taken him out of school every Thursday afternoon to attend plays, and they went together to the theatre on Saturdays as well. Neither of them could afford it, but it made life tolerable.

He spent years working at odd jobs in the theatre district and as a social director in summer camps, all the while writing highly unsuccessful plays. His ideas were good and he understood theatre, but his lack of training and education made his writing ponderous and awkward. He worked with George S. Kaufman, who in effect became a mentor-collaborator. Kaufman helped Hart sharpen his writing and achieve recognition. Even then it took Hart years to discover that writing theatrical comedy was his forté.

Damon Runyon

Runyon's attitude toward people might be summarized best by this quote: "There isn't much difference between the best of the worst and the worst of the best" (Weiner, 1948, p. xii). He grew up with his father in a hotel room, and while his father was well read, he was also well liquored. His father worked nights, so Damon roamed all day while his father slept and pretty much did as he pleased in the evening. When he went to school he was a good speller but didn't take to discipline. Damon became quite a storyteller as a youth.

During his adolescence and early twenties he wandered a great deal. In 1899 he served in the army and was wounded twice in the Spanish-American War. Later he even took to riding the rails as a bum for a couple of years.

By happenstance he ended up in New York and fell in love with the city. He became a sports editor for *The New York American* but found he was not a good straight reporter. His flamboyant style and the characters about whom he wrote led him to develop a readership. He began to report on a wide range of fascinating stories and eventually got interested in the New York underworld and

Broadway characters. His writing was not only informative, it helped readers experience the situations he described. For years his friends urged him to write fiction, and he finally gave it a try. He wrote by "opening his imagination and letting the life of Broadway stroll through" (p. 157).

Common Threads

What similarities can we find among these writers? All seemed to share a lack of close companions in childhood, a lack of mutual closeness with parents, a childhood spent in both urban and rural settings, and a certain remoteness from those around them leading them to become more an observer than a participant. Thousands of children have similar experiences but don't write or become recognized for their writing. There seems to be no reasonable hypothesis to explain why these individuals chose to write. Chance may have played a major factor. More than chance, however, persistence was a major contributor to their accomplishments.

MUSIC

The composers we have chosen to describe represent a broad sweep of musical talent ranging from classical to rock. With the exception of Mozart, all these men are twentieth century American composers. Mozart is included because he was so exceptional, and it seemed we could learn something from a brief review of his life and times. Some of these composers were also excellent performers; others, in fact, played very poorly.

We would like to preface this section on musical composers with some summary results from a series of interviews Schafer (1963) conducted with 15 British composers. He begins with the conclusion that "the most important factor emerging from any inspection of the creative process is its lawlessness" (p. 14). The composers Schafer interviewed all had creative intuition, which is described as precompositional planning that occurs in the mind and appears like a vivid dream in which the composer converts space into time. Only one composer in the group visualized written musical notes in the creative intuition stage. In the creative action stage the details are shaped after the form is fixed in the composer's mind. Intervals, rhythmic gestures, colors, and texture are added. Composers described this stage as mechanical rather than inspirational.

Of the composers interviewed, five composed at the piano, and five indicated they revised extensively. Five composers averaged six hours work during a given sitting, three averaged ten hours, five averaged less than five hours, and two indicated no regular composition pattern. In summary, the only generalization that could be made regarding work methods was that most composers were found to create using mental imagery involving spatial perceptions. This generalization is further supported by Farnsworth (1969) who, after an exhaustive study of composers, states, "All musicians have auditory imagery of more than average strength" (p. 183).

Wolfgang Mozart

There is no doubt that Mozart was pushed by his father into early performance. At three, Mozart picked out combinations and did conversions on the piano. At age four he played small pieces faultlessly from memory. By age five he had devised minuets and other pieces which his father wrote down. Whenever he showed a need for technical improvement, his father taught him. Mozart's father worked him hard, but the young Mozart never rebelled, although he constantly needed reassurance that he was loved. At age eight he began composing for a symphony and toured with his father who wanted to show off his child prodigy and make money as well. According to his biographer (Blom, 1935) his greatest accomplishments occurred when he produced three symphonies in a three-month period shortly before he died. In this three-month span Mozart completed the Symphony in E-flat Major on June 26, the Symphony in G Minor on July 25, and the Jupiter Symphony in C Major on August 10. His biographer comments:

> How these works had been shaping in his mind before they were put to paper is impossible to tell; . . . it is a puzzle how music of such lucid complexity could be carried in a man's brain without an immediate record, each equally great and entirely different from each other, during a period when the composer suffered from acute anxieties (p. 146).

Did Mozart think in music instead of words and mental pictures? Certainly music was the basis for his communication with both his father and older sister with whom he was very close. He did not communicate or relate very well with others, and he never seemed to feel secure or certain of being loved as a person. In music he soared above his emotional and social limitations. Possibly he withered and died because music alone was too fragile a bond with other humans to sustain life. Obviously this is psychological conjecture, but it should be considered a caution against pushing a young person in one field of study to the neglect of other aspects of human development.

Artur Rubinstein

Rubinstein begins his autobiography (1973) by noting that as a child he didn't talk but instead always sang. It became apparent that he had a musical gift when he would memorize his sister's piano lessons and thereby taught himself to play.

He was very single-minded regarding what he wanted to play. At age three he smashed both of the fiddles his father had given him to encourage him to play the violin someday. At three-and-one-half his parents brought Artur to Berlin for an interview and performance. The professor who heard the young musician recognized Rubinstein's talent but cautioned his parents not to push it but give him time to develop as a person. At age ten Artur began more intense piano instruction in Berlin. He was tutored in all subjects except math, which was avoided through mutual consent with his tutor.

From age 10 to 18 Rubinstein was completely isolated from his family. It wasn't until he was in his teens that he had any same-age peers with whom to associate. He describes himself during his teens as an extrovert who got along well with everyone. His one act of rebellion consisted of not practicing what he should all the time. Once he began playing concerts he began to practice in earnest, and he admits that he only studied and practiced well when there was a concert or recordings to prepare for.

In stark contrast to the European tradition of musical training exemplified by Mozart and Rubinstein, George Gershwin and Jerome Kern are two composers who grew up on the sidewalks of New York. They seemed to receive their education from the city as a whole, rather than from school and family.

George Gershwin

Gershwin grew up restless, energetic, and hating school. His one love was to roller-skate the streets of New York. As he grew up he liked the music he heard people sing or hum, but "music was for girls and sissies and he had to grow up to do man things" (Rushmore, 1966, p. 6). His biographer quotes Gershwin as saying he was really very indifferent to music until at age ten, while playing outside school, he heard Max Rosenzweig, an eight-year-old violin prodigy, play Dvorák's Humoresque for a school assembly. "It sounded so beautiful I had to meet the violinist and followed him to his home. It was like a flashing revelation of beauty" (p. 6). In effect, Max became George's mentor, although he was two years younger than Gershwin.

George became so enraptured with music that he began to teach himself how to play the piano, first picking out melodies with one finger and then learning to harmonize chords by trial and error. It wasn't until a few years later that he began piano lessons, when his brother, Ira, quit taking them. He pursued the piano in spite of the teasing from his friends. Poor grades in school had no adverse effect on him or his plans—he was going to do something with music.

Gershwin had a relatively poor musical background for a composer. He is quoted as saying he became a good pianist because, "while I only had four years of lessons I was an intense listener. I would go to concerts and listen not only with my ears, but with my nerves, my mind, and my heart. I had listened so earnestly that I became saturated with the music. Then I went home and listened in memory'' (p. 15).

At 15 he quit school and became a song plugger. In this job he played piano all day, selling songs to vaudeville acts. At the same time he realized he wanted to discover America's folk music and sell it to the public. In later years he would write his musicals by going to the location for inspiration—to Paris for *An American in Paris* and to North Carolina for *Porgy and Bess*.

Gershwin took up painting and studied under his cousin Botkin. One critic felt that had Gershwin lived long enough to develop his talent, he would have made his mark as a painter. Writing for an orchestra tested the limits of his formal training. Unlike most composers of orchestral music, Gershwin had no training on various instruments nor any background in music theory and composition. He actually worked from his own sense of composition. Critics felt his work was crude but obviously effective.

It seems that throughout Gershwin's career he required attention and reassurance. He seemed driven to excel but was never secure in the knowledge of how good his work really was. He constantly needed external validation. Would a more secure, better trained Gershwin have produced similar or better works? If he had lived longer would his skill have grown, or would he have shifted his energies and talent to art? For Gershwin, composition meant translating his experiences and feelings into music. It seems that he had the difficult task of creating from within and then hoping others would respond positively to his creations. For all his success, he never seemed to feel confident about his work.

Jerome Kern

Kern's mother had aspired to be a concert pianist. She transferred her drive to her children by beginning them on piano lessons before they could read or write. Jerome responded quicker than his brothers, so the family spent money on lessons for him. At age ten he was described by his biographer (Ewen, 1953) as ''quiet and self-centered, not able to make friends easily and not enjoying rowdy street games. Teachers accepted his lack of interest in any subject unrelated to music because he was so talented'' (p. 16).

Jerome proved himself worthless in his father's business, and finally he was allowed to go to Europe to study music. Because he was broke, it became necessary for him to write music for inexpensive shows that played in London for a few days or a week at most. He discovered that he had a knack for writing music for the theatre, a talent he didn't seem to have for ''serious'' composition.

Like Gershwin, Kern returned to the United States and began work as a song plugger. At age 25 he began to write successful Broadway shows. He was one composer who used the piano as his stimulus. His approach to composing was summed up in an interview he once gave. "If you wait for inspiration to light on your shoulder and gently poke cobwebs from your brain you had better change your profession. Even if a few hours at the piano do not result in a song hit you will get an idea, a striking combination of notes, a few bars from constant work" (p. 90). His method was to work and rework. He liked to cut his material until it seemed correct. Interestingly, he was a poor pianist. Like Gershwin he lacked the technical background required to compose lengthy, complex works, yet he could write songs that endured. Unlike Gershwin he knew what he liked and was rather indifferent to his critics.

Duke Ellington

According to his biographer (Vlanov, 1946) Ellington grew up in Washington, D.C. on baseball, movies, prejudice, and pride. He began piano lessons at age seven and practiced for the next seven years without enjoying the music or remembering much of what he learned. He did everything to avoid practicing in order to hang around with his friends. In high school his only interest was art, and he didn't study anything else. This single-mindedness was reflected in his failing grades. His artistic talent earned him a scholarship at Pratt Institute of Applied Arts in New York, which he rejected.

At age 16 Ellington became interested in music that "rang" for him and began composing his own music. In composing he drew upon mental images of color that corresponded to his moods. He translated these feelings into music. Using a player piano, he got tapes of a pianist named James P. Johnson. As he played the rolls over and over, he would put his fingers on the depressed keys until he could pattern his playing accordingly. For the next several years he led and played with a small jazz group. Later he began to orchestrate for other instruments, a skill he seemed to think came quite naturally. He made money painting signs by day and played his music at night.

Jazz composition allowed Ellington to translate his feeling for color into music. It seems likely that Ellington may also have listened to his compositions to see if they corresponded to the color image he was striving to achieve. When the sound didn't quite correspond to the mood, it's likely he corrected the composition accordingly. In essence he had an internalized system he used for both creating and monitoring.

Stevie Wonder

Stevie's biography (Haskins, 1976) offers some unique insights into the early perceptions of a blind child. Because Stevie's family didn't treat him differently, it wasn't until after he was three that he began to realize that he was different.

Since the age of two he beat on things to make sound, because sounds made him feel alive. He liked to mimic others and experiment with his voice. He developed his auditory and muscle memory so he could function as well as possible without sight. He comments that "there is a dependency on sighted people that is hard to accept, especially as one becomes a teenager and wants to be independent" (p. 15). He learned that his musical success led to loneliness because his peers were jealous and rejected him.

In a television interview in 1979 on ABC with Barbara Walters, Wonder indicated that he uses music to paint a sound picture which is then embellished or refined when words or phrases are added. He creates his music from the phrases, or the reverse, depending on whether he is stimulated by a sound, feeling, or words.

Common Threads

This section on musical composers may best be summarized with an interview of a colleague in music education at the University of Wisconsin. We asked him to comment on the identification of persons with potential musical talent. How does one develop this potential, particularly in the area of composition? He shared the following thoughts:

- Musical talent is most often seen in families with musical backgrounds. Economically advantaged backgrounds are necessary for private lessons.
- Musical talent is usually demonstrated behavior, and most teachers can readily identify the few who perform better than the norm.
- Most good composers were good performers first.
- Outstanding composers are those who can go beyond the prevailing norm but still produce something of lasting quality.
- Good composition requires getting the listeners' attention by doing the unexpected, but not turning the audience off. The composer must then create a sustaining tension, allow for a bit of relaxation, then resume the tension and provide a climatic ending.
- There have been no successful attempts at predicting creative musical genius into adulthood. It takes drive, commitment, some luck, and financial support to make it as a composer. A major decision is whether to go commercial (popular or TV) or remain serious. Many choose to keep music an avocational pursuit.
- While it is not possible to predict musical genius, it would be feasible to consider ways to provide musical opportunities across socioeconomic lines and provide more individual instruction (the basis of creativity) in music education.

THEORETICAL SCIENCE

Scientific theory is represented by three heavyweights, Einstein, Oppenheimer, and Wiener. Both Einstein and Oppenheimer are well known for their accomplishments. While Wiener is not as well known, his autobiography about his years as a child prodigy should prove meaningful to both educators and parents.

Albert Einstein

According to Clark, Einstein's biographer (1973), neither his father's nor his mother's side of the family was very distinguished. His father was described as a good-natured person who lived for good food and drink. His mother apparently enjoyed music and was ambitious for her son, but the exact nature of this ambition is unknown. Einstein's hometown of Ulm prided itself as a town of mathematicians, but when Albert was one year old his father's business failed and the family moved to Munich. As a child Albert was shy, withdrawn, and lonely. He enjoyed playing the violin but did not play it very well. At age ten, a medical student named Max Talmey befriended him and gave him books in science and math. Albert would work problems and every Thursday Max would go over the solutions with him. Max was in fact his mentor but could not direct Albert beyond the basics.

At age 13 Einstein abandoned his religion, had no friends, and did not feel a member of the community. To fill the void he turned to trying to understand natural phenomena to have something to believe in beyond one's daily existence. He was also seeking order in nature. Apparently he wanted to know how God created the world, wanted to know God's thoughts. He sought the law behind the law in striving for simplicity of understanding.

As a teenager he was expelled from the gymnasium for insolence. He learned to detest discipline from others but learned the virtue of self-discipline. It appears the lack of early stimulation and recognition served to suppress his exceptionality, but his thinking was neither stifled nor destroyed. He was immune to feelings of emotion and constantly challenged accepted beliefs. He engaged in considerable independent study. Somehow he managed to acquire various works and papers that were raising questions about scientific beliefs that had been accepted for generations.

Einstein was first and foremost an astute observer. He was unencumbered by fixed ideas, ideas that he might have acquired had he been better educated as a youth. He was highly perceptive and imaginative and this quite likely contributed to his being a troublesome student. While working at the Swiss patent office for seven years, he developed his observation, analysis, and writing skills and managed to complete his Ph.D. thesis. His thesis contained more math than physics and showed mastery but not originality. During his years at the patent office he published three noteworthy papers that proved to be the foundation for his later scientific achievements. He had no connections so he was able to secure only part-time work even after completing his degree.

Einstein searched for unity behind disparate phenomena and accepted a reality distinct from what could be seen. He used math and his conceptualization skills to develop his ideas because he lacked a laboratory and equipment to test some of his theories. Einstein tended to work in isolation and could concentrate on the task at hand to the exclusion of all else. He was not fast but worked nonstop. When his train of thought came to a dead end he turned to his violin. Sailing also helped him think, as the rhythm of the open sea had a soothing effect on him. (Oppenheimer discovered that the sea and the open spaces of the Southwest had the same beneficial effect for him.) While Einstein worked alone, once his ideas were formulated he needed to bounce his ideas off others. He enjoyed certain companions but had no emotional feelings for them.

Einstein used visualization effectively in formulating his theories. No clue exists to explain his conceptual capabilities or his drive to know, to understand. He was such a private person and was recognized so late in his life, that we have no detailed data about his childhood. His own children never achieved anything close to his level of accomplishment.

Robert Oppenheimer

Oppenheimer's biographer (Royal, 1969) tells us that Robert's father was a successful textile manufacturer who was an avid reader and an active member of the Society for Ethical Culture, a humanistic society in New York. His mother, Ella Friedman, was considered an intellectual and a gifted painter. As a child each of Robert's many interests were nurtured by his parents, who provided whatever was required in terms of time, opportunities, and materials. He had no peer relationships; his parents became his companions. He had a photographic memory and an exhaustive functional vocabulary. During his childhood and adolescence he traveled abroad four times with his father. Robert went to a private school that emphasized science and included laboratory time as early as fourth grade. By grade five he began individual work in elementary physics and also enjoyed literature and languages. He learned to type as a child and had a correspondence with several university geologists who didn't know his age.

Robert's peers considered him offensive and conceited, but he was somewhat tolerated because of his genius. He enjoyed being different from others and almost took pleasure in the teasing he received from peers. He disliked the piano but studied obediently for years because he would not question his parents about anything.

In his junior year in high school he was introduced to atomic theory. His father was convinced of his genius and hired a tutor to teach him a year-long chemistry course in six weeks.

Robert graduated as class valedictorian at 16. In addition to doing college level work in mathematics, chemistry, physics, Greek, and Latin, by that time he had mastered five foreign languages. He began Harvard at the sophomore level in all courses and was considered a disciplined student. He was a loner, but this did not disturb him. During his second year he changed his major from chemistry to physics. He was taking six courses, auditing four others, and wanted something to do with his free time. His brilliance was offset somewhat by his clumsiness in the laboratory. In fact it became necessary for the faculty to let him think through experiments and write them up rather than actually conduct them.

Oppenheimer took his doctoral examinations at age 23 in Europe. One member of the examining committee was heard to remark that the exam ended just in time, because Oppenheimer had begun to ask questions of the faculty. Upon receiving his degree he began to ask the question "Who am I?" At this time he began to seek out and relate better with others. His lectures were considered spellbinding but few students understood him. He found teaching difficult because teaching required him to slow down his mind to keep pace with his students.

Oppenheimer is perhaps best known for administering the disparate staff that built the atomic bomb. His later years were unsatisfying because he became a victim of McCarthyism. He maintains that he wasn't bitter and accepted the foibles of our society.

Norbert Wiener

Norbert entered college at 11, earned a bachelor's degree at 14, and a doctorate at 18. In his own words (Wiener, 1953), "Whatever conspicuousness one has as a prodigy has lost all importance in view of the much greater issues of success or failure in later life" (p. 3). At age six he found himself reading and understanding German without knowing how he learned it. It wasn't until age seven that he became aware that he could learn things much more quickly than the average person. Nevertheless, he experienced difficulty with handwriting, in arithmetic he had to count on his fingers, and he was not fast at learning multiplication tables or anything by rote.

Norbert was an omnivorous reader and longed to be a naturalist. His father brought him books from the Harvard library on light and electricity. His father also had a chemistry student tutor him in chemistry at age seven, the same time Norbert began studying biology and zoology. He reported that "it was the diagrams of complicated structures and the problems of growth and organization which excited me" (p. 50). He also admitted that he didn't understand everything he read but he could retain it for later use.

By age seven, grade placement in school proved difficult. His reading was well advanced, his handwriting was awkward and ugly, and his arithmetic was adequate but unorthodox. He devoured science and was fluent in German. He was placed in third grade where the teacher was tolerant of his infantile, temperamental behavior. Drill in fourth-grade arithmetic disgusted him, however, so his father removed Norbert from school and hired a tutor to start him in algebra. Deciding it was better to educate his son at home, the father repeatedly brought up Norbert's shortcomings. Norbert reports that what made him tolerate, even love his father, was "recognizing his exceeding ability in intellectual matters, his fundamental honesty and his respect for the truth" (p. 71).

By the time he was eight, Norbert discovered he was a misfit. His vocabulary set him apart from peers. He was clumsier than the children around him, due to poor muscle coordination and his defective eyesight. His eyes were so bad that once he had to go six months without reading. He was read to, however, so his lessons continued in math, chemistry, and language. "This period of ear training was probably one of the most valuable disciplines through which I have ever gone," he reported (p. 76).

He began college at Tufts. Writing was his most severe limitation. His life was divided "between the sphere of the student and that of the child" (p. 106). He graduated in mathematics. He would have preferred to concentrate in biology, but his fine muscle coordination was too underdeveloped to permit him to perform satisfactorily in the laboratory. He didn't realize he was a prodigy until he read newspaper accounts of himself after graduating from Tufts. He concludes that academic honors are worthless.

By age 14 Norbert had become acutely conscious of death. He became obsessed with studying the lifespan of great authors. Life was intolerable for a period, and he withdrew from his family. He became overwhelmed with the fear of death and felt increasingly isolated. His social clumsiness was misinterpreted as rudeness, so he was further isolated. He experienced a unique impatience resulting from "my mental quickness and physical slowness" (p. 128).

He noted that "not having an opportunity to overcome difficulties once I experienced them increased my lack of self-confidence" (p. 152). He describes his strengths as

> having a memory of rather wide scope and great permanence and a
> free-flowing, kaleidoscopic-like train of imagination which more or
> less by itself gives me a consecutive view of the possibilities of a
> fairly complicated intellectual situation. If I cram all my past ideas of
> what a problem really involves into a single, comprehensive impres-
> sion, the problem is more than half solved (p. 213).

Common Threads

A scientist must be able to remember, reflect, and correlate. The advantage of learning so much so early is that one has more time to be productive while others are still learning the language of science. In the case of a prodigy who is an efficient visual and auditory learner, anything requiring fine motor skills can sometimes be awkward and difficult. Writing, notetaking, and dissection, can be nearly impossible.

INVENTING

It is somewhat arbitrary to label Edison, Bell, Kettering, and Westinghouse inventors. They were applied scientists as well as innovators. Considering that Edison and Bell functioned in scientific isolation, their creations are all the more a magnificent tribute to the powers of the human mind and human motivation.

Thomas Edison

Edison's biography (Josephson, 1959) begins with a recognition that he was born into an inventive, technically oriented environment, rich in resources and ideas. It is a wonder he survived his youthful misadventures. At age six he burned down his father's barn, and he almost burned himself alive in order to see what fire would do. He received a public whipping from his father for his inquisitiveness. In fact, his father felt him not only wanting in common sense but thought he was just plain stupid. His mother, on the other hand, patiently answered all of Tom's questions.

Tom's mind worked in a decidedly visual fashion; he always drew designs before contriving a device. He also demonstrated little affect through most of his life. At age seven he witnessed the drowning of a friend, but he didn't report it to anyone for several hours because he had become involved in playing with something else. When he entered school at age eight, his teacher simply could not control him. After a few days the teacher labeled Tom as "addled," whereupon Tom stormed out of school and became his mother's charge. His mother, a former teacher, taught him reading and math. He took to reading quickly and was soon enjoying the classics. He never did learn to spell. His mother concluded that you couldn't teach Tom. He had to be inspired and stimulated, and then he would learn in his own way and at his own pace.

At age nine he read R. G. Parker's *School of Natural Philosophy*, which described and illustrated various experiments. Tom tried all of them in turn. Learning then became a game of discovery. His mother next obtained a copy of the *Dictionary of Science,* and he continued to learn through experimentation.

By age ten he was spending all his money on chemicals, scraps of metal, and wire. He is quoted as saying, "My mother was the making of me, she understood me, she let me follow my bent" (p. 22).

Thomas so dominated his agemates that he seldom had any companions. He could not resist playing practical jokes for which he was whipped by his father. His "experiments" led to constant messes and complaints from his mother. Although he and his family were living in poverty, he was allowed to spend the little he had for materials and to set up a laboratory in the family cellar. The frequent explosions in the cellar would lead to bitter family arguments; his father would threaten, and his mother would protect him.

At age 12 Tom went to work selling newspapers on the train that ran 70 miles or so from his hometown to Detroit and back every day. He was fascinated with Morse's telegraph, as was Alexander Bell. Telegraphy played an important part in both their lives. The trainman allowed Tom to set up a lab in the baggage car so the young Edison could have something to do during the long layovers in Detroit. This arrangement ended with the inevitable explosion.

In 1860, at age 13, Tom began to grow deaf. He said his loss of hearing allowed him to concentrate better. At this time it would be accurate to describe him as poor, undereducated, and lonely. He had no friends and was really shut off from almost any social interaction. The result was intensified self-study, beginning with his discovery of the Detroit library. He began to frequent the library during train layovers, during which time he started to literally read through the entire library. He is quoted as saying that *"Newton's Principles* gave me a distaste for mathematics from which I have never recovered" (p. 33). His isolation gave him an opportunity to think things out, and even later he always kept his own counsel.

At age 14 he decided to become a telegrapher because he could hear the loud clicking and telegraphy would allow him to travel while guaranteeing him a job. At the same time he was intrigued by printing and thought about becoming a journalist. At 15 he bought type and a rudimentary press, and ran his own paper from the baggage car of the train. He developed a subscription list of over 400 persons, but the frustration of not being able to spell finally got the better of this enterprise. Later the same year he saved the stationmaster's daughter from being hit by a train and in gratitude he was offered a chance to learn telegraphy. The next day he arrived for his lessons with a set of instruments he had made.

As a tramp operator Edison traveled thousands of miles in the Midwest, South, and East. With his earnings he bought books and materials with which he could tinker and experiment in his spare time. He was usually fired from his job because he didn't accept discipline and was careless and inattentive. As a telegrapher he was a good receiver but never became a good sender. He was always trying to improve the equipment or office procedures. Neither this nor his love for practical jokes was appreciated, and invariably he was dismissed.

At 16 or 17 Edison invented a repeating or recording system that could handle the press of inputs during peak periods and then play back and decode these messages during slack time—the forerunner of the phonograph he was to develop. However, his machine broke down during heavy transmission and he was forbidden to use it.

At age 19 he decided he no longer wanted to be a telegrapher. He wanted to be an inventor like Samuel Morse. The question was how to pursue this career and stay alive. In 1867 he taught himself Spanish so he could go to Brazil, but that didn't pan out. For something to do, he then taught himself to read and write French. Finally he decided that Boston was the place to go and be an inventor, so off he went. Working at odd jobs during the day and "inventing" at night, Edison survived on catnaps and scraps of food. Again, like Bell, he was driven by the problems or possibilities of multiplex telegraphy (the sending of two messages simultaneously over one wire). Ten years worth of experiments on this problem usually resulted in his being fired.

When Edison was 22 a group of Boston investors decided to finance his work as a full-time inventor. After failing to sell an automatic vote counter to the state legislature, Edison turned to making practical inventions. He adopted a philosophy regarding invention: you didn't invent anything that required people to change their behavior unless it would save time, energy, or money. When he failed to demonstrate the effectiveness of his multiplex system, he left Boston and headed for New York. There he formed a partnership with a trained engineer named Franklin Pope, and together they developed the first electrical engineering service. Western Union bought up their inventions and Edison became wealthy. This meant he could spend even more money on materials and could expand his experimentation. After a couple of years he went to work for Western Union and received $40,000 for his first major improvement. This was too much money to spend in his usual way, so he decided to go into the manufacturing business. It took him only 30 days, back in 1870, to spend all this money on equipment.

Working for Edison must have been an interesting experience. He would stop his workers in the middle of a project or an order so he could play with an idea and get their reactions. He paid bills only when pressed and never developed a business sense. In fact, he didn't want to be bothered with the business end of manufacturing. He and his employees would generally spend their time experimenting, and only when money ran out would they do contractual work for Western Union. It was not unusual for Edison and most of his employees to work 60 hours straight when they were trying to unravel a new problem.

How did Edison go about his work? He would study the history of any technical device he was going to develop. He would observe the process at great length and from every perspective. Then he would plan everything down to the smallest detail in his head so he could recall it when needed. This process is all the more remarkable when we realize that at times he had as many as 44 projects going at once, with a different team of employees working on each, all under his direction and relying solely on his verbal instructions.

In 1875 Edison began experimenting with an electric arc based on exposure to carbon points. He undertook this project because he was still trying to solve the problem of multiplex telegraphy. Lights and lightbulb were not even part of his concern at this time.

Edison placed great value on serendipity. He believed that an inventor's mind always must be alerted to greater things than the task at hand. In developing the phonograph he was really seeking a way to record telegraph messages at 200 words per minute, a goal he had been trying to reach for over ten years. In fact, he was always fascinated with repeating devices and the storage of input.

Edison is well known for his quotation that genius is "99 percent perspiration and 1 percent inspiration." It is worth noting that Edison knew how to learn from the prior work of others, and he could generalize his own work on a specific project to other tasks or problems. In developing the lightbulb it was necessary for him to develop a higher vacuum than had previously existed, improve upon the incandescent element in order for it to resist tremendous heat before giving light, and regulate the current flow.

Although completely self-taught, Edison's theoretical knowledge excelled that of graduate engineers and most, if not all, of their university instructors. Edison was not a random tinkerer. His efforts were distinguished by his power of observation, his imagination, and his clear-cut reasoning. Edison, like many other eminent persons in various fields of endeavor, saw himself striving against the unknown elements of nature. He set impossible time limits for himself and then achieved them. When he solved a problem he did not rest but went on to attack larger problems. For example, after the discovery of the lightbulb he turned his attention to developing a complete power system.

Edison personified the power and drive of a highly imaginative, self-directed individual who believes in himself. His personality was marked by perseverence, a willingness to take risks and make sacrifices, and a disregard for social niceties and even basic needs. His power of observation, his memory, and his efficiency combined with his humor and his divergency to make him a human dynamo.

Alexander Graham Bell

The young Bell was favored with considerable practical knowledge regarding sound (Waite, 1961). His father was an elocutionist who also worked with stutterers and others in need of speech therapy. His father developed a system of writing sounds to show pupils the shape of the lips and tongue for each sound. Alex and his two brothers helped with various experiments in visible speech. As a boy, Alex could manipulate his dog's jaw to produce human-sounding words. Later, using reinforcement techniques, the dog was taught to make these sounds on its own. As a youngster Alex tried to develop a talking machine by reproducing a diagram prepared years earlier by a German baron. He and his brother liked the idea but developed their own talking machine by copying nature.

Although Alex was inventive and fascinated by sound, he was doing very poorly in school, particularly in mathematics and geography. He was sent to Edinburgh to live with his grandfather. This man made learning come alive for Alex, but also made him aware of his shortcomings as a student. Bell came out of this year "ashamed of his ignorance" and determined to study so he could go to college. Shortly after this both of his brothers died of tuberculosis and the family moved to Canada. At 23 Alex's own health had recovered sufficiently and he began to consider his future. Through his father's connections he went to Boston and began teaching "visible speech" in a school for the deaf.

At the same time Bell became intrigued with the telegraph and noted how inferior the American system was to the European. He became almost addicted to trying to discover a way to send more than one message over the wire at a time. He was trying to discover a way to develop a harmonic or multiple telegraph. Like Edison, and most eminent persons, Bell would work to exhaustion by simply forgoing sleep. He received financial support from his future father-in-law and, just as important, began working with Thomas Watson who knew electronics and was an expert with apparatus and equipment.

Alex quickly realized that he did not have the electrical knowledge he needed to move ahead with his idea of "sending speech over a wire," so he taught himself everything he could from books and discussions. His biographer suggests that Bell's ignorance of electricity actually helped him, since he may otherwise have concluded that his quest was impossible.

Actually a sequence of serendipitous happenings led Bell and Watson to discover that the secret to sending speech was having a continuous, undulatory undercurrent instead of the intermittent current that marked the telegraph. Bell was working with some chemicals near the wire, which just happened to be open. Watson just happened to be in the other room near the receiver when Bell spilled some chemicals on himself and on the wire and exclaimed loudly in reaction to the mess he had made. Watson heard the exclamation and came running in to ask what happened. The two men then put the events together, realized that the chemicals had changed the current from intermittent to direct, and that by coating the wire they were able to change the nature of the current and transmit verbal messages. Would this discovery have been inevitable as Bell continued to test and exhaust the possibilities? Possibly. After all, Bell and Watson were responsible for having all the necessary materials in the right place at the moment of discovery.

How can Bell be described? Like so many other eminent persons, he benefitted from early opportunities to experiment and learn from his experiments.

He was knowledgeable about human sounds and therefore had a natural theory to guide him. He was energetic and driven by a single idea. He was also patient while pursuing many ideas at once. In fact, all four inventors we are discussing were always pursuing many ideas at once, and as these ideas ebbed and flowed they enhanced one another. In his later years Bell developed the first prototypes for the hydrofoil and experimented with solar energy. He simply didn't live long enough to develop either idea and he was frustrated that he had never had the opportunity to get into manned flight.

Charles Franklin Kettering

Kettering (Boyd, 1957) is not as well known as either Edison or Bell, but only because his breakthroughs were not as striking as those that resulted in the invention of the lightbulb, the phonograph, and the telephone. Kettering was the prime developer of the battery and the self-starting ignition system for cars. Regarding invention and his ignition system he said, "All human development, no matter what form it takes, must be outside the rules; otherwise we would never have anything new" (Boyd, p. 76). He was instrumental in the formulation of General Motors and served as vice-president in charge of research.

As a youngster he was good with his hands and interested in nature. He broke his right arm and quickly learned to use his left hand. He used to "write different things with both hands simultaneously by thinking quickly back and forth from one hand to the other" (p. 13). He was especially good in math and science and was stimulated more by taking on the things he couldn't master than by pursuing things that came easily.

Kettering kept having to drop out of college because his eyes kept failing him. He too learned by listening, which child prodigy Norbert Wiener noted as very significant.

In a commencement address at Ohio State University 25 years after he graduated, Kettering summed his philosophy:

> There are a few things you need to understand. First is you are going to be a servant of somebody or something . . . next, being a good servant implies two things; willingness to work and to learn . . . and if you pack your bag for the eventual journey . . . put your ego on the bottom (p. 47).

Although he was good with his hands, Kettering, like Bell, was an idea man. Just as Bell had Watson as an assistant, Kettering had an assistant, Bill Chryst, who did all the detail work needed to develop Kettering's ideas.

George Westinghouse

Two years before his death Westinghouse attributed his lifetime of success to the following (Prout, 1972):

> My early greatest capital was the experiences and skill acquired from the opportunity given me, when I was young, to work with all kinds of machinery, coupled later with lessons in that discipline to which a soldier is required to submit, and the acquirement of a spirit of readiness to carry out the instructions of superiors (p. 11).

In essence, early hands-on experience, learning that he could survive in the Civil War, and recognizing the importance of having goals and a sense of purpose underscored his self-analysis.

Between the ages 34 and 44 Westinghouse took out 134 patents and organized over 80 companies in the United States and Europe. He became immersed in electronics and was very involved in problems of energy including hydropower, natural gas, and the steam turbine. Among his contributions were railroad air brakes, automatic switches, and the manufacture of power through the use of alternating current.

Westinghouse can be described as having astute observational skills, almost total recall, and an ability to adapt to meet changing circumstances. Over his lifetime he took out over 400 patents, including one for the development of natural gas. He did not create anything new, but rather used his initiative and imagination to carry the crude developments of others through to a highly functional end. Perhaps it is most fitting to describe him as the master adapter.

LETTERS AND PHILOSOPHY

It is very difficult to classify eminent people when their accomplishments are so broad and diverse as the persons described briefly in this section. Certainly George Washington Carver and Luther Burbank are scientists first of all. Yet their contributions extended far beyond their scientific research. It is no less difficult to decide how to classify a Martin Luther King, Jr., or a John Muir or a Ralph Bunche. The reader is therefore asked to not make too much of the groupings in this chapter, but rather consider these eminent persons as individuals qualified to make their mark in many fields of endeavor.

George Washington Carver

Carver was born around 1860, the son of a hired girl and a free black. His was a family of poor farmers living in dread of avenge-seeking whites. At age five he and his mother were abducted. His father hired a hunter to get his mother back, but he could only find George. The mother he really never knew was reported to have had almost total recall, as did George.

As a boy George gained a reputation for having a green thumb. He would collect and grow samples of any plant he could find in the woods. A childhood case of whooping cough left him with a speech impediment; he was also undersized due primarily to lack of proper nourishment.

As a small boy George was once allowed into a rich man's house where he saw a painted portrait. He was much taken with the idea of painting and learned to make his own colors and painting materials. He was extremely shy and his only friend was his half-brother. He taught himself to read from old books and pamphlets.

Around the age of eight George left his farm home and went to live about eight miles away. The midwife who brought him into the world took him in. He proved to be a real asset because he could iron clothes so well. He began attending a one-room school that had 75 other students. When he wasn't doing chores, he was reading. He learned to cook and wash and mend clothes. All the time he was taught not to aspire beyond the limits appropriate to blacks at that time.

George seemed guided by curiosity and self-confidence all his life. Between the ages of 8 and 16 he lived by himself and earned a living by washing clothes and ironing, sometimes hiring out as a cook and dishwasher. He moved around a great deal, usually choosing to move to a place where he could go to school and learn something he didn't know.

His biographer (Holt, 1943) describes Carver as having almost a compulsion to recreate anything he watched others construct. He spent a great deal of time alone, and he constantly asked himself questions about the earth, stones, plants—anything he saw and didn't understand. By the time he was 18 or 19 he was six feet tall. He not only lost his stammer but performed in local dramatics. At 25 he had a laundry business and continued going to neighborhood Negro schools until finally he thought he was ready for college.

He left his business with no material assets or money and went to Highland University where he had been admitted by mail. When he arrived he was informed they didn't admit blacks. Carver worked for a time at a nearby fruit farm. In 1886 he left to try homesteading in Kansas. He became an expert builder of sod houses and started a desert nursery, but his crops couldn't come in given the poor condition of the soil. He continued to study whatever books he could find. He also continued to paint and even received some art instruction from a nearby settler.

After two years Carver gave up homesteading and headed for northeast Iowa. For a few months he ran a traveling laundry to help make ends meet. He was befriended during this time by a Mrs. Milholland who gave him encouragement and tried to provide some stability for him. His chief joy during this period was to travel through the countryside collecting plant specimens. He would classify them and go to any library he could get into to learn more about them.

Mrs. Milholland pushed him to continue his education, so at age 30 Carver walked the 25 miles to Simpson College in Indianola, Iowa. He had no math and little training in writing. He lived in an abandoned shack on the edge of town and did other students' laundry to earn a livelihood. A friend of his art teacher, a Mr. Liston, befriended him, and other students brought him old furniture for his shack. He began to think better of himself because his teachers and fellow students showed him so much respect. He learned he could have "human aspirations" and no longer needed to keep his aspirations within "proper" bounds. He pursued piano and vocal lessons, played on the college baseball team, and kept up his collecting, his laundry business, and his studies. His singing voice was considered so good that he was offered a scholarship at the Boston Conservatory of Music.

His art teacher worried that he couldn't make a living with his art, so after graduation she arranged for him to go to Iowa State to study agriculture science. He chose Iowa State because of his love of plants. He hoped he might someday classify plants according to their commonalities for instructional purposes. In other words, he chose agriculture because he felt he could make a contribution in that area.

At Iowa State, James Wilson, Dean of Agriculture and Director of the Experimental Station, became Carver's friend and mentor. During this time his artwork also received recognition. He was continually torn between his personal desire to paint and his desire to be of service to others. His philosophy is represented in a quote from Tennyson, a quote he often repeated (p. 189):

> Hold you here, root and all, in my hand,
> Little flower—but if I could understand
> What you are, root and all, and all in all,
> I should know what God and man is.

In 1896, at age 36, Carver received his masters degree. He wasn't a social crusader and realized that he would have to direct his energies into science if he were to serve his people. His first and only position was as the chairman in the newly created agriculture department at Tuskegee Institute in Alabama. Because he had no funds, he had to make all his equipment. When he got "stuck" he would come up with a solution, no matter how complex the problem. He developed a simplified system of botany so that students could discriminate accurately and as quickly as possible from among a large variety of plants.

Carver learned and taught by demonstration. He was always very good with his hands and could construct anything no matter how complex, after someone showed him how. He ended up teaching economics, crop rotation, and canning, and even developed better cotton strains. World leaders came to visit him, but until the day he died at age 83 he remained pretty much the same person that first came to Tuskegee.

Luther Burbank

During Burbank's lifetime he created or improved over 800 plants, the result of thousands of experiments, the majority of which failed (Kraft & Kraft, 1967). He had as many as 3,000 experiments going on at one time, with many taking years to complete. To gain an appreciation of Burbank's accomplishments, one needs to realize that during his productive years, every three weeks he produced something new, something that had never been seen on the earth.

Burbank's formal education ended at 15 when he went to work as a factory mechanic. He proved to be very good with his hands and his mechanical inventions proved to be so creative and functional that he could earn $16 per day doing piece work when the going rate was 50¢ a day.

His poor health caused him to leave factory work. By chance he developed the Burbank potato (named after him), which he in turn sold. He received enough money from this venture to move to California and continue experimenting. With adequate funds, the success of the Burbank potato, and his chance reading of Darwin's theory he was on his way.

Susan B. Anthony

According to her biographer (Harper, 1969) Susan had an exceptional memory and an insatiable appetite for learning—particularly those things considered beyond a woman's capacity. This attitude and drive can be attributed partly to her father's influence. He raised his children to think of themselves as persons who should value their independence above all else. He even built a school over his store so that the immediate members of the family could receive an unrestricted education, including teaching the girls division (unheard of at that time). At age 29 Susan was not ready to accept the standard "woman's" career—teaching—simply because she was a woman. Her father encouraged her ambition by having her join him in his insurance business.

It is hard to explain the accomplishments of a social reformer. The cause must be right for the time, and the individual must have the drive and skills needed to be an effective leader. Anthony was probably one of the very few skilled woman orators of her time. This, along with her business experience, helped her achieve a prominent role early in the women's movement.

John Muir

John Muir, like Andrew Carnegie, was just entering his teen years when he was uprooted from his native Scotland and landed in America (Muir, 1912). Carnegie settled in Pittsburgh and eventually went into business, and Muir settled in the woods of Wisconsin and went on to become a naturalist. In reading their biographies one is struck by the freedom they experienced in not having to fit into the expectations or morés of their birthplace. This combined with a sense of excitement and newness and discovery that seemed to characterize the young adolescent. Obviously thousands of teenagers were uprooted from their birthplace and abruptly set down in the United States without reaching similar heights of achievement. Interestingly, most of these people made a go of it and several achieved eminence, possibly *because* the adolescent immigrant viewed a new language, new customs, and new challenges not as obstacles but as opportunities.

Muir was completely taken by nature. There was nothing that failed to stir his interest. He was a hard worker and he was also inventive. In his teens he constructed clocks made entirely from wood; it was in the interest of showing these at the State Fair in Madison, Wisconsin, that he came to the city and university at age 15. He won a prize for his clocks and fell in love with the college campus. When the university president encouraged him to enroll, he did so even though he hadn't been to school since age 11. Muir graduated in four years, teaching in a neighboring community during the winter and harvesting in the summer to pay his way. He then engaged in 50 years of botanical and geological exploration and conservation efforts.

Margaret Mead

Like Susan B. Anthony, Margaret was greatly influenced by a supportive family (Mead, 1972). She was raised by her well-educated grandmother and her social scientist parents. Interestingly, everything she learned as a child she learned in an historical perspective; both her grandmother and parents always encouraged her to consider the broader perspective. When Margaret was a child her parents moved to New Jersey so her mother could finish her own Ph.D. Margaret learned the observation method and the importance of detail from her father, a professor at the Wharton School of Finance in Philadelphia. From her mother she learned to take pride in herself and the meaning of commitment. Margaret felt her grandmother had the most decisive influence. Margaret's grandmother exposed her to the joy of learning and taught her to learn both deductively and inductively.

According to her grandmother, nature was the most important teacher to teach Margaret. Because the grandmother valued the ability to do things with one's hands, Margaret was taught as much as possible through demonstration. Her grandmother, unlike her mother, felt comfortable as a person; Margaret identified with the grandmother and felt good about herself.

Margaret's first college experiences were disappointing because the school was primarily social. In her second year she transferred to Barnard College which provided the serious environment she originally expected. She had intended to be a writer but she couldn't write creatively. She rejected politics because at the time there was no future for a woman in politics, and above all she wanted to make a contribution. Finally, a senior seminar taught by the anthropologist Franz Boas attracted her attention. Then Ruth Benedict, the teaching assistant, encouraged her to enter the field.

Margaret married in 1923 but kept her maiden name. Samoa was one of two choices she had for her field work. The rest of her accomplishments are known so well that they do not need to be described here.

Ralph Bunche

On the surface, Ralph Bunche seems like a modern-day George Washington Carver—only his area of endeavor has been government and education. His early years were spent knocking around and moving, but always the steady hand of his grandmother was there to guide and support him (Mann, 1975). His family managed as best they could, but the economy, health problems, and racial barriers made things difficult. Bunche credits a sixth-grade teacher with exciting his interest in school. Then when he was only twelve, his father left home, his mother died, and the uncle who was supporting the family shot himself. Ralph remembered it was like being orphaned three times in one year.

When he entered high school his teachers were going to put him in the commercial track. His grandmother insisted he be in college preparatory. He was the only black in his high school and graduated as valedictorian. He learned the printing trade by working nights. His grandmother encouraged him to enter UCLA, and during his college days he was a member of the national champion basketball team, a debater, on the student government, on the staff of the newspaper and college yearbook, held outside jobs, and graduated as class valedictorian. He received a fellowship at Harvard, became an assistant to the president at Howard University, and was the first black American to receive a Ph.D. in political science.

He prided himself on his ability to break down racial barriers quietly. He was a proud man with tremendous energy and resourcefulness. He wrote well and was a good researcher. He assumed a leadership role in the United Nations and worked effectively in the U.S. State Department. Always he received steady support from his grandmother. He had to believe in himself when someone else believed in him so much.

Martin Luther King, Jr.

King's temperament was described as a cross between his quick-tempered father and his more placid mother. He was always a good student and graduated from high school at 15. His early career goal was to be a physician in order to better serve the black community. In college he changed his major to sociology in order to enter law school. Then toward the end of college he accepted the call to the ministry.

Early in his ministerial studies he was attracted to the writing of Walter Rauschenbusch, especially *Christianity and the Social Class* from which King concluded after reading, "that any religion which professes to be concerned about the souls of men and is not concerned about the social and economic conditions that scar the soul, is a spiritually moribund religion only waiting to be buried" (Miller, 1968, p. 17). Ghandi's writing and success in India attracted King, and he also studied Niebuhr's critique of pacifism and nonviolence.

King's definition of leadership, as he applied it to himself, included a broad range of elements: commitment, a philosophy for guiding behavior, taking risks, courage in the face of fear, being able to command attention and teach others your perspective, leading by example, communicating effectively in words and deeds, and gaining the involvement of other leaders—which may prove more difficult than rallying followers. He knew also that leadership requires the right circumstances, favorable publicity, and a knowledge of how to use the media. He recognized how important it was to understand law and the government in order to function well within the system. And most important, he knew the value of knowing one's own motives and fears and the motives and fears of others. King tried to lead along these lines. He was a reluctant leader at first, but as people turned to him he had to become more assertive. He admitted to living in fear for himself and his family and would have preferred not to have been a social reformer.

G. Stanley Hall

This noted psychologist commented, "My autobiography in some respects is more like the expensive coffin a Chinaman makes and elaborates, with much output of time and money, and then decides to sell because he wants to use in his own lifetime what it may bring" (Hall, 1923, p. 4).

What Hall learned about his life in writing his autobiography he sums up rather succinctly:

> I never should have realized how much I owe to my parents and how in all my "thun and haben" I have simply reproduced their lives, with a few amplifications offset by grave shortcomings in which I have

fallen below them; how deeply I am indebted, body and soul, to the country farm life of my early years; how early all my very fundamental traits were developed so that despite all changes in environment I am yet the same in every basal trait that I was in childhood or even infancy, in which everything in me was preformed, how relatively isolated my life has really been despite all its associations (p. 7).

Obviously Hall subscribes to the theory that as the twig is bent so grows the tree—at least as he reviews his own life. Regarding his inclination to become a psychologist he writes, "If gossip is the foreschool of psychology I was raised in a favorable atmosphere for there were incessant discussions of real motives and much analysis of personality, and endless criticism which, on the whole, favored public and private morals" (p. 13).

Hall lived his life as a critic. He broke ground by setting up the first experimental psychology lab, founding the *American Journal of Psychology* in 1887, and organizing the American Psychological Association. His most difficult task was to break from the era's philosophical traditions and his own religious orientation.

John Dewey

His biographer (Coughlan, 1973) states that Dewey formulated his ideas by mediating between the core of evangelicalism he derived from his mother and the intellectual life presented by his family minister. His father was considered well read, and family friends included many faculty at the University of Vermont. Dewey remembers himself as a "shy, self-conscious little boy who had been taught not to take the world at face value"—his mother's view (p. 6). John was considered by others to be quiet and a follower. His way of establishing himself as an independent person, free of his mother, was to be outdoors and join with his brother and his friends. Both he and his brother were considered bookworms. Although John was younger than his classmates he was not thought to be precocious.

In his junior and senior years at college he became interested in the philosophical writers who presented ideas that were in sharp contrast to those on which he had been raised. After graduating at age 19, he went to teach in Oil City, Pennsylvania. After two years he returned to teach in his home state of Vermont, but when he found himself with a class of 35 boys whom he couldn't control he lost interest in teaching school and directed his effort into the study of philosophy. He was highly influenced by psychologist G. Stanley Hall and by philosopher George Morris. Dewey studied at the University of Michigan with Morris and was asked to take his place when Morris died shortly after Dewey completed his graduate work.

In 1894 Dewey went to the University of Chicago and founded the Laboratory School. He left in 1904 after an argument with the university president. He went to Columbia where he remained until he died in 1952 at the age of 93.

POLITICS

A great deal has been written about persons who hold high public office, particularly the presidency. The paths to the presidency have been many and varied. Some of these men, such as Theodore Roosevelt and Franklin D. Roosevelt, strove to put themselves in a position to become president. Robert Taft, on the other hand, did all the right things in order to follow his father into the White House, but lacked the warmth or personality to convince his own party and the electorate to vote for him. Eisenhower had a good press as a result of World War II, and Kennedy and Johnson were the first presidents to rely heavily on television. Hubert Humphrey never achieved the presidency although he strove mightily. Also included in this section is George Marshall, the great World War II general and formulator of the Marshall Plan.

Theodore Roosevelt

Teddy's father was an energetic, outgoing, confident, well-lettered man who directed his energies into business affairs and social welfare (Morris, 1979). Theodore was a sickly child who suffered from asthma through his teen years. While his asthma almost killed him, his father would not let him baby himself, so days of suffering were followed by days of intense activity. Teddy's very delicate health, combined with his inquisitive mind, led him to be an observer of everything around him, a person so well read that even during the presidency he read at least one book a day. As a child he also discovered nature and enjoyed the outdoors—particularly the wide open spaces as contrasted with the confines of New York City.

By age nine both his observations and writings demonstrated methodological arrangements of classifications and patient indexing. He constantly brought animals and insects into the house. His mother was rather indifferent to what he did, but his father more or less encouraged him. In this same year the family left on a year-long grand tour of Europe. Teddy recorded each day in his diary. Most days he was either seasick or suffering from asthma, but his father insisted they move on.

When Teddy was 12 his father told him unless he developed his body, his mind would be wasted. Teddy then went into weight training and took long walks. Although he built himself up, he still was rather frail. During these years his education was provided largely by tutors. He excelled in languages, history, and literature. Mathematics was not a strong point. When he was 15 the family embarked on another trip through Europe and North Africa.

When Teddy entered Harvard his goal was to become a natural historian. His father had established the Metropolitan Museum and the Natural History Museum. But during his sophomore year the death of his father was followed by the rather quick demise of the family fortunes. He paused to rethink his plans.

Teddy graduated from college and married at age 22. At the same time he began Columbia Law School, completed the research and writing of the book he began as his senior thesis at Harvard, became involved in Republican politics at the ward level, and was elected to the New York state legislature. In his second term at age 24 he was elected minority leader, but he resigned within a year after his wife and mother died of natural causes on the same day. He then began his sojourn to the West and took up cattle ranching in North Dakota. At 28 he ran unsuccessfully for mayor of New York.

Between the ages of 28 and 30 he organized a group of environmentalists who led the fight to develop legislation to protect both animals and the land. He initiated a successful publication. He campaigned for Harrison, researched and wrote the first two volumes of *Winning of the West* (a book widely acclaimed for its scholarship), and edited and wrote several short pieces for magazines. He became Civil Service Commissioner in Washington and found himself in the center of controversy by enforcing the existing legislation. Through all this he managed to take his annual hunting trips to the West.

After six years in Washington he moved on to become Police Commissioner in New York City. After some initial success, he ran upon bad times politically. Finally, he managed to obtain the position of assistant secretary of the Navy and then ran the Navy Department. He went on to become a hero as colonel of the Rough Riders in the Battle of San Juan Hill. Later he became governor of New York, then vice-president of the United States. He succeeded the assassinated McKinley.

Outspoken, daring, energetic, demanding, and commanding, Roosevelt wanted to be president and worked toward that goal continually. It is obvious he enjoyed winning a good fight and he would take on anything. At the same time he learned from his mistakes. He reversed his position on many politically sensitive issues when he found that people suffered as a result of a position he was defending. Few eminent persons retained their boundless childhood energy to the same extent as Teddy Roosevelt.

Franklin D. Roosevelt

Franklin's family always did what was proper and appropriate (Freidel, 1952). To them politics was "dirty" business. In fact, the family wasn't too happy about sharing a name with Franklin's fifth cousin President Theodore Roosevelt, and made it clear that the relationship was distant. Franklin's self-assured mother was the driving force in the family. Franklin spent most of his first 14 years in the company of his parents, whether it be at home on the Hudson, traveling to Europe, or summers in Campobello. His mother took responsibility for his training and discipline, and his early education was largely at the hand of tutors. As a child he was interested in bird collecting and bird watching and enjoyed sailing with a passion. He wanted to attend Annapolis. His parents, however, directed him toward Groton, Harvard, and law school, and he obeyed.

When Franklin went off to Groton at age 14 his life changed abruptly. He went from being the center of his parents' attention to being a fringe member of the group. In his second year he gained a little confidence and began to assert himself. Both at Groton and at Harvard he was a satisfactory but not brilliant student. After Harvard he entered Columbia Law School but had no enthusiasm for studying. He studied law for three years and quit after passing the state bar examination. He practiced law for three years but enjoyed politics more than the law.

In 1910, his home county beckoned him back to run for the state legislature. He found that he enjoyed campaigning for a senate seat as a Democrat in a Republican county. In 1913 he became assistant secretary of the Navy, and during his seven years in this position he gained administrative experience and an understanding of federal government.

This position built his confidence and taught him how to use the press. He viewed himself as a person who got things done during World War I. He was also impressed with the value of personal diplomacy, and he felt he could handle just about anyone on a one-to-one basis. Although he had felt stifled in the legislative branch of government, he felt comfortable with the idea of being an administrator and president. His ability to put himself in a position to be nominated and elected is a story in itself.

Harry S Truman

Harry Truman was a Johnny-come-lately to politics (Daniels, 1950). In 1922 the political king-maker in Missouri asked Truman to run for county judge (in effect, county administrator), and he was defeated. In 1926 he ran again, successfully. His resourcefulness in getting roads built and in financing a county courthouse led to his being perceived as an honest and capable man. At age 50 the state political machine asked him to be a candidate for U.S. Senator. Surprisingly he won and was reelected in 1940. During his tenure his work as chairman of the Senate Committee investigating war-time contracts was highly regarded. When Truman was asked to run as vice-president with Franklin Roosevelt, it was assumed that Roosevelt would not live out his term of office. Truman was thus psychologically ready for the presidency.

Truman could be described as a political late bloomer. Through the age of 40 he had no goals as such, other than to make it at whatever he was doing. He tempered his honesty with political reality.

Robert A. Taft

If ever an individual was molded to the presidency, it was Taft. He not only had his father as a model, but he followed in his father's footsteps as far as he was able. His grandfather had earned a law degree, and his father and uncles had all graduated from Yale, his father second in his class. Taft's biographer (Patterson, 1972) writes that Robert was trained for success but received little affection from either parent. He was obedient to a fault.

As a young boy Robert was bashful and had few if any friends. He studied with a tutor and because of his father's governmental positions he spent time in the Philippines and in Europe. By age 13 he preferred books to spending time with other children. He was expected to excel in school and he always did. Robert was an excellent debater who remembered everything he read. He was consumed with studying at Yale. Nevertheless, he didn't enjoy learning, although he was an excellent "rote" learner who disliked dealing with abstractions. He never did anything that wouldn't contribute to his knowledge, and he avoided social involvement.

He was largely unaffected by the fact that his father was president of the United States during his years at Yale; certainly his classmates seemed unimpressed. He graduated first in his class at Yale and at Harvard Law School. He was singular in purpose and more directed to excel than even his most motivated peers. It is hard to estimate his intelligence because he worked so much harder and more diligently than his classmates. Taft prided himself on his ability to totally control his emotions and concentrate. His life was emotionally flat, and this was communicated in his bid for the presidency.

Taft's biographer hypothesizes that either consciously or unconsciously Taft had to follow a career map laid out by his father. The route would be unique to the times and circumstances, but the goal would be the presidency. Robert Taft's intense commitment to following the pattern is an example of what can happen when attitude and behavior are convergent.

Apparently his first real feeling of personal accomplishment—possibly because he was out from under the shadow of his father—came when he assisted Herbert Hoover with the Food Relief Mission after World War I. When he returned to Cincinnati, Taft seemed to have lost his uncertainty. He entered the state legislature in 1921, the same time his father became chief justice of the U.S. Supreme Court. In 1939 Robert ran successfully for the U.S. Senate and in 1940 unsuccessfully sought the Republican nomination for president. His unwillingness to bend, his conservatism, and his rather stoic personality combined to keep him from gaining the Republican nomination for president.

George Marshall

For years George Marshall was an unsung hero (Payne, 1951). It wasn't that he was without pride or a need for recognition. Rather, he toiled for years in obscurity. He was a career military man when the military was not valued by American society. Later when Roosevelt wanted him to take over the visible direction of the Allied victory in Europe, Marshall felt it was of great psychological importance to keep Ike in the forefront.

Marshall was a student of history who had the "misfortune" of graduating from Virginia Military Institute instead of West Point. But in spite of this "handicap," he later became Army chief of staff. He had a long history in the military. He was commissioned a second lieutenant in 1902. Ten years later he made first lieutenant and received his first recognition when, without notice or preparation, he stepped in and took command during a simulated war game. His performance was so spectacular that the commanding general wrote in his report that Marshall was America's greatest military genius since Stonewall Jackson. Four years later Marshall was old enough to be promoted to captain.

In World War I Marshall was put in charge of American troops who arrived in Europe with no training. Again he proved his leadership. His broad comprehension of all factors—men, terrain, equipment, and the enemy—prompted him to ask questions which in turn produced the information he needed to formulate complete, concise orders that were easy to follow. Despite his effective leadership, at 37 he was too young to be promoted.

In 1924 Marshall was assigned to China and made lieutenant colonel. His years in China made him more speculative and contemplative. In 1933 he became commander of the Eighth Army and received a 15 percent pay cut. At age 55 he was considered too young to be promoted to brigadier general, the next rank. Finally in 1939 Roosevelt named him chief of staff on the day that Poland was invaded by Germany. He was charged with building an army, preparing military tactics for a war in Europe and Asia, keeping up morale, and preparing himself to deal effectively with Congress and the president. He accomplished his goals by breaking with tradition and selecting men like Eisenhower for command positions. He ignored the age-in-grade system that had victimized him throughout his military career.

In 1947 he was appointed secretary of state and in effect became the chief of staff during the Cold War. He formulated the highly successful Marshall Plan which incorporated economic, human, and political issues.

Marshall was the consummate organization man. His quiet nature hardly gave evidence of his tremendous vitality. He was noted for his ability to concentrate, raise comprehensive questions, and process information with great facility. He could effectively juxtapose information generated through convergent and divergent information processes.

Dwight D. Eisenhower

There was nothing particularly unique about Eisenhower's boyhood (Childs, 1958). He was a typically active, athletic Midwesterner. He decided to go away to school only because his friend was taking the entrance examination to Annapolis. As it turned out Ike was too old to be admitted to Annapolis, but he qualified for West Point and accepted the appointment. During his childhood and throughout his years at West Point, one overriding characteristic emerges: his reluctance to commit himself completely to any course of action; he always held part of himself in reserve.

At West Point his adaptability was considered his strongest suit. He graduated 95th in a class of 164. His personality was a great asset as people liked and trusted him almost immediately. He served under General Fox Conner in Panama. Conner served as a mentor, guiding Eisenhower's reading and discussing with him various philosophies of military science. Conner also got Ike into Command and General Staff School in 1925. There Ike graduated first in a group of 275 officers. Still a major at age 45, he served on MacArthur's staff in the Philippines.

Just five days after Pearl Harbor, General Marshall brought Eisenhower to Washington as assistant chief in the War Plans Division. Marshall had Ike draw up plans for the defense of Hawaii, the Aleutians, New Guinea, and Australia. Eisenhower also outlined a cross-channel invasion of Europe. Recognizing Eisenhower's self-confidence, the quality of his work, and his agreement with Marshall regarding European strategy, Marshall advanced him over 366 senior officers and made him commander of the European Theater of Operations.

Eisenhower's biography gives the impression that he was passive regarding the major events surrounding his rise to eminence. While no one individual designed the tactics for the war in Europe, Eisenhower was able to hold the plan together without allowing his own ego to spill over into the situation. His external demeanor usually remained calm and reassuring regardless of how much strain and uncertainty he was experiencing. He looked and behaved the leader.

John F. Kennedy

Kennedy was regarded as an underachiever in school (Dollen, 1965). As a boy John was fascinated with ideas but careless over facts. He was a very poor speller and could not grasp foreign languages. Interestingly, the political blood came from his mother's side of the family; her father, "Honey" Fitzgerald, was the first Catholic mayor of Boston.

John was sent to boarding school in Connecticut in seventh grade. It was his first time away from home. His parents received constant reports on his poor achievement, and teachers were concerned that young Kennedy would not apply himself. There were also complaints about his room at school being disorderly.

Kennedy graduated from prep school in 1935, 64th in a class of 112. His peers recognized his energy and determination and voted him most likely to succeed. He enrolled at Princeton but had to leave because of jaundice. After a year in Arizona he decided to attend Harvard. He was an average student there and reasonably popular. His interests were broad and universal and he appeared to concentrate in no one area.

After spending the summer of 1937 in Europe he became interested in politics and people and decided to major in political science. Professor Arthur Holcombe became Kennedy's mentor and encouraged him. About this time his father became ambassador to Great Britain, and John spent six months as a diplomatic courier. His senior thesis at Harvard entitled *Why England Slept* was later published. In the book he analyzes both democracies and dictatorships and shows an understanding of the strengths and weaknesses of each. After graduation he began business school at Stanford but left and spent several months in South America.

It is written that John's older brother Joe had been the object of the family's presidential aspirations. When Joe died in military service it fell to the next oldest brother, John, to assume his place. His grandfather's political connections in Boston and Massachusetts and his father's connections and money helped him secure the support needed for a seat in the U.S. Congress. His three terms in Congress were marked by absences and no major legislation. He was personally ambitious but not a party regular. He was, however, able to gather good people around him. Kennedy defeated Lodge in the U.S. Senate election. A back injury and a long recuperation period gave him time to author *Profiles in Courage* for which he received a Pulitzer Prize.

How many parents state that one of their children will be president someday and see the prophecy fulfilled? Living up to family expectations can be a strong stimulus.

Kennedy had personal drive but did not seem ambitious like Humphrey, Johnson, or even Roosevelt. Somehow Kennedy communicated that he would be competent and willing to serve without demonstrating an intense personal need to be president. His greatest accomplishment lay in achieving the presidency and convincing a somewhat disillusioned generation that he and they had something worthwhile to offer.

Lyndon B. Johnson

His biographer (Kearns, 1976) begins by noting that Johnson's gift of leadership rested in his ability to understand, persuade, and subdue. Johnson operated on the assumption that the power he gained made good works possible and that good works should bring love and gratitude.

From childhood Lyndon lived more in terms of the way he wanted to picture life than the way things actually were. He did not appreciate disagreement or contradictory feedback. His memory was selective and inflative. His parents had little in common, and his mother concentrated all her attention on Lyndon. In fact, she seldom left him alone and played games in such a way that he would always win. Lyndon could read and spell by age four, in part a result of the conditions his mother placed on their relationship.

At age five he began associating more with his father and imitated his father's gregariousness. Lyndon was a troublemaker in school. After graduation from high school he and some friends roamed through the West and California for a year. When he returned he worked on a road gang and clerked for a criminal lawyer. Finally he gave in to his mother's wishes, and with her tutoring passed the entrance examination for Southwest Texas State Teachers College.

Shortly after entering college he developed a knack for organizing and taking charge behind the scenes. He edited the college paper and had himself appointed as assistant to the university president. In addition he was a member of the debate team. After graduating with honors he taught school and then went to work on the staff of a U.S. Congressman from Texas.

Apparently Johnson developed an astute skill of "psyching out" situations, systems, and people through observation and questioning. Once he understood a situation he acted to put himself in a position of control because he believed everyone would benefit from his leadership. Always he tried to direct resources in order to benefit others who would in turn be appreciative of his efforts. He was effective at manipulating powerful persons and circumstances, particularly in the United States Senate. He was, however, unable to accept limitations on his personalized system of control, particularly in international affairs. He would likely take only slight offense at being labeled a "wheeler-dealer" but would be highly offended if accused of acting for personal gain. Always he perceived himself as a powerful instrument for doing good.

Hubert Humphrey

Unlike Johnson, who discovered the joy and satisfaction of political maneuvering early in life, and unlike some who were "programmed" for high public office, Humphrey admitted he would have followed in his father's footsteps as a pharmacist if the opportunity had presented itself (1976). Humphrey's father taught him to love political debate and discussion, but when he was growing up there was little if any thought given to public office. He went to the University of Minnesota at his father's insistence, and when he married in 1932 he was still uncertain of his future. In 1935 he attended his sister's wedding in Washington, D.C. and indicated that he found Washington so exciting he intended to get into Congress someday. He later graduated with a major in political science and took his master's degree at Louisiana State University. Returning to Minneapolis he took a job working for the trade unions and began studying for his Ph.D.

Union members wanted him to run for mayor, but he lost that election. By then, however, he had been bitten by the political bug and realized he would have to build up the Democratic party in Minnesota if he or any other Democrat were to be elected. He worked to establish a new party coalition in Minnesota, and to make ends meet he taught at Macalester College. In 1945 he ran successfully for mayor.

As mayor and later as a U.S. Senator Humphrey managed to reform the city, build a political party, generate considerable national legislation, and more than adequately represent the liberal wing of the Democratic party. He was always a champion of social welfare. Always considered a decent and loyal party man, he liked to think of himself as the great healer. Humphrey's drive, optimism, and buoyancy set him apart.

Common Threads

The men described in this section were not humble men. They were confident and self-directed, but not without faults. Some came to their presidency well read and well traveled. Others brought a sparse intellectual and geographical background. What can one learn from studying U.S. presidents? First, that there is no one presidential personality type. Second, that chance plays a significant role in success. Third, that the individual seeking the presidency feels up to the demands of the office.

BUSINESS–FINANCE–ADVENTURE

Carnegie, Ford, Rockefeller, Baruch, and Lindberg were alike in that they were all "first" but in different areas of endeavor. Some came from humble beginnings; others were helped by important family connections. All these men braved different frontiers. Today the frontiers are more elusive. Will personal initiative be rewarded so handsomely for tomorrow's achievers?

Andrew Carnegie

Carnegie had the good fortune of arriving in Pittsburgh at the beginning of his adolescence (Wall, 1970). His father was an unemployed weaver in Scotland, and while the loss of his trade and the move literally killed the elder Carnegie, the break with the past provided Andrew a golden opportunity that he pursued. Andrew was self-taught and was so appreciative of the books that were made available to him as a teenager that much of his fortune later went to the building of public libraries throughout the United States, the British Isles, and Canada.

Andrew was raised with the Scottish motto, "Take care of your pence, and your pounds will take care of themselves." As a child he convinced his parents to let him stay out of school for three years. At age eight he began school in a one-room class with over 150 other pupils. Needless to say, discipline was harsh and instant.

In 1848, when Andrew was 13, the family set out for America. Andrew shared his mother's excitement and none of his father's doubts about leaving. Andrew enjoyed the excitement and adventure of the ship and became a favorite of the crew. He arrived full of self-confidence and with a sense of freedom to carve out his own path. He worked for a short while in a textile factory and learned bookkeeping. Working as messenger boy for the telegraph, he learned about the city and gained the confidence of influential persons. Next he learned telegraphy and was the first in the office to take messages by ear. He was so clever that people used to stop by and watch him take messages. He was given increased responsibility and by his late teens he had become secretary and telegrapher for the superintendent of the Pennsylvania Railroad. In his job he became familar with the business world and was able to discern why particular businesses were strong or weak. He learned about shipping costs and the importance of management and was at the center of the communication and transportation industries. Combining his knowledge with his personal ambition, it was only a matter of time before he made his first investment.

Early in his rise it was significant that Thomas Scott, the man under whom Carnegie worked, moved up the management hierarchy of the Pennsylvania Railroad and took Andrew with him. During the Civil War Carnegie was charged with organizing communication and transportation from Washington through Virginia. When Scott was made assistant secretary of war, Carnegie became responsible for nationwide transportation and communication.

At 26 a neighbor persuaded Carnegie to invest in the Pennsylvania oil fields. Within a year he had made his first million. He stayed with the railroad several years more, but between 1865 and 1875 he invested widely and successfully.

Through a series of stock manipulations he formed United States Steel. All the while he maintained heavy investments in transportation, communication, oil, and later finance. Carnegie was the first one-man conglomerate. It is worth noting that other than the oil industry, he understood every aspect of each business in which he invested. He used the knowledge gained from one area of endeavor to make inroads in other areas. He considered the 2,300 libraries he founded just payment for what he owed society.

Henry Ford

As a boy Henry Ford was always tinkering and taking things apart (Nevins, 1954). He shaped tools that made work easier. He grew up on a farm but disliked the repetition of farm life. He was highly energetic and liked novelty. At age 13 he went to Detroit and saw a steam-driven car; he could remember everything the owner told him about how it operated. He took watches apart and put them back together, and in turn learned how to repair watches for which he made his own tools. At the Centennial Exposition of 1876 he saw seven internal combustion machines being demonstrated and was inspired to develop what was to become known as the automobile.

Each step in developing a self-propelled vehicle required him to master some new bit of knowledge, whether it was combustion or electricity. He learned to hire people to do the things he couldn't do, such as making the carriage. Once he accepted the fact that he couldn't excel or master all aspects he made rapid progress. Much of his early work on the automobile took place while he was employed by the Edison Illuminating Company in Detroit; he used much of his income for experiments.

Ford was a tireless worker, and each problem was seen as a challenge. In 1896, at age 33, he completed his first car, having built it from scratch. By test driving he quickly learned what was lacking, and went on to develop such features as the cooling system.

Ford was not the first to conceptualize the essential elements of the automobile. However, he developed a car that was clean in design, strong, and required fewer repairs than those developed by his contemporaries. At least 55 other people and companies were manufacturing self-propelled vehicles at the same time, and many of these people had superior technical backgrounds and better finances.

Why was Ford so successful when others failed? First, Ford was able to get the men he needed to make the car function and help the company grow. Many of his business associates stayed with him indefinitely. Second, Ford benefitted greatly by recognizing his limitations, particularly in the business area. Ford had the final word on design and engineering, but a coworker managed the business affairs. Later the company would fail when Ford was unable or unwilling to adapt to changing times and insisted on maintaining outmoded economic policies. Third, Ford was driven by his goal of developing the "best" motor car. His eventual success was due in part to the car's reliability and success in racing. These elements, plus a little bit of luck and his ability to capitalize on some major scientific breakthroughs in electrical and metallurgical engineering allowed Ford to accomplish what many other had tried.

John D. Rockefeller

Young Rockefeller was a serious, industrious boy who saved every penny he earned. He even kept a ledger of his earnings, starting with his first income as a boy and continuing through all subsequent transactions until his finances grew beyond his ability to accurately record. According to his biographer (Winkler, 1929), Rockefeller learned the value of having money earn money when as a boy he hoed tomatoes for ten days and received $3.50. He realized he would have earned more had he loaned out $50 at seven percent. From that time on, making money work for him became his life rule. He earned his fortune because he saved the money made from shipping transactions and invested it in oil just when the oil boom was beginning. What made Rockefeller different was that he continued to invest, acquire, and manage until he was in control of Standard Oil. Once his fortune was made he built a financial empire by maintaining his control of oil production and distribution. He was one of the first modern corporate managers who could do it all: he built, developed, and maintained.

Bernard M. Baruch

In his autobiography (1957) Baruch describes himself as a shy and fearful child with an ungovernable temper and a dread of speaking in public. As he grew up he was challenged by his parents to outdo others. It took him years to learn how to control himself and select those areas in which he could excel, leaving to others what he could not do well. As a child he lived in rural South Carolina and enjoyed the status and benefits that come with being the town doctor's son. When he was 10 his family moved abruptly to New York City following the death of his father's friend in a duel. His first recollection of New York involved having to wear shoes all the time.

At 12 or 13 he first experienced prejudice directed at him because he was a Jew. He entered City College of New York at age 14 because there was no public school after eighth grade. He had wanted to enter West Point but during the physical it was discovered he was totally deaf in one ear. As he grew stronger and taller he became less combative and more confident. Nevertheless, he was suspended from CCNY for hitting a student who insulted his mother. He spent the next several months hanging around gyms learning to box; he wanted to be able to take punishment if his temper was going to keep getting him into trouble.

About this time his mother took him to a phrenologist who suggested that Bernard would be best suited for finance or politics. To this end his mother got him a job with one of his father's patients as an office apprentice in a stock company. Baruch made his first investments a few years later, but these were total failures. He learned the hard way that it was important to know the companies in which one was investing, rather than taking other people's word for things.

His guidelines for becoming a successful speculator included astute observation, getting all the facts, forming a judgment about those facts, and acting in time. When he earned his first million dollars his father reacted by saying, "So what!" This so disturbed Baruch that he began to seek meaningful ways to contribute to the well-being of others. He continued to prosper and in time served in the federal government in various capacities.

For Baruch the stock market became a testing ground. His father convinced him that he should be concerned with making socially worthwhile investments as well as economically sound ones. During World War II he applied himself toward solving the most complex problems involving money, materials, and politics.

Charles A. Lindbergh

Lindbergh grew up in Minnesota, appreciating the freedom afforded by an open and friendly countryside (Ross, 1964). His father was financially comfortable and well known, having been elected to the U.S. Congress in 1907. In 1917 he campaigned for the U.S. Senate on a strong antiwar platform and was defeated. Charles' mother was his father's second wife and considerably younger. She taught Charles and enjoyed his spirit of adventure. Interestingly, as a child Lindbergh had a phobia of the dark and feared falling from high places—strange fears for a person who later flew across the Atlantic relying on dead reckoning.

As a youth Lindbergh equated freedom with flying. He entered the University of Wisconsin and was rumored to have kept a machine in his room for tinkering. He lived with his mother who had moved to Madison to teach school. He hated writing and wrote poorly, and he was frustrated by the lack of practicality in engineering school. After two years of relatively poor scholastic performance, he left college. He barnstormed and took flying lessons. At the time he took up flying the average life span for an aviator was 900 hours.

The planning and preparation for his trancontinental flight was equivalent to that needed for a military campaign. The slightest miscalculation would end in failure and death because he had left himself no margin of error. His accomplishment was all the greater because it was primarily a one-man operation.

SUMMARY

The common denominator that unites all the eminent people profiled in these pages is their motivation to know and to be productive. For some the commitment came early; for others it came late in life. Some individuals realized personal satisfaction and social recognition together, whereas many achieved personal meaning long before their achievements were publicly acclaimed. Nearly all struggled and saw early failures as an inspiration to try harder. Some were pushed along by parents, others were drawn along by mentors, and some experienced both and others experienced neither. Some were narrow and others broad in their accomplishments. These individuals defy stereotyping.

REFERENCES

Atkinson, J. W. Motivational determinants of risk-taking behavior. *Psychological Review,* 1957, *64,* 359–372.

Atkinson, J. W., & Feather, N. T. (Eds.). *A theory of achievement motivation.* New York: Wiley, 1966.

Baker, C. *Ernest Hemingway: A life story.* New York: Charles Scribner's Sons, 1969.

Baruch, B. M. *Baruch: My own story.* New York: Henry Holt and Co., 1957.

Blom, E. *Mozart.* London: J. M. Dent and Sons, Ltd., 1935.

Blotner, J. *Faulkner: A biography.* New York: Random House, 1974.

Boyd, T. A. *Professional amateur—The biography of Charles Franklin Kettering.* New York: E. P. Dutton & Co., 1957.

Champigneulle, B. *Rodin.* London: Thames and Hudson, 1967.

Childs, M. W. *Eisenhower: Captive hero.* New York: Harcourt, Brace, 1958.

Clark, B. H. *Eugene O'Neill: The man and his plays.* New York: R. M. McBride & Co., 1929.

Clark, R. W. *Einstein: The life and times.* London: Hodder and Stoughton, 1973.

Coughlan, N. *Young John Dewey.* Chicago: University of Chicago Press, 1973.

Covington, M. W., & Omelich, C. L. Effort: The double-edged sword in school achievement. *Journal of Educational Psychology,* 1979, *71,* 169–182.

Daniels, J. *The man of independence.* New York: J. B. Lippincott Co., 1950.

Dollen, C. *John F. Kennedy, American.* Boston: Daughters of St. Paul, 1965.

Donaldson, T. C. *Walt Whitman: The man.* New York: Francis P. Harper, 1896.

Ewen, D. *The story of Jerome Kern.* New York: Henry Holt and Co., 1953.

Falk, S. L. *Tennessee Williams.* New York: Twane Publishers, 1961.

Farnsworth, P. R. *The social psychology of music.* Ames: Iowa State University Press, 1969.

Freidel, F. B. *Franklin D. Roosevelt: The apprenticeship.* Boston: Little, Brown, 1952.

Fuller, B. *Ideas and integrities.* Englewood Cliffs, N.J.: Prentice-Hall, 1963.

Gropius, W. *Scope of total architecture.* New York: Harper and Brothers Publishers, 1955.

Hall, G. S. *Life and confessions of a psychologist.* New York: D. Appleton and Company, 1923.

Harper, I. H. *Life and work of Susan B. Anthony.* New York: Arno and The New York Times, 1969.

Harris, T. F. *Pearl S. Buck: A biography.* New York: The John Day Co., 1969.

Hart, M. *Act one: An autobiography.* New York: Random House, 1959.

Haskins, J. *The story of Stevie Wonder.* New York: Lothrop, Lee and Shepard, 1976.

Hellman, L. *An unfinished woman: A memoir.* New York: Bantam Books, 1969.

Holt, R. *George Washington Carver.* New York: Doubleday and Co., 1943.

Humphrey, H. H. *The education of a public man: My life and politics.* New York: Doubleday and Co., 1976.

Josephson, M. *Edison.* New York: McGraw-Hill, 1959.

Kearns, D. *Lyndon Johnson and the American dream.* New York: Harper and Row, 1976.

Kraft, K., & Kraft, P. *Luther Burbank: The wizard and the man.* New York: Meredith Press, 1967.

Kruglanski, A. W. The endogenous—exogenous partition in attribution theory. *Psychological Review,* 1975, *82,* 387–406.

Mann, P. *Ralph Bunche, U.N. peacemaker.* New York: Coward, McCann, and Geoghegan, 1975.

McClelland, D. C., et al., *The achievement motive.* New York: Appleton, 1953.

McClelland, D. C. Managing motivation to expand human freedom. *American Psychologist,* 1978, *33,* 201–210.

Mead, M. *Blackberry winter: My early years.* New York: William Morrow and Co., 1972.

Mertins, L. *Robert Frost.* Norman: University of Oklahoma Press, 1965.

Miller, W. R. *Martin Luther King, Jr.* New York: Weybright and Talley, 1968.

Morris, E. *The rise of Theodore Roosevelt.* New York: Coward, McCann, and Geoghegan, 1979.

Muir, J. *The story of my boyhood and youth.* New York: Houghton-Mifflin, 1912.

Nelson, B. *Arthur Miller: Portrait of a playwright.* New York: David McKay Co., 1970.

Neutra, R. *Life and shape.* New York: Appleton-Century-Crofts, 1962.

Nevins, A. *Ford, the times, the man, the company.* New York: Charles Scribner's Sons, 1954.

Nicholls, J. G. Effort is virtuous, but it's better to have ability. *Journal of Research in Personality,* 1976, *10,* 306–315.

Patterson, J. T. *Mr. Republican: A biography of Robert A. Taft.* New York: Houghton-Mifflin, 1972.

Payne, R. *The Marshall story.* New York: Prentice-Hall, 1951.

Penrose, R. *Picasso: His life and work.* New York: Schocken Books, 1962.

Prout, H. G. *A life of George Westinghouse.* New York: Charles Scribner's Sons, 1972.

Ross, W. S. *The lost hero: Charles A. Lindbergh.* New York: Harper and Row, 1964.

Royal, D. *The story of J. Robert Oppenheimer.* New York: St. Martins Press, 1969.

Rubinstein, A. *My young years.* New York: Alfred A. Knopf, 1973.

Rushmore, R. *The life of George Gershwin.* New York: The Crowell-Collier Press, 1966.

Saarinen, E. *Search for form.* New York: Reinhold Publishing Co., 1948.

Schafer, M. *British composers in interview.* London: Faber and Faber, 1963.

Sohn, D. Affect-generating powers of effort and ability self attributions of academic success and failure. *Journal of Educational Psychology,* 1977, *69,* 500–505.

Sullivan, L. H. *The autobiography of an idea.* New York: Press of the American Institute of Architects, Inc., 1924.

Sullivan, L. H. *Kindergarten chats and other writings.* New York: Wittenborn, Schultz, Inc., 1947.

Summerfield, J. D., & Thatcher, L. (Eds.). *The creative mind and method.* New York: Russell and Russell, 1964.

Vlanov, B. *Duke Ellington.* New York: Creative Age Press, Inc., 1946.

Waite, H. E. *Make a joyful sound.* Philadelphia: Macrae Smith Co., 1961.

Wall, J. F. *Andrew Carnegie.* New York: Oxford University Press, 1970.

Weiner, B. Achievement, motivation, and the education process. *Review of Educational Research,* 1972, *42,* 203–215.

Weiner, E. *The Damon Runyon story*. New York: Longmans, Green & Co., 1948.

Wiener, N. *Ex-Prodigy: My childhood and youth*. New York: Simon and Schuster, 1953.

Winkler, J. K. *John D: A portrait in oils*. New York: The Vanguard Press, 1929.

Wright, F. L. *An autobiography*. New York: Duell, Sloan and Pearce, 1943.

Chapter 6

Sequence of Development in Two Talented Individuals

In the previous chapters we presented our definition of talent and talent potential, offered ideas about why and how giftedness develops, and took brief glimpses into the lives of some eminent persons. In this chapter we present two fairly detailed case studies of persons identified in ninth grade as talented. GIFTS staff have maintained regular contact with these people over a 20-year period. Connie and John are among 600 persons being studied on a longitudinal basis.

The material on Connie and John is edited from two case studies originally written by Dr. Nicholas Colangelo while he was a research assistant in GIFTS. Both case studies are based upon materials gathered on Connie and John during their four years (grades 9–12) of participation in GIFTS programs, on follow-up questionnaires completed the first five years after high school graduation, and on personal interviews conducted every three years after that. The personal interviews covered Connie's and John's growth and development from childhood to the present day—approximately the first 35 years of their lives.

These case studies allow readers to test some of the ideas presented in previous chapters against a whole life perspective. While reading about these two "typical" talented people, keep in mind the material already presented and test your own ideas and thoughts in order to come to a personal understanding of how talented persons develop.

CASE STUDY OF CONNIE

Connie is presently a second-grade teacher. She views herself as very enthusiastic and dedicated and states "teaching is my vocation." Connie sees teaching as more than a job; it is a life style. The feeling that teaching is a very important element of her life was very evident during personal interviews. It seems that teaching has opened an array of discoveries about herself and her abilities, including a realization of creative talent. "I remember myself as the child who at the end of art period had a blank paper in front of me," she says. Encouragement from her husband and the opportunity to teach have helped Connie test herself. She sees the way she's decorated her classroom as one of her accomplishments.

Connie came out of the mold of "traditional" teaching. However, her own interests and enthusiasm have led her to try new ideas and develop a "learning center approach" in her classroom.

Some of the themes evident in Connie's life are enthusiasm and a keen perception about herself. Her senior-year GIFTS report reads, "Connie's zest for living and the prodigious enthusiasm she generates toward each task she undertakes is nothing short of remarkable."

Early Childhood and Elementary School

Connie was the oldest in the family, followed by two sisters and a brother. She recalls getting along well with her siblings. She states that it was hard being the oldest because "she was expected to do everything well." She remembers herself as a "deliberate type" instead of impulsive. In early childhood Connie had a friend who made her feel "second best," and Connie remembers, "I always compared myself to her."

She recalls that her father did not trust the children and would often ask what she was doing. Her mother "defended" the children and seems to have been closer to Connie. In her tenth-grade essay Connie writes, "I never was too close to my father, and so my mom has been extra close." Her family was not a "talking family," and Connie remembers keeping many things to herself. One incident in particular stands out for her. As a little girl she became involved in mixing colors down in the basement. When her parents found out, they did not like what she was doing. She recalls they did not seem to understand what she was trying to do.

Connie's brother was born mentally retarded and eventually became a ward of the state. Connie recalls her mother "going through a lot" over Johnnie. For Connie there was some feeling of not getting enough attention because of Johnnie, but she learned many things, too. In her ninth-grade essay she reports, "I learned a great deal about human nature because of him." Connie often displays this sensitivity and empathy for others.

The family often had picnics in the backyard. They did not travel much because her father did not have a car.

School did not seem much of a problem for her and she enjoyed it. She had no trouble reading and "liked books right away." She recognized in these early school years that she was not one of the "dummies," but neither did she see herself at the top. She received good report cards consistently and this pleased her parents. She recalls an incident in third grade when the teacher did not like her because she was lefthanded. What seems to stand out most about this is that her father "stuck up" for her on this issue. Connie remembers it felt good to get so much support from her dad. In fifth grade she first realized that she was "bright."

Junior High School

Connie did not have to change schools and attended the same school for eleven years. Her most striking memory of this period is that in eighth grade she received all As. "This was really exciting. It was just the kind of recognition I needed." This seemed to signal an "awakening" for her; she felt confident of her abilities. During these years she got along very well with others.

High School

In high school Connie had a reputation for being very studious. Her many school activities included student council secretary, coeditor of the school newspaper, girl's athletic association, and pep club.

There was a shortage of money in her family, so in addition to her schoolwork and activities Connie held two jobs. This range of activity extended her energies to the limit. At one point she remembers working so hard she became physically ill.

However, being busy and active was a way of life for her. "I like being busy; I thrive on it." Her deliberateness led her to approach tasks in a very organized manner. She was able to do many things at once because she knew how to organize her energy. (This trait is also evident in her teaching.)

Connie remembers her high school years as a time when she pushed herself to achieve. External approval and recognition seemed very important. "I was measuring myself on other people's standards. It seemed like getting the A was all important." She wishes that at this time in her life someone would have told her to relax. She had many girl friends in high school but claims she had little social life with boys. "I think I scared them off, probably because of my high grades and drive for achievement."

She recognized that her family was not in a financial position to put her through college. Thus it was one of her goals to earn a scholarship, which she did.

GIFTS—Grades 9–12

Connie was selected for the GIFTS program in ninth grade. This experience was very enjoyable for her as well as enlightening. First, GIFTS exposed her to a university setting, and she was so excited by that atmosphere that she "knew" she would attend school there. Also GIFTS helped her investigate future plans after high school. It further served to help her to think about herself.

For a time Connie was insecure about her abilities. "My success was from hard work and not native ability," she stated. However, the activities at GIFTS helped her gain confidence in herself and appreciate her many strengths. The introspective essays she wrote gave her a chance to express her personal side, and her excellent scores on the verbal and math tests gave her evidence of her ability. (See Exhibit 6-1.)

From her writings, it seems that GIFTS opened new horizons and gave her opportunities to express her enthusiasm about some of her ideas. GIFTS, she wrote, "stimulated me to my full capacity and caused me to utilize what I have." Her personal essays indicate an overriding optimism about life. In her senior essay she wrote, "I have faith in the future, for the future brings along so many wonderful experiences and the possible fulfillment of so many dreams." She went on to say, "I love life and am doing my best to make the most of every opportunity. I guess this is the key to my personality. Sometimes even I wonder where I get the energy. There's nothing I really dislike doing."

Connie's essays at GIFTS were further distinguished by their length and her keen perceptions about herself. Some of these reflections included: "Somehow or somewhere I've lost my sense of humor. I guess I take life too seriously. This is an obstacle I hope to cross soon for I value it highly" and "I consider everyday a new challenge to be met and a new opportunity to be taken. I hope I can meet these challenges and make the most of the opportunities that come along." In reference to her youngest brother she wrote, "Through little Johnnie I think I've learned much about human nature. I don't think I'm nearly so self-centered." This indicates an awareness of how she can be affected by others around her.

Her own sense of competition and a developing sense of personal achievement were showing. In her senior report her counselor wrote, "She is a highly motivated young lady who strives to excel not only in the competitive sense, but for her own personal satisfaction. She personifies many of the qualities we associate with a truly superior student." This striving for personal satisfaction rather than external rewards continued to mark Connie's personality and is strongly evident in her present attitude about herself.

Connie expressed concern at GIFTS over what field to pursue after high school. Because she was able to do so many things well, she found it difficult to narrow the choice. She wrote, "The field of chemistry sounds so interesting but so are many other fields—I'm becoming more and more confused about what I want to do." Counselors at GIFTS recommended that she investigate Integrated Liberal Studies (ILS) as a first-year program because it gave her a broad background plus flexibility. She began college in the ILS program.

Exhibit 6-1

Cumulative Test Record
Connie
Testing Period: 1959–1963

Test	Form	Grade	Percentile	Norms
SCHOOL AND COLLEGE ABILITY	1A	9		9th graders
Verbal			96–99	
Quantitative			96–99	
Total			98–99	
DAVIS READING				
Level of comprehension	1A	10	95	11th graders
Speed of comprehension	1A	10	99	11th graders
STEP SOCIAL STUDIES	2A	9	99	10th graders
TERMAN CONCEPT MASTERY	T	12	79^2	70^b
WISCONSIN INVENTORY GIFTS STUDENTS*				
Verbal score (number right out of 100)	I	11	58^2	60^b
Quantitative score (number right out of 50)	II	11	36^2	33^b

* This test has been made up from items which have proved to be most difficult for students at GIFTS over a four-year period.

[2] Raw score

[b] GIFTS student average

Summary Comment on Cumulative Test Record

Connie's test performances on standardized tests place her within the top five percent of her norm group. Because of the newness of the WITS verbal and quantitative tests taken by Connie last year, we were unable to give an accurate interpretation. According to our established norms, Connie's performance on the verbal test was about average, and her performance on the quantitative test was slightly above average. This year, on the difficult Terman Concept Mastery test, her performance was above the average for GIFTS seniors.

College

Connie received scholarships that allowed her to attend the University of Wisconsin—Madison. College was an exciting time, and Connie was active in school, especially after the first year. Scholastically she graduated with a 3.65 grade point (out of a possible 4.0) and was elected to Phi Kappa Phi honor society.

Connie married in her senior year and this seemed to complement her life. Both she and her husband enjoyed their studies. As she states, the discovery of being loved opened her to even more of the world and herself.

Post College

After college Connie and her husband moved to Chicago where he pursued his studies in theology and she took a secretarial job. This was an unhappy time for her because her job did not require enthusiasm or talent. Given her abilities and her eagerness to make a contribution, it stands to reason that a nondemanding job would cause her problems. In addition, though not as important (by her account), she felt somewhat of a "failure" because she was not earning a good salary. Her need for financial success seems consistent with the fact that she had to be so aware of finances during high school and college.

Present

Connie is continually developing and growing as a person. She seems to be integrating many of her best qualities. She is more self-confident, and her life is now guided more by "internal standards" than by the "standards of others." She has developed her own system of self-evaluation. "I know when I'm doing a good job," she says. "I feel I can solve problems if I have some."

She claims that what she likes best about herself is "the feeling that I know what I'm doing and doing it well." Teaching is central to her life. In her own words, "I have found my place." A career is important to people like Connie; it is not just a job but a way of life.

Connie is constantly "learning." Recently she received her driver's license. This meant more freedom for her and also represented going beyond some previous restrictions. (You will recall that her family did not have a car.)

She has been married several years but has not felt ready for children. She has felt she needed more time for herself first. "I did not want to apply my needs to my children," she stated. She is clear about what it all means to her: "Wanting a baby means I feel good." She believes she is now much closer to making children a part of her life.

Connie still looks to the future with optimism and enthusiasm. She is not certain of the exact direction but feels some change is imminent. She has thought about setting up a private school to test some of her ideas about education and teaching. Always she is concerned about her effectiveness as a teacher. Connie appears to be continually developing and recognizing her many superior abilities.

CASE STUDY OF JOHN

John is a minister. He is characterized by himself and his colleagues as the "intellectual" on the staff. Most philosophical and theological questions are brought to him, yet he also acts as an advisor to youth and to university students. He views himself as a strong teacher and is considering moving to a teaching position in the next two or three years. What is extremely important to John is maintaining a wide range of intellectual and people-oriented activities. Currently he is thinking of pursuing a Ph.D. in systematic theology.

John sees himself as basically satisfied in his field. He believes he is building a solid foundation in theology and counseling. He is committed to his profession, one he chose deliberately and not by chance. In his own words, "There are no other options I want."

In his work he is his own best critic. He feels most comfortable with intellectual issues and sees some "defects" in his role as a counselor. However, he feels he has become much more sensitive to his parishioners and is happy about his progress in this area.

John describes his interests as "catholic," with much variety. He reads broadly and tends to read several things at once, often not completing any one book. He views himself as a "contextual thinker"—that is, he is interested in how things relate. His interest is in common themes rather than specific ideas. Much of his thinking about the church and other topics takes the form of imagery, and his sermons tend to be infused with poetic images. His scientific background is evidenced in much of his thinking, but he is more interested in the culture of science than the mechanics. He is interested in how the scientist goes about his work. He wants to know the data but looks for the larger interpretation. This habit of viewing things in a larger and usually more humane perspective is important to keep in mind when considering John's change from science to the humanities.

In discussing how he performs his tasks, John admits he is not well organized. He tends to put things off and does things at the last minute—a trait from his public school days. As he states, "I can be easily interrupted from my work." However, he always gets the job done.

When talking about career choices, John says, "I can't put my finger on a good sound career pattern. I can't recall reasons why I went to a particular school." He feels he has become more self-accepting and has formed his own identity. He also thinks his life has become more deliberate in the sense that he is in control of much of what happens. He states, "People don't make rational systematic choices—we have to have a certain amount of spontaneity." While allowing for spontaneity, John is definitely not the type who sits back and lets things happen to him.

He views himself as happily married. He has given considerable thought to how he would raise children, but he and his wife have decided not to begin their family yet. John gives the impression of having a well thought out value system. He views himself in the traditional Christian model where the criteria are "love thy neighbor" and "practice what you preach."

In his free time John enjoys such activities as reading, television, camping, cross-country skiing, canoeing, solitaire, and "straightening things up."

In speculating about his future John states, "It's open but frought with hazards." He is optimistic about the possibilities for himself and the world. His optimism will endure so long as people are willing to work toward improvement and not believe that things will "just get better." He strongly believes the church has an important role in helping to humanize the environment. He sees himself as actively participating in this by offering people a sense of hope and helping them see the necessity for sharing.

Early Childhood

John remembers himself as a very verbal child. He would hear jokes or stories and he could remember these and pass them on. Sometimes he would hear "dirty" jokes and repeat them for the family, not understanding what he was saying. The family used to laugh about this and John did too, enjoying the attention.

John also had a very active imagination, much of which seems to have left him as he entered junior high school. He would make up stories to himself "with connected ideas." He had vivid images of whatever he would make up. Sometimes he would talk himself to sleep. He did not share these fantasies with others as he realized they were made up and private.

His father would read the Sunday paper to the children with great animation and John loved this. John's father also taught him much about nature and passed on an appreciation of the environment. John recalls learning a great deal from both his parents. His mother had an artistic bent and would take the children to museums, concerts, and other cultural events. This was quite rare for the small town in which they lived. In recalling his parents, John sees they supported him and were always most concerned that he do or be whatever he wanted. They would teach him and give him attention, but they also allowed him a lot of freedom.

John got along well with his siblings. His parents had a good marriage, and the home was very stable

Elementary School

John was always a top student. He was conscious of competing with others. He recognized the academic achievers in his class and compared himself only with them.

He remembers being curious and reading a lot in science. He became interested in music and joined the junior high school band. He particularly enjoyed going to the junior high school for rehearsals with the older students.

While in school he never regarded himself as an "egghead," nor did his friends ever regard him in this way. When teachers would ask a question he would not get called on since it was assumed he knew the answer. Sometimes he would answer anyway, talking out of turn. He wanted others to realize that he knew his stuff, and he remembers feeling somewhat arrogant about his intellectual abilities. He hated to give the wrong answers. His favorite subject was science and he remembers having very poor handwriting.

He got along with other students and with his neighborhood friends. He did not choose friends on the basis of intelligence. (This did, however, occur in high school.) He disliked being second in anything. He was not as interested in team sports as in individual sports.

Junior High School

John already had exposure to junior high school through the band, so the transition was not very difficult for him. He enjoyed changing teachers for each class. He did some reading on his own but he did not have to work particularly hard to do well. Projects and assignments were done at the last minute, but successfully. He remembers his parents did not overly praise him for his good grades and academic ability. He feels they cared but did not give too much attention to his achievements. John remembers sometimes wanting more from them than was given.

Socially he was on the boundary of the most popular group in grades seven and eight. In ninth grade he was elected president of the student council. John remembers himself as more of a loner in ninth grade.

His vivid childhood imagination was not very evident at this time—at least not in the same way. Sexual fantasies dominated his imagination during these years.

High School

John was very active in high school. Among his activities were president of the student council, debate club, National Honor Society, football, swimming, and band. The hobby he most remembers is stamp collecting, a hobby he continues to this day. Most of his reading was for pleasure.

Socially, he had a steady girlfriend. Again he was not a member of the most popular group. He wanted to be, but only on his terms. He did not care for drinking and refused to succumb to peer pressure on this issue. He spent most of his time with his girlfriend. John remembers feeling tinges of loneliness during these years.

His favorite subjects were science and math, particularly chemistry and physics. The science classes and science teachers were the most stimulating. In particular he recalls an excellent chemistry teacher and credits this teacher as inspiring him to start his own college career in chemistry. Role models have been important to John throughout his life and seem to have some impact in career planning. When it came time to choose a career or college, John recalls that his parents wanted it to be his choice. He remembers his father wanting him to go into chemistry but only if that was what John wanted.

English, French, and history were John's least favorite subjects. He recalls there was no imagination exercised in teaching these classes and so he was not enthusiastic. In general, he felt his high school classes were not challenging; he did not have to work very hard to do well.

John recalls his high school years as pretty narrow in terms of thinking about his own interests. He was not very aware of his budding humanistic interests and did little to explore them at this time. He remembers being tracked into science and math because he was always strong in these areas. His high school guidance counselor did nothing to help him explore career opportunities in fields other than science. He entered college as a chemistry major with little thought other than the fact that he was good in this area and chemistry was a "status" field. Since science was most interesting to him in high school, he assumed the same would hold true for college.

In thinking about college, John considered the United States Naval Academy and the University of Wisconsin—Madison. He chose Wisconsin because he had some exposure to the university through the GIFTS program and because the university had a good science department.

GIFTS—Grades 9–12

John was selected for the GIFTS program in ninth grade. When asked why he was selected for the program, he replied, "because of good grades, high test scores, and being active in student activities." John seemed to be aware of his intellectual ability beginning in elementary school. In high school he had a clear sense of being one of the more intellectual students. This group enjoyed a unique camaraderie. In John's words, "We were highly skilled and inventive hell-raisers."

John enjoyed his participation in GIFTS. What he recalls as most influential was simply exposure to the Madison campus, which helped in his decision about which college to attend. Also GIFTS got him to think more about himself. In his senior essay John wrote that GIFTS had presented many new ideas, had helped him see himself as a superior student, and had helped him make his final decision concerning a career.

Some comments made by John's ninth-grade teachers describe how he was viewed during this period:

English/Journalism—very capable. Inclined to procrastinate at times and rely on the ease and quickness with which he can work.
Social Studies—an excellent, sharp mind. *Tremendous* potential. Things come almost too easy for John.
Biology—often becomes interested in things on his own and carries them out to satisfy his own curiosity.
Algebra—a lot of ability going to waste. If John ever finds a purpose in life, he will be a powerhouse.
French—John is a superior student, but seems to come by this without too much effort. He is inclined to be rather "lazy" and content to do what is required of him and stop there. He can be rather "cocky."
Band—his initiative runs about parallel to the interest that he takes in a matter.
Physical Education—he has the problem of not thinking before he acts in many cases.

The GIFTS reports on John seem to include uncanny indicators of things to come. (See Exhibit 6-2.) It seems many of John's diverse qualities were recognized. While it was agreed that he would pursue chemistry and physics, he did express interest in the humanities, particularly literature. The GIFTS reports indicate that John had an unusually deep sense of personal meaning about his future; whatever he chose to do would have to be very meaningful to him.

The reports also state that while chemistry was his occupational choice, there were other possibilities that he had not considered thoroughly. His interest in literature, debating, music, and social problems suggested a number of different areas. A line in his senior year report is worth quoting: "Clergyman has been suggested by others, but John has discarded the idea."

The GIFTS material indicates that John was becoming aware of himself in many areas, but because he was bored with the way humanities were presented in high school, he made no effort to think about this area when considering a career. The only career exploration he did was in science.

Exhibit 6-2

<table>
<tr><td colspan="5" align="center">Cumulative Test Record
John
Testing Period: 1958–1962</td></tr>
<tr><td>Test</td><td>Form</td><td>Grade</td><td>Percentile</td><td>Norms</td></tr>
<tr><td>SCHOOL AND COLLEGE
ABILITY TEST</td><td></td><td></td><td></td><td></td></tr>
<tr><td> Verbal</td><td>2A</td><td>9</td><td>96–99+</td><td>9th graders</td></tr>
<tr><td> Quantitative</td><td></td><td></td><td>99+</td><td></td></tr>
<tr><td> Total</td><td></td><td></td><td>99+</td><td></td></tr>
<tr><td>DIFFERENTIAL
APTITUDE TEST</td><td></td><td></td><td></td><td></td></tr>
<tr><td> Abstract reasoning</td><td>—</td><td>—</td><td>—</td><td>—</td></tr>
<tr><td> Verbal reasoning</td><td>—</td><td>10</td><td>97</td><td>10th grade
boys</td></tr>
<tr><td> Numerical ability</td><td>—</td><td>—</td><td>—</td><td>—</td></tr>
<tr><td> Space relations</td><td>—</td><td>—</td><td>—</td><td>—</td></tr>
<tr><td>DAVIS READING TEST</td><td></td><td></td><td></td><td></td></tr>
<tr><td> Level of comprehension</td><td>1A</td><td>10</td><td>96</td><td>11th grade
boys</td></tr>
<tr><td> Speed of
  comprehension</td><td>1A</td><td>10</td><td>96</td><td>11th grade
boys</td></tr>
<tr><td>WATSON–GLASER
CRITICAL THINKING</td><td>2M</td><td>11</td><td>99+</td><td>High school</td></tr>
<tr><td>STEP SCIENCE</td><td>2A</td><td>9</td><td>98–99+</td><td>9th graders</td></tr>
<tr><td>TERMAN CONCEPT
MASTERY</td><td>T</td><td>12</td><td>100[a]</td><td>60–69[b]</td></tr>
<tr><td>WISCONSIN INVENTORY
GIFTS STUDENTS</td><td></td><td></td><td></td><td></td></tr>
<tr><td> Verbal score (number
  right out of 100)</td><td></td><td></td><td>—</td><td></td></tr>
<tr><td> Quantitative score
  (number right
  out of 50)</td><td></td><td></td><td>43</td><td></td></tr>
</table>

[a] Raw score
[b] GIFTS student average

Summary Comment on Cumulative Test Record
  John's performance on tests taken at GIFTS this year seems to be considerably above the average for seniors in the GIFTS program. His performance on the Terman Concept Mastery Test—a very difficult test on the recognition of antonyms, synonyms, and verbal

Exhibit 6-2 continued

analogies—was among the top quarter of GIFTS seniors over the past two years. The WITS quantitative test score is also above the average for GIFTS seniors.

Generally, John's test performances compare favorably with the upper one to three percent of his class. (Note that his performances on the Davis Reading Test and Watson-Glaser Critical Thinking Test are compared to a norm group one grade level above John.) There is no significant difference between performances on the WITS verbal and quantitative tests.

College and Seminary

John's study habits had to change when he began college. Fear of new surroundings prompted him to study harder. A "radical" change occurred during his first semester when he dropped chemistry as his major. He felt it was too narrow a field and was not worth his putting in all of his time. He realized that his interests were people oriented; he had a greater curiosity about subjects he had not considered interesting before. He switched to general humanities and finished college with a B.A. in history.

His college career was successful and he remembers these being "most enjoyable years." He graduated with a 3.94 grade point average out of 4.0. He was active in honor societies, religious organizations, intramural sports, and service organizations.

The college years seem to depict a rapidly expanding focus on people and a pursuit of the humanities. These interests prompted John to attend a school of theology after graduation. He felt that theology offered a broad human perspective. He believed that teaching theology would satisfy his intellectual desires.

In the seminary two very important things happened. John found that there was a split between the intellectuals, (he counted himself in this group) and those who were "people-oriented." It seemed that others believed a person could not care about and work with people and pursue an intellectual career at the same time. But during John's seminary internship he was supervised by a minister who exemplified the combination of intellect and service John hoped to achieve. This role model helped John see what he wanted from his life's work—a combination of intellectualism and service to people. This experience more than any other helped John finalize his career choice. He saw the ministry as a vocation that would satisfy his own desires and hopes.

Present

When speaking about his career John states, "My work is extremely satisfying, challenging, and provides the opportunity for continual learning and development." Since high school John has been aware of his own intellectual curiosity and broad interests. Politically and socially his thoughts have moved from the more traditional to what he calls "the left."

John's career path changed several times. Memories of high school counseling, other than the trips to Madison, are vague. "I don't think there was any significant official counseling," he says. In reflecting about his career development John writes, "I think, at any rate, that the most significant factor for me has been encounters with personal models of involved lives—people who have exhibited both intellectual and personal/ethical commitments in integrated and sustaining and joyful life patterns."

John sees his career as a way of life and not simply an occupational role. He has much of his life vested in the ministry. As he says, "It is a dimension of my self-identity, though not the sole shaper of my identity. I feel that I have been able to shape my career to fit my personal life style."

While John presently feels satisfied about his career, he is thinking of how to improve himself through further schooling in theology. He may eventually teach.

SUMMARY

John and Connie are both talented individuals, yet they are very different. John has always been self-sufficient, a free thinker, while Connie only recently achieved a degree of self-reliance. Their backgrounds are quite different, yet not so different as one would imagine. In fact, they grew up in the same town with John one year ahead of Connie in the same school system. The early support each received from family and teachers differed markedly, and perhaps this accounts for their "personality" differences. These differences are becoming less marked as time goes on. As you may have already deduced, John and Connie are now husband and wife.

SUGGESTED READINGS

Ginsberg, G., & Harrison, C. *How to help your gifted child.* New York: Monarch Press, 1977.

Hauch, B. B., & Freehill, M. F. *The gifted-case studies.* Dubuque, Iowa: William C. Brown Co., 1972.

Sears, R. S. Sources of life satisfaction of the Terman gifted men. *American Psychologist,* 1977, February, 119–128.

How to Plan and Implement Programs to Foster Development of Talent Potential

In Section Three we discuss the what, why, where, when, and how of planning and implementing programs designed to help those with talent potential perform to their fullest capacity. Appropriate sequencing of events is discussed, and the relevance of each event is analyzed and explained.

Chapter 7
Organizing Programs for the Talented

How does one identify which students are talented and potentially talented and therefore qualified to participate in specially designed educational programs? Identification can prove more difficult than anticipated. Many school systems begin a special program by identifying gifted pupils before seriously considering program objectives and instructional resources. If students are selected first, program goals either must be designed to accommodate that population or students must accommodate themselves to whatever program goals are established later. In the work GIFTS has done in planning programs with over 100 school systems, we have found that failure to establish program goals before identifying pupils has been the single greatest obstacle to implementing and sustaining successful special educational programs for the talented.

In this chapter we discuss such organizational issues as establishing program goals, determining student identification criteria, and assessing student needs.

WHERE TO BEGIN

Although it may seem that identifying program participants is the first logical step in initiating a program for talented pupils, identification should in fact come much later. Because "talent" can be defined in many ways, the selection criteria must, to a large degree, reflect the goals of the program. More precisely, what is to be done for the students should largely dictate what characteristics to look for in screening possible participants. Because there is certain to be a wide range of learning needs represented in the group, establishing program parameters is essential for a manageable and successful program. Even if special

We wish to acknowledge the contributions Dr. Phyllis B. Post and Mr. Narciso Aleman have made to portions of this chapter.

programming is eventually individualized, limited resources necessitate setting some parameters as to the "type" and number of student participants.

If you make the mistake of trying to program for all the disparate needs of talented students, you will end up with a nonintegrated, hit-or-miss program, with limited resources being dissipated through indiscriminate use. Experience has shown that the best type of program is one that facilitates the achievement of specified objectives for individuals within the context of systemwide goals. This educational strategy is likely to be useful to more students over a longer time period.

DEFINING PROGRAM GOALS

There are three major issues that must be resolved when program goals are being established: (1) What is to be accomplished? (2) How many students will participate? and (3) How long will it take to achieve program goals?

It must be decided whether programming is to be directed at enriching students' conceptual development, affective development, or both. Attempting to achieve either one or both requires different approaches. For example, a conceptual program could be implemented by taking students out of the classroom for a period of time each week for individual or small-group instruction, requiring appropriate instructional materials and a knowledgeable teacher. A program designed to meet the affective needs of students could involve group or individual counseling and the classroom teacher's increased awareness of the unique needs of talented students; here the human interaction skills of the teacher and counselor would be of prime importance. The approaches could be integrated or pursued separately if both conceptual and affective goals are decided upon.

It should also be decided whether a program is structured to meet the overlapping needs of many students or the idiosyncratic needs of individual students. Given limited available resources, individually-oriented programs require comprehensive individual assessment and programming. This kind of program is capable of serving fewer students than one that focuses on broader goals.

There are additional program considerations when deciding on the type and number of students to include: (1) teacher and community support; (2) the number and type of resource people available in the school and community; (3) the amount of money available for purchasing materials, field trips, etc.; (4) student and parental attitudes; and (5) resources available for parent and teacher training. We have observed that if teachers do not have adequate knowledge or time to prepare, they appear "afraid" of talented youngsters and are likely to opt for insignificant short-term "enrichment" activities. Thus, teacher knowledge and attitudes are major factors to assess when deciding how many students should participate and what special learning needs will be met.

When deciding how long it will take to meet program goals, you must take into consideration the point of initial intervention and the criteria used to determine if student goals have been reached. The stage of development at which students are selected should be a function of program goals and the concentration of resources available to achieve program goals. The greater the concentration of resources, the more rapidly the hypothesized outcomes should be achieved. A planning committee should accept responsibility for making a long-term commitment to pupils through the various levels of school. For example, if it has been decided to begin a program for kindergarten children, will the commitment end at the elementary school level? Will next year's kindergarten children be included? Will children participate for varying lengths of time based on needs, accomplishments, and resources? Will transfer students and newly identified students be added to the original group? If a program is initiated later, in junior high school, will previously identified elementary pupils automatically be included? These questions suggest the need for continual reassessment of program goals and pupil accomplishments. Working toward long-range program objectives requires coordination and communication among all schools within the system.

RECOMMENDED PHASES OF PROGRAM DEVELOPMENT

In initiating any program, certain tasks best occur within a given timeline. The following summary is a modification of the outline developed by Kaplan (1974).

Phase I—Planning
- designating leadership
- formulating a planning committee
- reviewing the research, literature, models
- assessing existent local conditions (Force-field Analysis)
- understanding program criteria, requirements
- developing philosophy, goals, objectives (Program Goal Attainment Scaling and Value Clarification)
- defining program dimensions: prototypes, materials, personnel, evaluation
- formalizing a written plan

Phase II—Preparing
- communicating and publicizing the program development
- allowing for reaction and revision
- obtaining formal approval and commitment
- assigning roles and responsibilities

- coordinating and devising forms and procedures for identification and certification of program participants (Individual Goal Attainment Scaling)
- orienting students, parents, educators
- developing curriculum and related materials
- planning evaluative procedures

Force-field analysis and goal attainment scaling (as identified above) are useful methods for dealing with some elements of Phases I and II. These methods are described in detail below.

Force-field Analysis

In assessing local conditions the objective is to identify facilitators and barriers affecting the implementation of a systemwide program. One efficient technique for this type assessment is a force-field analysis. In addition to helping the committee identify specific positive and negative factors, the analysis can be developed to the point where consideration is given to maintaining or enhancing positive factors and minimizing or overcoming negative factors. Force-field analysis is usually used at the programmatic level, but a mini force-field analysis can be employed when designing programs for individual students in pursuit of established objectives. In effect, using force-field analysis with individuals results in the development of a curriculum guide when a timeline or plan for implementing specific practices is included.

Force-field analysis is a technique based on the following assumptions: behavior can best be understood in relation to the physical, social, and psychological circumstances or forces surrounding a situation, and these forces can be changed to increase the likelihood of accomplishing desired program goals and individual objectives.

Principles of Change

The sources of resistance within persons and within institutions can be summarized in a few concise principles. These are not absolute laws but are based on generalizations that are usually true and likely to be pertinent.

A. Who brings about the change?
   1. Resistance will be less if administrators, teachers, board members, and community leaders feel that the project is their own, not one devised and operated by outsiders.
   2. Resistance will be less if the project clearly has wholehearted support from top officials in the system.

B. What kind of change?
3. Resistance will be less if participants see the changes as reducing rather than increasing their present burdens.
4. Resistance will be less if the project is in accord with values and ideals that have long been acknowledged by participants.
5. Resistance will be less if the program offers the kind of new experience that interests participants.
6. Resistance will be less if participants feel that their autonomy and their security are not threatened.

C. Procedures in instituting change:
7. Resistance will be less if participants have joined in diagnostic efforts leading them to identify the basic problem and agree on its importance.
8. Resistance will be less if the project is adopted by consensual group decision.
9. Resistance will be reduced if proponents are able to empathize with opponents, to recognize valid objections, and to take steps to relieve unnecessary fears.
10. Resistance will be reduced if it is recognized that innovations are likely to be misunderstood and misinterpreted, and if provision is made for feedback and for further clarification as needed.
11. Resistance will be reduced if participants experience acceptance, support, trust, and confidence in their relations with one another.
12. Resistance will be reduced if participants are helped to revise and reconsider after experience indicates that changes would be desirable.

D. Climate for change:
13. Readiness for change gradually becomes a characteristic of certain individuals, groups, organizations, and civilizations. They no longer look nostalgically at a Golden Age in the past, but anticipate their utopia in days to come. The spontaneity of youth is cherished and innovations are protected until they have had a chance to establish their worth. The ideal is seen as possible to achieve.

How to Conduct a Force-field Analysis

There are four steps in conducting a force-field analysis. These steps are listed here and explained in detail below.

1. Write a goal statement or objective.
2. Identify, usually through brainstorming, positive and negative factors affecting movement toward the desired goal or objective.
3. Rank the relative strength or importance of the factors identified.

4. Rate the goals and objectives as to the relative ease of increasing positive factors and decreasing negative factors.

1. Problem/goal specification: Think about a problem that is significant in your setting. Respond to each item as fully as needed so that others will be able to understand the problem.
   a. I understand the problem/goal to be specifically that . . .
   b. The following people with whom I must deal are involved in the problem: Their status of involvement is . . .
   They relate to me and to the problem/goal in the following manner:
   c. I consider these other factors to be relevant to the problem/goal:
   d. I would choose the following aspect of the problem/goal to be changed if it were in my power to do so (choose only one aspect):
2. Positive and negative factors affecting movement toward problem/goal:
   a. If I consider the present status of the problem/goal to be a temporary balance of opposing forces, the following would be on my list of forces providing thrust *toward* change:

   _____ 1. _____
   _____ 2. _____
   _____ 3. _____
   _____ 4. _____
   _____ 5. _____
   _____ 6. _____
   _____ 7. _____
   _____ 8. _____
   b. The following would be on my list of forces *opposing* change:

   _____ 1. _____
   _____ 2. _____
   _____ 3. _____
   _____ 4. _____
   _____ 5. _____
   _____ 6. _____
   _____ 7. _____
   _____ 8. _____
3. Relative strength or importance of identified factors:
   a. In the spaces to the left of the numbers in Item 2a quantify the forces on a scale of one to five. Use the following criteria:
      1—It has *almost nothing* to do with the thrust toward change in the problem/goal.
      2—It has *relatively little* to do with the thrust toward change in the problem/goal.

3—It is of *moderate importance* in the thrust toward change in the problem/goal.

4—It is an *important* factor in the thrust toward change in the problem/goal.

5—It is a *major factor* in the thrust toward change in the problem/goal.

b. Fill in the spaces to the left of the letters in Item 2b to quantify the forces providing counter-thrust to change. Use the same ranking system.

4. Diagram the forces of thrust and counter-thrust quantified in Question 3 by drawing an arrow from the corresponding degree of force to the status quo line. For example, if you rated the first force on your list in Item 2a as a 3, draw your arrow from the 1 in the lefthand column to the 3 position, indicating thrust toward the status quo line.

THRUST   COUNTER-THRUST

	1	2	3	4	5	5	4	3	2	1	
1											1
2											2
3											3
4											4
5											5
6											6
7											7
8											8

STATUS QUO

After completing these four steps, the next step is to develop a plan for enhancing positive factors and countering negative factors. Nonexisting factors can be judged as either positive (for example, no organized resistance) or negative (no organized support). It takes a certain amount of creativity to identify the not-so-obvious factors.

Prior to finalizing a course of action it is important to identify how much time, effort, and resources will be required by everyone involved to carry out a particular plan. A plan is completed and ready for implementation after specifying *who* is going to do *what, when,* and *where.*

5. Detail a strategy for decreasing two or more counter-thrust elements from your list.

6. Detail a strategy for increasing two or more thrust elements from your list.

Goal Attainment Scaling

Goals and objectives emerge from the values of those who take the initiative in developing special programs for the talented and potentially talented. While there may be universal agreement that special programs are needed, when choices have to be made or priorities established, values come into play. Studies and statistics are employed selectively to support established views or values. The earlier that leaders' values can be clarified and hidden agendas made public, the more efficiently program priorities or goals can be developed and student objectives established. There are numerous books and workshops available to help those interested in value clarification.

There are also several techniques and procedures for specifying program goals and objectives for individual students. We recommend a modification of the goal attainment scaling procedure developed by Dr. Thomas J. Kirsuk and Robert E. Sherman (1976). It is an efficient planning and evaluative technique. The procedure was originally designed for evaluating patient outcomes in community mental health programs.

The purpose of goal attainment scaling is to determine the extent to which goals have been achieved and to determine the effectiveness of techniques and procedures used to achieve the stated goals. There are three steps involved:

1. Goal determination by teachers, the student, and possibly the parents.
2. Student participation in individually designed programs or group experiences that help the student attain specified goals.
3. Followup of each student to assess relative accomplishment of the goals and scale values set prior to special programming.

Goals are described in terms of behavioral outcomes or products. Examples of behavioral words which are generally understood by most persons to mean the same thing include:

- to write
- to solve
- to construct
- to list
- to identify
- to compare
- to complete
- to increase
- to smile
- to differentiate.

More ambiguous words that are open to many interpretations include:

- to know
- to understand
- to appreciate
- to enjoy
- to believe.

A goal statement is not complete until it describes what a student will *accomplish* under what *conditions* as measured by what *criteria*.

The goal attainment scale is used with individual students. When it is used properly, the student is not judged against some arbitrary or general measure. Rather, the student *is* compared against what can be realistically "expected." That is, the "expected" level is set specifically for each student, and that student is judged on standards and in areas that are relevant to his or her case.

In addition, the "expected" level reflects a particular time frame. That is, it conveys what it is reasonable to expect from that student six weeks from now, three months from now, or whenever it seems appropriate to look at the attainment of a goal or series of goals.

Once the major goals for the program—and eventually for the individual students—have been selected, each goal may be placed on a goal attainment scale. An example of such a scale follows.

Outcome	Goal
Most unfavorable outcome	
Less than expected success	
Expected level of success	
More than expected success	
Most favorable outcome possible	

The scale is intended to be a systematic arrangement of specific possible outcomes. It represents a continuum of observable measures, from the "worst anticipated outcome" to the "best anticipated outcome." The "expected level of outcome" appears at the middle level of the scale.

To derive a goal attainment score, the goal attainment scale is weighted as follows:

Outcome	Goal
Most unfavorable	1
Less than expected	2
Expected	3
More than expected	4
Most favorable	5

A goal attainment score for the individual would be determined by adding the achievement level for each goal and dividing by the number of goals. A mean of three would indicate "expected achievement." Less than three is unsatisfactory, and more than three would be considered exceptional.

A goal attainment follow-up guide frequently will be scored by someone other than the person who constructed it. Consequently, precise descriptions and clearly discriminated levels are essential for accurate follow-up and evaluation.

Kirsuk and Sherman have organized their comments on construction of goal attainment follow-up guides. They call these *"The Ten Commandments of Goal Attainment Follow-up Guide Construction"* (1976, p. 18).

1. Include at least three scales (goals) on a follow-up guide.
2. Fill in at least three levels for each scale (goal). The expected level should be filled in, as should at least one level on each side of the expected level.
3. Include only one variable or goal on each scale.
4. Be sure to quantify the performance criteria to the extent possible.
5. The student's behavior at the beginning may be at any of the five levels. Avoid terms like "better than when the program began."
6. Avoid variables (goals) which are too general or vague to be adequately scored at follow-up.
7. The levels on a scale should not overlap each other.
8. If the information needed for a scale's follow-up scoring is to be obtained from a source other than the student, the special source of information should be listed.
9. No "expected" level should be so high that there can be no "better than expected" level. No "expected" level should be so low that there can be no "less than expected" level. There should usually be a possible outcome for all levels of the scale even if some are left blank.
10. Avoid having two blank levels adjacent to each other on the scale.

Goal attainment scaling has special advantages that could prove useful.

1. *Student-Specific:* In proper use of the goal attainment scale there is no set number of goals and no list of predetermined subjects to be included as goals. Whatever goals seem appropriate to the needs of the student may be incorporated into a goal attainment scale.
2. *Fair Measurement:* In proper use of the goal attainment scale the student is not judged against some arbitrary, across-the-board measure. Instead, the student is compared to what could be uniquely "expected" for this student. The "expected" levels are determined specifically for each student so he or she is judged on standards and in areas relevant to the individual.

3. *Guide Construction:* Goal attainment scales and goal attainment follow-up guides have been constructed by a wide range of persons: clinical psychologists, social workers, psychiatrists, administrators, teachers, psychiatric nurses, and students themselves. The teacher, the student, or both, can build the goal attainment scales and follow-up guide. Even parents or other involved persons could construct scales and guides.

Exhibit 7-1 is an example of a follow-up guide. The behaviors also describe the goals, so in effect they serve both the purpose of setting objectives and providing an evaluation tool. Of course, programming comes in between.

It may prove helpful to keep in mind that *goals* are inclusive statements that provide a general direction and broad parameters within which educators and students function. *Objectives* are specific, measurable outcomes to be accomplished by individual students within a specified time. Once again, the six dimensions in writing performance objectives include specifying:

1. WHO (will perform the activity)
2. DOES WHAT (behavior/product)
3. WHEN (time specific)
4. UNDER WHAT CONDITIONS
5. HOW MUCH/HIGH (amount of change, level of attainment)
6. HOW MEASURED (criteria and naming the evaluation if feasible).

Exhibit 7-2 outlines specific responsibilities for faculty, staff, and students. The responsibilities listed are only suggestions. In a particular school district the responsibilities should be reassigned as appropriate. Again, these responsibilities are a modification of those suggested by Kaplan (1974). We would also suggest certain parental responsibilities, including to:

- provide support and stimulation at home
- become a mentor for talented children
- enlist the support of community members who can serve as resource persons for the talented, providing unique learning experiences for them
- become a member of a Parent Advisory Council or other decision-making groups.

STAFF INVOLVEMENT

An often unanticipated problem is determining the persons who should be involved in (1) setting objectives; (2) defining identification criteria; and (3) participating in the actual selection process. The long-range consequences of staff selection can be significant because active participation usually indicates

Exhibit 7-1 Example of a Follow-up Guide

		GOAL ATTAINMENT FOLLOW-UP GUIDE Scale Headings		
Weight-ing	SCALE 1: Employment	SCALE 2: Interpersonal Relationships	SCALE 3: Leisure Time	SCALE 4: Self-Concept
1	Student continues without a part-time job.	Student avoids all groups because he is made apprehensive in group situations.	Student continues without any leisure time activity except TV.	Continues to state there is nothing likable about himself.
2	Student has had a few different jobs, averaging less than four weeks on any of them.			Only occasionally states something negative about himself.
3	Student is employed part-time and has held a job 30 days.	Student sometimes indicates mild discomfort when in group situations, but does not purposely avoid groups.	Student has made some attempts to find leisure time activities which might interest him.	Says something positive about himself occasionally.
4		Student feels no discomfort in groups.		
5	Student has had a part-time job more than 60 days and indicates satisfaction with the job.	Student seeks out or tries to join at least one group.	Student has developed a new interest (art, music, hobby) which occupies his leisure time and keeps his interest.	Usually can say something positive about himself.

Exhibit 7-2 School District Roles and Responsibilities

COORDINA-TOR	TEACHER	STUDENT	PRINCIPAL	CENTRAL OF-FICE STAFF
	Classroom:			
Design, develop, coordinate, and evaluate the program.	Provide an enriched individualized program for the gifted.	Attend regular or specially scheduled programs or events.	Become knowledgeable about the unique needs of the gifted.	Provide the necessary staff to implement and support all identification,
Develop and implement curriculum (techniques, materials) related to enriching the total program.	Assist students in planning, organizing, and evaluating tasks.	Complete selected tasks. Communicate and share learning experiences	Become acquainted with gifted students in the school.	program development, material acquisition, in-service training,
Prepare financial, statistical, and descriptive reports as needed to develop, maintain, and account for the program.	Screen, develop, and provide appropriate materials for the gifted. Evaluate pupil progress. Interpret the program to parents.	with peers, teachers, and parents. Practice decision-making skills. Develop self-awareness and understanding.	Stimulate interest in and concern for the gifted. Urge teachers to provide qualitatively differentiated programs for the gifted in their classrooms.	publicity, evaluation, and related procedures that are required to provide a qualitatively differentiated program for the gifted and talented.
Coordinate identification and certification procedures.	*Itinerant:* Support classroom teachers and building principals in their relationships with the gifted and talented.	Participate in planning and evaluating learning experiences within the program.	Cooperate with district personnel in identifying the gifted and implementing programs for them.	Define and coordinate the requisite roles and responsibilities of the school board, super-intendent, psychologist,
Serve as a consultant and resource to the staff, students, and parents involved with the program.	Provide an enriched		Encourage and assist teachers in securing appropriate	psychometrist, counselor, and classroom teacher.

Exhibit 7-2 continued

COORDINA-TOR	TEACHER	STUDENT	PRINCIPAL	CENTRAL OF-FICE STAFF
Participate as part of the Educational Services staff. Promote public relations activities at the local, county, and state levels.	extension of the regular curriculum for gifted students in intra- or extra-classroom settings. Demonstrate diverse methods of instruction appropriate for the gifted, such as problem solving, independent study, etc.		instructional materials for the gifted. Meet regularly with parents to explain the program to them. Work cooperatively with other personnel in objectively evaluating the program.	

a greater personal commitment. Uninvolved staff members may become passive and even defensive. It is essential, of course, to involve those upon whose expertise the program will later depend. Beyond that, interest may be a good criterion for determining initial involvement.

It is wise, however, to include everyone who is interested in each of the three steps mentioned above. While it is desirable to have everyone's input, there is reason to think that more inclusive involvement is of greater importance in the actual identification process than in the setting of objectives or the determination of identification criteria. These later two processes take time in simply working through different beliefs and opinions until agreement can be reached.

Although a completely homogeneous group would defeat the purpose of bringing together people of different perspectives, a group that is too heterogeneous or too large might make eventual consensus almost impossible. The best group to accomplish the twin tasks of setting objectives and determining selection criteria is likely to take the form of a small committee consisting of an administrator, a counselor or school psychologist, several interested teachers from various grade levels and subject areas, and a few community members. It might also prove helpful to include three or four high school students who are recognized as gifted in different areas of endeavor.

In carrying out the actual selection of pupils, it is ideal to involve the entire staff. Selection of pupil participants generally involves two steps: (1) a pool of possible students is created, a procedure often called student nomination; and (2) students from this pool are then selected for participation in the program.

Because nomination criteria generally include both standard measures of a given student and subjective evaluations by teachers, counselors, or parents, it is helpful to include many staff members during this process. This enhances the reliability of the information obtained. Subjective nominations should be open to any staff member wishing to be involved. It is important to provide those making nominations with nomination guidelines and a definition of talent and talent potential. This results in a better informed, more fully involved community. Students, peers, and parents require special preparation if they are going to be involved in the nomination process. Which person's involvement will be most useful in data collection will depend on the selection criteria being used. If historical developmental data are sought, parent involvement is essential. If psychomotor information is to be included, all teachers (not just physical educators), must be educated concerning how physical talent is displayed in the classroom.

Once nominations have been obtained, along with the first round of information, it is time to begin the difficult process of narrowing down the candidates. Again, at this time it may be wiser to involve the small group of interested staff who developed objectives and criteria, since the criteria are best applied by those who developed them. The addition of one or two outside members at this time could, however, serve as a check on the group's tendency to become overly consensual. In any case, if you follow the general rule of applying criteria before names and personalities of identified pupils become known, this will make the inherently difficult screening process somewhat easier.

PROCESS OF IDENTIFICATION

An essential issue in this process involves considering to what degree the process should be primarily logical or primarily intuitive. There are advantages and disadvantages to each approach. While a scheme that is logical, carefully planned, and strictly adhered to is easier and quicker, there is greater danger of missing some students whose talent potential is manifest in an unanticipated manner. On the other hand, a process that relies totally on individual intuition is time-consuming to implement. Exhibit 7-3 compares and contrasts these two possible schemes for identifying the gifted.

Probably the most difficult and controversial task in establishing a program for the gifted involves defining the criteria for selecting students. In essence,

Exhibit 7-3 Two Schemes for Identifying the Gifted

Objective	*Subjective*
1. Supply faculty with a list of characteristics, behaviors, and definitions of talent. Ask them to think of students who fit the definition and rate these students on the characteristics and behaviors. Invite additional comments on reasons why teachers selected particular students.	1. Make lists on characteristics and definitions of talent available to faculty. Ask them to nominate students they think are talented either on the basis of the information supplied or their own intuition. Invite additional comments on reasons for their choices.
2. First-round elimination accomplished by taking only those nominated and for reasons that seem to fit with established program objectives.	2. Consider all nominations, and eliminate only those who seem not to fit the global definition of talent.
3. Gather information based on observations and pupil products for all those students remaining in the pool.	3. Gather information based on observations and pupil products for all those students remaining.
4. Second-round elimination based on predetermined schema for weighing selection criteria.	4. Review each nominee with regard to program objectives and selection criteria. Consider intuition of nominators and others on committee as well as factual information. Make decisions by arriving at consensus or taking votes, until desired number of students remain in the pool.
5. Gather further information by using assessment instruments in order to individualize program to the extent possible.	
6. Third-round elimination based on further weighing, until desired number of students remain in the pool.	

determining selection criteria is the equivalent of defining talent or talent potential, because those selected will become known as the talented. There is no universally accepted definition of talent and even less agreement regarding what constitutes talent potential. Nonetheless, it is the job of those making the selections to consider all the subjective and intuitive definitions as well as all the definitions in the literature and boil these down into a set of observable and measurable traits by which students will be identified. The many dimensions of talent that need to be considered include: creative skills; analytical ability; depth in one content area; breadth of skill across many content areas; verbal, social, or mathematical exceptionality; persistence; motivation; task commitment; ability to accept responsibility for self; and ability to integrate ideas.

Identifying Talented Children from Minority Cultures

Special thought must be given to criteria for identifying talented children from minority cultures. We have observed that gifted children from these groups possess talents valued and nurtured within their own subcultures—talents that frequently go unrecognized in school. At home the child's behavior may be supported and rewarded; in the school the child may be ignored or treated as a misfit. Being ignored and rejected creates the groundwork for eventual segregation from the educational and economic opportunities of the majority culture.

In addressing these problems, the Foundation for Exceptional Children in 1974 hosted a conference entitled "Talent Delayed—Talent Denied: The Culturally Different Gifted Child" (Gallager, 1974). The conferees agreed that the definition of gifted was too narrow and that there were a host of barriers encountered by culturally different gifted children. These barriers included various aspects of the curriculum, system procedures, and most important, the attitudes and values of decision makers.

Defining Multicultural Talent

As a first step in broadening our definition of talent, GIFTS staff have conferred with educational and spiritual leaders, family members, and students representing three minority cultures: American Indian, Mexican, and Puerto Rican. (The Afro-American culture extends beyond the scope of our current work, and there is some question over how to best differentiate or identify unique talent manifestations in the black culture.)

A three-day meeting was held separately with each cultural group. A synthesis of the valued and exceptional behaviors reported at these meetings follows. These reports represent concerns of specific members within each minority culture and do not necessarily represent the concerns or values of the minority culture in general. One may question the need to have two separate approaches (Mexican and Puerto Rican) for the Spanish-speaking population. We found that the concerns and values of our cultural representatives clearly supported the need to differentiate between some aspects of Mexican and Puerto Rican talent. Currently we are attempting to substantiate or modify these general guidelines, based on data obtained from the children, their families, and teachers.

Puerto Rican. Some values that are an integral part of the Puerto Rican culture include respect of the land, the culture, and the elders. Before the 1950s, life for Puerto Ricans was tied to survival. This preoccupation with survival meant close associations with the land and its crops. Curriculum materials should make note of the various conditions that reflect present socioeconomic reality for this group, including single parent families, economic needs, and unemployment. Puerto Rican children in the U.S. must be prepared for the harsh realities of life found in the inner core of large urban areas: discrimination, drug abuse, and crime.

The following phenomena point up some apparent differences between the Puerto Rican subculture and the dominant middle-class Caucasian culture:

- Education is reflected not so much in formal schooling as it is in being respectful and behaving properly.
- Puerto Rican children may lower their heads when addressed directly by adults. In school this may be interpreted as obstinacy or defiance.
- In Spanish there are formal and informal pronouns and verb conjugations used to address elders or strangers. It is difficult to make the English transition when addressing teachers.
- Competition within the family, or with one's peers, is not valued.
- There may be a differentiation of responsibilities at home based on sex roles. This may be incompatible with responsibilities and expectations in school.
- Career decisions and career goals are made with the important approval of parents.
- The family counsel is used in decision making.
- The extended family assists, in decreasing degrees, in the moral and economic support of adolescents.

Mexican-American. Schooling represents the first betrayal of the Mexican-American child by the parents. The child is told that school will be an enjoyable experience in which they will learn a great deal and have fun. Consequently, the child looks forward to going to school because parents would never lie. But one of the first things the teacher tells the child is: "Juanito, here we are going to speak English and you will behave in this manner." The child begins to feel that perhaps there is something wrong with the language spoken by the parents; otherwise, why would this nice person prohibit it?

Mexican-Americans find themselves in a complex dilemma because they are caught between two dominant cultures: the United States culture that stresses consumerism and the traditional Mexican culture of their forefathers that stresses cooperation and conservation. Mexican people are more closely related to the American Indian culture; they value cooperation and place less value on individualism.

Mexican families develop respect for elders, the law, and authority. While these attitudes are beneficial within the cultural context of the Mexican community and the extended families, they lend themselves to manipulation by others. Moreover, such attitudes create a certain vulnerability. In the home environment the Mexican child is expected to be cooperative, patient, unobtrusive, obedient, and to wait for direction or instructions rather than assume individual initiative, self-direction, or engage in self-indulgence. In the school, however, the same child is expected to take the initiative and compete, even against friends.

Talent among Mexican children can be most easily identifiable in language manipulation. Mexican children who speak both Spanish and English may demonstrate a facility to manipulate both languages to convey more subtle and finer meanings. A second sign of talent potential is the use of "calo," a street language spoken by young people. This language may be interspersed with anglicized Spanish words or vice versa. A third sign may be the creation of entirely original words using both languages in new combinations. Children who ask a great many questions are sometimes considered talented. However, such questions are usually discouraged by overworked parents, especially as it becomes increasingly difficult for parents to answer those questions.

School systems are individually oriented and therefore, Mexican, Puerto Rican, and American Indian children may have a difficult time in these systems. Delinquent behavior can be indicative of frustrated creative talent, a result of a conflict in values between home and school.

American Indian. American Indian children also find themselves caught between the school that places high value on independence and the home and community that place high value on interdependence. The extended family and the relationship to the Universe and the Natural Order place the American Indian in a state of perpetual interdependence with all living things and natural matter. But the school reinforces the importance of independence in many ways, including the classroom seating arrangements. According to the American Indian way, everyone would be seated in a circle so that everyone could see one another's face. But schools seat pupils behind one another so that pupils can see only the back of one another's heads; the only face pupils see is that of the teacher. Such a seating arrangement reinforces independence from peers and dependence on the teacher.

The expansion of the commercial/industrial interests and the expansion of settlements has limited and in many instances infringed upon the lands once designated as "reservations" for the various woodland tribes in Wisconsin. A lack of jobs and opportunities has forced many Indians to migrate to the urban areas of Wisconsin. Many of these tribal members return to the "reservation" to maintain their tribal status, but these trips become less frequent for the young Indian who has grown up in the urban areas. Economic conditions affect the familial relationships, and the tribal values and traditions are bombarded by the mass "culture" of the United States consumer society.

The loss of language and isolation from the youth are two major problems concerning adults. With the loss of language, the loss of identity seems only a breath away. Right hemispheric functioning, which is receiving an increasingly positive treatment in the literature, is the basis of American Indian expression. Yet most teachers do not understand right hemispheric manifestations, and therefore suppress and in some instances penalize American Indian students. Some initial data that we have collected indicate that a sense of humor is highly valued among the tribes interviewed.

American Indians consider Earth to be the best teacher. They deem it necessary to have a personal relationship to Earth Mother. It follows that if they accept the Earth as their Mother and they walk upon her, then they do so with a great deal of care and caution. American Indians believe that no human being can surpass as an educator.

"Red Power" is the sum of all things and interactions. Red Power does not mean only Indian Power. Red Power is Love. Red Power is for all peoples. The blood of all people is red. The love of all people is red. Love is the basis of all interaction and therefore the basis of teaching. Another basic value is collective decision making. For thousands of years the American Indian has decided matters collectively through discussion.

SELECTION CRITERIA

There are numerous assessment models that address many of these dimensions. However, more specific "content" assessment is required when determining course content. The selection process is further specified in order to help identify the number of students the program has been designed to serve. There is no foolproof method or set of criteria by which the best possible selection can be made. Those persons establishing a program must decide which criteria are most valuable and recognize and accept that value judgments are necessary in order to establish a successful program.

It is estimated that three to five percent of any school population exhibits talent potential. This means that not everyone with talent potential can be included in a program. This limitation must be accepted. Identification tools and techniques include teacher observations, counselor observations, parent input, pupil products, and different standardized assessment instruments (including verbal, written, and behavioral measures).

Whatever tools and procedures are used, one rule of thumb can be applied in selecting these procedures: include those that can be observed or measured with some degree of consistency or reliability. While it is desirable to include different criteria and different kinds of data to measure each criterion, there is also a risk of generating too much data. This can happen when there is no planned procedure for weighting the data that is obtained. Without a weighting procedure, it can be difficult—if not impossible—to make sense of the accumulated information. It is always best to determine the relative importance of each kind of data before any information is gathered.

You may want to use the following two-step procedure. First, clearly outline how the data that is collected will be used in the identification procedure. This provides a check against gathering data that cannot be used. Second, construct a hierarchy that shows which criteria are to be considered during each successive round of eliminating possible candidates.

INDIVIDUALIZED ASSESSMENT

If it is the goal of education to facilitate development of the total person's potential—affective as well as cognitive, personal as well as social, process as well as product development—then educators must be willing to recognize diversity of needs, both between individuals and within individuals. Each student has strengths that require encouragement, additional stimulation, and positive reinforcement—and weaknesses or deficiencies that require supplemental instruction. This suggests a need for comprehensive assessment.

Most assessment done in the schools is designed to differentiate among students with a wide range of interest and capabilities. Most tests used for this purpose are standardized achievement tests, based on nationally determined norms. These tests are not designed to measure such criteria as divergent thinking skills, ability to visualize, self-esteem, or independent thinking. Moreover, talented students typically score at the upper ranges on these achievement tests, thus limiting the tests' usefulness in assessing their learning needs.

The Case Study Approach

A case study approach seems essential in assessing talented students for program purposes. Clearly, there are a great many variables that are important in assessing each student's strengths and weaknesses, interests, and learning style. Educators need to be aware of *what* a student does or produces, as well as *how* a student thinks.

In doing individual case studies the following points should be kept in mind:

1. Use multiple methods of data collection. Assessment in any one area should never be based on only one sample—whether it be a sophisticated test, an informal interview, or a structured observation. Each of these measures is based on assumptions that may or may not be valid.
2. Use multiple theories when deciding what data to collect and how to interpret that data. Different theories of development, intelligence, emotion, and behavior provide different viewpoints. Be careful to look at data from several theoretical perspectives.
3. Make sure Points 1 and 2 are carried out by involving several persons in the construction of a case study and in the interpretation of the data.

In addition to knowing each student's behavior, cognitive style, and feelings, educators must also be concerned about the forces that influence behavior, cognition, and emotion. In a very broad sense, these influences can be broken down into internal forces and external factors. Perceptions, habitual emotional responses, and associations that occur inside a person are examples of internal forces that help determine that person's behavior. One's culture and the emotional and intellectual climate of the home and school are examples of external factors. Both the internal and external variables interact in an ongoing, dynamic process, necessitating an ongoing and dynamic assessment program. At GIFTS we have found that the case conference format is especially useful. It involves the active, ongoing participation of the student, parents, and teachers and produces communication and trust. It helps the pupil achieve self-understanding, social understanding, and self-direction.

We have outlined various phases in developing a program for gifted students. These include establishing program objectives, selecting identification criteria, identifying pupil participants, individual assessment, and staff involvement. A workable program for talented students requires careful consideration of each of these phases. If the school succeeds, you should observe children who are motivated, intense, articulate, interesting, demanding, restless, independent, risk takers, and possibly creative. If the special learning needs of this group continue to remain unmet, it can be estimated that 5 to 10 percent will move toward maximizing their potential, 20 percent will adjust to the prevailing norm, another 20 percent will become poor achievers who are likely to drop out— along with the 50 percent who will just fade away.

INSTRUCTIONAL CONCERNS FOR DEVELOPING TALENT

Teachers of children with talent potential often express deep concern and uncertainty over which instructional approaches are "correct" or best. Teachers typically feel a great responsibility for providing opportunities and guidance that will help youngsters recognize, appreciate, and develop their gifts.

Teachers' concerns are reflected in the questions they raise during interviews and discussions with GIFTS staff. Typical questions include:

- "How can I get beyond feeling insecure and intimidated in order to help a child whose conceptual skills and knowledge may actually surpass mine?"
- "How do I help talented adolescents respect and develop their talent and still participate in a peer group that values sameness and conformity?"
- "How can I cope with a youngster who asks penetrating questions about the way I teach and about the course content?"

Gifted adolescents acquire formal operational thought, or the capacity to envision abstract or symbolic alternatives, at a younger age than their peers. With the acquisition of formal operational thought, these young people begin to conceptualize what ideally or symbolically *could be* rather than what *is*. They compare what they are being taught with their newly formulated conception of what they should be learning. Courses and teachers are often found wanting. Talented youngsters may respond to a teacher's ideas and assertions with highly developed and sophisticated counterproposals. Being challenged by an inexperienced, impatient adolescent can be an unsettling experience for some teachers. Teachers may be surprised; some may be offended. They may find themselves implicitly discrediting or discounting their experience and wisdom, forgetting that even the brightest adolescent—one whose academic knowledge and ease in assimilating new information is exceptional—cannot possibly have acquired the wisdom that comes from years of living.

In addition to academic talent, gifted children may demonstrate exceptional abilities in social skills, physical prowess, or artistic expression, each of which may heighten the potential for dissonance between that child's performance and what the teacher expects of a "normal" child.

The talented adolescent may demonstrate exceptionality in one area, but normal or even retarded development in other areas. This imbalance may result in highly sophisticated behavior in one task and strikingly immature behavior in another situation. It is obvious that teachers of the gifted and talented must demonstrate special understanding and must be able to function more as a learning consultant than a dispenser of information and an evaluator of pupil performance. The necessary skills are described in some detail below.

Above all else, talented children are typical in their need for love, acceptance, security, challenge, guidance, and opportunities for self-expression—all the basic elements of support and stimulation that generally foster individual development (Dunlop, 1958). Talented adolescents experience the same concerns earlier than their peers. Talented adolescents begin to focus their energies on autonomy and personal identity issues and begin to consider their future roles as adults (Erikson, 1968).

Given all these special concerns, it is no surprise that teachers ask how they can best help their talented children fulfill their potential. Since the most popular instructional guides are based on expectations derived from studies of "normal" or average children (Ross, 1979), the teachers of gifted and talented adolescents find few guidelines that focus on the special needs of this group.

ESTABLISHING TEACHER GOALS

Terman (1954)[6] identified three attributes associated with the successful use of intellect in gifted adult males. Those males rated most successful and satisfied with their use of intellectual talent were also rated highest on qualities of "self-confidence," "task persistence," and "integration toward goal." It would seem that these attributes would apply to talented adult females as well. Teachers and parents can best ensure the successful realization of a child's talents and future life satisfaction by fostering the development of that child's self-confidence, task persistence, and goal direction.

The literature on human development also suggests that teachers should help adolescents acquire a psychologically androgynous self-concept. The word *androgyny* is derived from the Greek roots *andros,* meaning male, and *gyne,* meaning female. Androgynous individuals, whether male or female, incorporate into their self-concepts and behavior those positive attributes and qualities traditionally called "masculine" as well as those traditionally called "feminine." Interpersonal competence is increased when men and women possess both sets of characteristics (assertive and understanding, strong and gentle, independent and nurturing), because then they can act as warranted by the situation (Bem, 1977).

The androgynous perspective enables individuals to develop their talents and interests on the basis of individual preferences rather than from a sex-typed, socially prescribed bias. For example, an adolescent boy with an androgynous self-concept would feel more comfortable about showing an interest in such "nonmasculine" pursuits as ballet, nursing, child care, or needlework, rather than developing himself only in those areas that are socially approved for his sex. An adolescent girl with an androgynous self-concept would feel more at ease in showing interest in such "nonfeminine" pursuits as engineering, mechanics, or carpentry. Adolescent boys and girls who choose to pursue nontraditional interests are likely to encounter at least some social disapproval, often unconsciously conveyed by "well-meaning" parents, teachers, and/or peers. However, androgynous, talented adolescents, are better able to cope with such disapproval and maintain their self-esteem, especially given their wider range of psychological behaviors including being assertive, sensitive to others, and self-expressive. In general, the androgynous self-concept and the social skills that accompany androgyny lead to more effective and more satisfying interpersonal relationships and to more satisfying lives. In addition, an androgynous perspective may help talented young people realize their potential for responsible, intelligent leadership in this rapidly changing, complex society. Such leadership will assuredly require the enhanced flexibility and interpersonal effectiveness that comes from a blending of traditionally "masculine" and "feminine" perceptions and behaviors.

Teachers need to reassess and determine their own values and goals in providing instruction for the talented. How does a teacher value independent, responsible students who want a say in their learning and evaluation? These students can be perceived either as agents of chaotic disruption or as mature persons who can become catalysts for personal growth and development among other students. Teachers may find it useful to:

- clarify their understanding of and goals for the talented individual.
- consider how student talents can be used to aid in the development of others.
- Decide what kind of teacher-pupil relationship they want and can achieve with the gifted child.

Sharing these assessments with talented pupils and asking for their input can open lines of communication, promote negotiation of mutual expectations, promote the expression of feelings and trust, and engender a mutually rewarding and perhaps enlightening learning experience for both student and teacher.

CREATING AN EFFECTIVE TEACHING STYLE

The present literature suggests that successful parent-adolescent relationships—ones that encourage adolescent self-esteem and the use of parents as valued resources of wisdom—are those that feature a democratic parenting style (Elder, 1975); frequent explanations of rules and requests (Miller & Swanson, 1960); along with warmth, limit setting, and respect for individual expression within those limits (Coopersmith, 1967). Effective teacher-pupil relationships should feature the same elements.

Elder (1975) notes three basic parenting styles or approaches that are typically assumed in the parent-child relationship: (1) the autocratic or dictatorial mode, where the parent presumes all of the decision-making responsibility and thus all the power in the parent-offspring relationship; (2) the permissive or ignoring/laissez-faire mode, where the parent gives most or all responsibility for decision making (and thus power) to the offspring; and (3) the democratic or participatory mode, where the parent and offspring share decision making and thus power.

Each of these three approaches may be accompanied by frequent or infrequent parental explanations of rules of conduct and demands for action.

Previous research had demonstrated that modeling or conformity to parental rules is most typical of democratically reared adolescents who often receive explanations. Nonexplaining autocratic and permissive parents are least apt to be modeled (Elder, 1975). Frequent explanations of rules and demands tend to make parental regulations seem right in the eyes of adolescents, and this has been associated with resistance to temptations in adolescent boys (Miller & Swanson, 1960). Nonexplaining parents are apt to undermine children's self-confidence; these children are likely to doubt their ability to make their own decisions as well as display a diminished desire for independence. The frequency of explanations has been shown to be least common with the autocratic parenting style and most common with the democratic parenting style.

The parent-child literature is cited here because it puts the emphasis on a one-to-one relationship—the same kind of highly individualized approach the teacher needs to adopt when working with the gifted and talented. In contrast, the education literature is oriented to working with and instructing students as a group in the classroom environment.

Classroom observations by GIFTS staff have led us to conclude that classroom teachers adopt similar styles. Within the democratic or participatory decision-making style, teachers may further the development of a student's self-esteem, independence, and creativity by negotiating clear learning objectives and the logical consequences that will ensue if the student fails to assume responsibility. When democratic instructional practices are employed, adolescents often feel more responsible for and accepting of the consequences of their actions since they have participated in the planning. When objectives and behavioral expectations are clearly defined, students have a set of criteria against which they can measure their progress, behavior, and judgments. Limits provide students with the security of structure and the knowledge of what is expected of them.

Coopersmith (1967) has found that children with healthy self-esteem live in families where limits are set and there is respect for individual expression within these limits. In late childhood and adolescence there is a need for psychological "space" so that young people can try on different styles of self-expression in order to find a style that best "fits" their idiosyncrasies. Teachers who are able to accept individual differences within prescribed limits will create a receptive and supportive learning atmosphere—one in which talented students can struggle to establish their personal identity and still retain a sense of internal security.

Teaching talented pupils can be both challenging and rewarding. One major task that confronts teachers is to review and reestablish priorities in educating these students. A democratic learning environment encourages talented students' growth toward satisfactory adulthood. Teacher flexibility and adaptability seem imperative.

REFERENCES

Bem, S. On the utility of alternative procedures for assessing psychological androgyny. *Journal of Consulting Psychology,* 1977, *45,* 196–205.

Coopersmith, S. *The antecedents of self-esteem.* San Francisco: W.H. Freeman & Co., 1967.

Dunlop, J.M. *The education of children with high mental ability.* In W.M. Cruickshank & G.O. Johnson (Eds.), *Education of exceptional children and youth.* Englewood Cliffs, N.J.: Prentice-Hall, 1958, pp. 147–188.

Elder, G.H. *Parental power legitimation and its effect on the adolescent.* In J. Conger (Ed.), *Contemporary issues in adolescent development.* New York: Harper & Row, 1975, 147–161.

Erikson, E.H. *Identity, youth, and crisis.* New York: W.W. Norton and Co., 1968.

Gallager, J. Talent delayed—Talent denied: The culturally different gifted child. *A conference report.* Reston, Va.: The Foundation for Exceptional Children, 1974.

Kaplan, S.N. *Providing programs for the gifted and talented: A handbook.* Ventura, Ca.: Superintendent of Schools, 1974.

Kirsuk, T.J., & Sherman, R.E. *Goal Attainment Scaling,* (mimeo), 501 Park Avenue, Minneapolis, Minn. 55415.

Miller, D.R., & Swanson, G.E. *Inner conflict and defense.* New York: Holt-Dryden and Co., 1960.

Ross, A.O. *The gifted child in the family.* In N. Colangelo & R.T. Zaffrann (Eds.), *New voices in counseling the gifted.* Dubuque, Iowa: Kendall-Hunt, 1979.

Terman, L.A. The discovery and encouragement of exceptional talent. *American Psychologist,* 1954, *9,* (6), 221–230.

Chapter 8

Model Education Programs

In this chapter we define conceptual development and present a model program for facilitating conceptual development. The program focuses on specific elements of cognitive and affective growth. We take a developmental approach to programming, based on the general outline of program organization presented in Chapter 7.

In order to present a model educational program certain assumptions are necessary. A program cannot be conceived in a vacuum; in order to succeed it must be based on knowledge of the school, community, and the population it will serve. Individuals or groups involved in the development and implementation of programs for the talented cannot accept programs designed for other locations and populations—or those that are considered generally applicable—without first making a careful analysis of local concerns and characteristics. The program presented in this chapter is but one example of a possible program. Like any other model, it must be evaluated according to local needs and resources. In this instance, expedience is served by moving carefully, starting small, and building upon success.

The model program we present here focuses on conceptual development. The authors realize that conceptual development is but one aspect in the whole spectrum of human growth. But because conceptual development has a pronounced affect on most other areas, it was selected as the topic for this chapter.

CONCEPTUAL DEVELOPMENT AND THE TALENTED

Human development encompasses intellectual, social, physical, and psychological growth and is marked by many transitions. When youngsters become better able to discriminate, differentiate, and generalize, one assumes there has been corresponding growth in understanding or responsibility taking. Development progresses through a sequence of stages. Self-centeredness emerges into social awareness and social concern. Dependence emerges into independence. Subsequently, individuals strive to realize the full extent of their personal potential. Talented and potentially talented youngsters experience faster rates of development than their peers and require programming that is paced to this accelerated rate. If there is no opportunity to sustain conceptual development, optimal development can be hampered, impaired, or blocked entirely. The formulation of goals for enhancing conceptual development, combined with specific methods of educational intervention, can provide both a practical and theoretically sound approach to assessment and educational planning for children with talent potential.

Before discussing conceptual development further, it may prove helpful to define what we mean by "concepts" and explain their importance in educating talented youth. Kagan (1966) states: "Concepts are viewed as the distillate of sensory experience and the vital link between external inputs and overt behavior" (p. 97). The importance of conceptual development to our present discussion was perhaps best explained by Klausmeier (1974):

> In connection with concepts as mental constructs, it is noted that each maturing individual attains concepts according to his unique learning experiences and maturational pattern. In turn, the concepts he attains are used in his thinking about the physical and social world (p. 4).

It can be seen that conceptual development is fundamental to most areas of human growth and behavior. It seems unquestionable that everyone develops at his or her own rate. The problem encountered by many talented and potentially talented students is that their advanced level of conceptual development often places them at odds with teachers, with the school's curriculum, with other students, and even with their parents. Remember, conceptual level is not the same as ability level or academic achievement level. Conceptual level describes how a student learns, not how much a student has learned or is capable of learning. Some children learn best in a structured environment distinguished by clear, concise instructions and teacher-parent support. Other children learn best with less structure, in an environment characterized by self-initiated learning activities.

If one concludes that the talented are conceptually different from their agemates, then it would naturally follow that these differences have specific implications for program design. Essentially, a curriculum designed for talented students should place greater stress on meeting the unique learning needs of children who are conceptually advanced, yet still exhibit physical and social skills more characteristic of their chronological age. It is relatively simple to identify a child who is learning at a faster rate than peers. It is more difficult to identify the conceptual level within which the individual is functioning. Assessing conceptual level is not only more complex; it is essential in designing instructional programs.

Page's (1979) comments at the Hyman Blumberg Symposium are particularly cogent to this discussion. Page cited physiological studies and cumulative information gathered from standardized tests to argue in favor of the idiosyncrasy of mental traits and processes, rather than a belief in general intellectual ability. This line of thought raises serious doubts about the appropriateness of insisting that talented persons achieve equally well in all curricula areas. Perhaps what is needed is an approach that allows talented students to pursue areas of special ability or interest while accepting more typical or "average" performance in areas where talent is not demonstrated.

Acceleration in a particular area is of great importance when considering curricular activities that go beyond the basics. Our interpretation of the literature and discussions with colleagues in art and music education lead us to share their conclusions that talented musicians and artists will demonstrate their special talents given the opportunity to perform before someone capable of evaluating their "performance." Music and art educators also stress that if the school is going to take responsibility for developing these artistic talents, pupils will require individual and sustained instruction. In order to sustain a special program in the arts, schools may have to tap the broader community.

One fact that perhaps needs emphasizing is that the talented are no different from other pupils in their need to develop effective writing skills, oral communication skills, and such coping skills as good study habits and effective decision making. Moreover, the study of history, current events, and futuristics should not be neglected. As a preface to our discussion of program development for the talented we share these thoughts from Page (1979):

> To be intellectually defensible, a program for the gifted must not be equally appropriate for the less gifted. . . . The gifted are innately different in ability from the average, and this innate difference by itself is not adequate to assure the maximum contribution to society or to their own fulfillment (p. 209).

The lack of appropriate curricula, both in terms of pace and quality of instruction, often lulls talented pupils into becoming ineffective students, who fail to fully develop their own capabilities and interests. Getzels and Thelen (1969) suggest why the talented may become ineffective learners. They hypothesize that a relationship exists among teacher and pupil personalities, the structure of the subject to be learned, and the learning situation. They describe certain subjects as well-arranged bits of information to be presented in a sequential fashion.

Subjects that fall into this category include mathematics, science, languages, and history. Personality is involved in learning such prescribed, ordered information only to the extent that the teacher's personality influences the manner of presentation and subsequent student evaluation. Subjects requiring more personal involvement include music, art, and creative writing.

Getzels and Thelen (1969) created a paradigm to illustrate the relationship between information acquired by students and the amount of personal involvement the student has with the material learned. We have modified their paradigm somewhat so that it is consistent with the present discussion. (See Exhibit 8-1.)

On the left of the paradigm, personal involvement is minimal, with the information flowing directly from the teacher or textbook to the student. The information is encoded pretty much intact by the student, requiring only efficient data acquisition and memorization skills and a minimum of personal involvement. This type of mental activity is predominantly convergent and left hemispheric in nature, and it requires only the lowest levels of cognitive and affective functioning, according to Bloom's (1974) taxonomy. As one moves toward the right, learning becomes more dynamic, interactive, and subject to hypothesis raising and testing. Personal characteristics of the learner become increasingly important and the necessity for structured content is minimized. This type of mental activity is more divergent and right hemispheric in nature and it involves the higher levels of cognitive and affective functioning, again according to Bloom's taxonomy.

One implication that can be drawn from this perspective is that talented students—by our definition, conceptually advanced—will be challenged and stimulated more by courses structured along the right side of the paradigm. All courses can be taught in this manner to some degree, but unfortunately the talented seldom experience this instructional mode. A course that allows the potentially talented person to become involved in the learning process would also stimulate the development and demonstration of potential, thus making identification of talent easier and more valid.

Another issue that relates directly to conceptual development and our definition of talent concerns those students whom we refer to as pseudotalented. The appearance of being talented may be the result of early, concentrated, planned or unplanned training or attention. In a child's early years it is difficult to determine the extent to which she or he has genuine talent potential. Perhaps the youngster is just very well taught or conditioned. Under appropriate environmental conditions, those with genuine talent potential will continue to develop and perform in an exceptional manner through adolescence and adulthood. The pseudotalented will usually show signs of stress or regression toward the norm in junior or senior high school—that is, if the curriculum is sufficiently demanding and appropriately structured.

Exhibit 8-1 The Interaction between Subject and Student Involvement

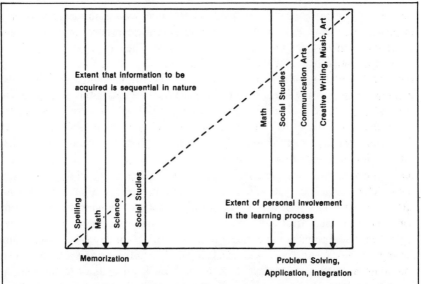

Extent that information to be acquired is sequential in nature

Creative Writing, Music, Art

Communication Arts

Social Studies

Math

Extent of personal involvement in the learning process

Spelling

Math

Science

Social Studies

Memorization

Problem Solving, Application, Integration

Source: Getzels, J.W., & Thelen, H.A. The classroom as a unique social system. In N.B. Henry (Ed.) *The dynamics of instructional groups.* Yearbook of the National Society for the Study of Education (59), Part II, p. 70.

PROGRAMMING ISSUES

The theoretical ideas set forth can best be summarized, and provide a transition to specific programming ideas, by summarizing the results of a study conducted in the Palo Alto, California school system (Lundy, Carey, & Moore, 1977). The purpose of the study was to determine how to effectively program for academically talented (conceptually advanced?) students. The students tested three or more standard deviations (IQ 145+) above the mean on either the Binet or Weschler Intelligence Tests. Talented pupils in four grade levels were matched by sex and age with a like number of high-average pupils: 30 each in grade three, 38 in grade five, 20 in grade eight, and 23 in grade 11. Fifteen questions were developed, and these served as the basis for individual interviews with the two groups of students.

The academically talented identified four dimensions that affected their learning.

1. *Teacher's instructional style*—Discovery learning and problem solving were most valued by students. This type instruction was promoted through

class discussion, projects, stimulation, and learning games. Secondary pupils learned best when activities were clearly related to class purposes. Elementary age pupils enjoyed human interaction and learning games more. It would appear secondary pupils are more product or goal oriented and elementary pupils more process oriented. The highly talented preferred learning at their own, self-directed pace.

2. *Peer context*—This involves a preference among talented high school students for sharing ideas with others. Elementary age pupils preferred pursuing a subject alone or with a few others—but socializing was not as important. About half the pupils in both elementary and secondary levels liked to teach others. Talented pupils, unlike their less talented peers, liked discussions that elicited different opinions.

3. *Independence and decision making*—At all levels the highly gifted expressed a desire to self-direct a part of their learning. A lack of independence (possibly reflecting a lack of confidence in the student's judgment) is particularly frustrating. Gifted students also express frustration in not being able to pursue a topic or project in sufficient depth because of time restrictions and lack of materials. Repetitive drill is boring after a concept has been learned; in fact, it is so noxious it generalizes to the concept being learned (e.g., multiplication), making it almost equally noxious.

4. *Variety*—The talented detailed two types of variety they appreciated: activities within a subject, and a variety of instructional methods employed by the teacher. Workbooks were not appreciated, particularly when they served as the basis for individualized, self-paced instruction.

Essentially, talented students make a case for being taught differently. It is necessary too to recognize the great variation in individual preferences and the differences between elementary and secondary pupils. It becomes apparent that many factors must be considered when designing and implementing programs for talented and potentially talented students.

A MODEL PROGRAM FOR CONCEPTUAL DEVELOPMENT

With the preceding foundation, we will proceed with outlining a "typical" program designed to foster the conceptual development of talented youngsters. This exercise is a hypothetical construction intended to illustrate the organizational sequence presented in Chapter 7. Readers would be wise to note the suggested methodology while evaluating the applicability in their own setting.

The first task is to survey community and school attitudes toward and support for programs specifically designed to foster the conceptual development of talented children. This survey can be carried out by designing appropriate questionnaires or by conducting interviews with a sample representing all facets of the school and community (e.g., teachers, administrators, counselors, other school staff, politicians, parents, professionals, clergy, action groups, and club members). Some sample questions could include:

1. Is there a need for special programs for talented children?
2. What special needs of the talented are currently not being met?
3. Do programs for the talented exist? If so, please describe.
4. Would you be willing to participate in the planning of programs for the talented?
5. Would you help implement programs for the talented?

You can expect a wide range of responses to questions such as these. Some people would express belief in the need for such programs and promise to actively support them; others would be unalterably opposed to any type of special "elitist" programs for the talented. The range of responses can help you identify community and school attitudes. More specifically, the responses can be used to develop a force-field analysis of the thrusts and counter-thrusts to program development. In fact, information from such a survey is useful in many aspects of both Phase I and Phase II of program development (see Chapter 7).

Formation of a planning or steering committee is facilitated by knowing the attitudes one would like to see represented by the committee, although it does seem preferable to include persons representing all prevailing attitudes.

Once the committee is formed, two of its initial tasks are (1) consolidating and broadening program support and (2) establishing program parameters and goals. Force-field analysis, goal attainment scaling, and values clarification are all useful activities in this process.

There are several possible strategies for increasing popular support for programs, including:

1. Informational/educational programs via local media (e.g., television, radio, and newspaper).
2. Programs presented for local action groups and interest groups (e.g., parent-teacher association, teachers' meetings, Junior Chamber of Commerce, and Rotary).
3. Enlisting the aid of respected persons to spread the word to their constituencies.
4. Special events such as talent shows, science fairs, and art exhibits.
5. More recognition of the special achievements of the young (e.g., publication of deserving reports and poetry, exhibitions of the art of young people in schools, libraries, and government buildings).

Establishing program goals and parameters is facilitated by selecting or developing an organizing developmental theory. Suppose that after evaluating the

utility of many developmental theories, the committee concluded that Klausmeier's (1974) Conceptual Learning and Development (CLD) model was the
most useful means of determining conceptual development levels in children
from preschool through grade five, and that Hunt's (1971) model and assessment
procedures were the most useful for assisting conceptual development in grade
six and beyond. Obviously such conclusions must be based on knowledge of
these theories. For purposes of illustration, we provide an explanation of each
theory.

Klausmeier's (1974) CLD model depicts four levels of conceptual development through which a child progresses. The sequence of level acquisition is
invariant, but the acquisition rate depends on the interaction between the individual and the environment. The four levels as identified and explained by
Klausmeier (p.17) are:

Concrete Level
a. Attained when the individual becomes aware that the object of
current attention has been encountered on a prior occasion.
b. The first step is attending to the object and forming an internal
representation of it.
c. The individual must then discriminate this object from others and
compare it with a representation recalled from memory.

Identity Level
a. Attained when an object that has been encountered before is recognized as the same one when observed from a different perspective
or sensed in a different modality.
b. Whereas concrete level functioning involves only the ability to
discriminate an object from others, identity level functioning requires discrimination of various forms of the same object from
others and generalizing the various forms as the same.
c. Klausmeier states: "Generalizing is the new operation postulated
to emerge as a result of learning and maturation that makes attainment at the identity level possible."

Classificatory Level
a. Attained when two different objects from the same class of objects
are treated as the same—for example, treating the family parakeet
and a robin in the back yard as birds.
b. The individual need not be able to explain why the two objects are
the same.
c. This level also includes the ability to classify examples as members
or nonmembers of a class of objects, but does not necessitate having
to explain the basis for grouping them.

Formal Level

a. Attained when the individual can name the concept or object and its defining attributes.
b. The individual must also be able to state whether particular examples of the concept belong to a specific set and why these examples are included or excluded in terms of defining attributes.
c. Klausmeier states: "Discrimination of things on their global and diffuse stimulus properties, which is essential at the concrete level, changes to discrimination of more specific and abstract properties at the identity and classificatory levels. However, at the formal level the individual must be able to discriminate and label all the defining attributes of the concept."

Hunt's (1975) approach includes analyzing the person in situation (P), the environment the person is experiencing (E), and the consequences of the person's interaction with the environment (B). In Hunt's formulation, learning styles are equated with conceptual levels. Conceptual levels (P) are matched with the degree of environmental structure (E) required to enhance learning (B) and promote continued development. Hunt's model thus considers both cognitive complexity (which is defined in terms of differentiation, discrimination, and integration), and interpersonal maturity (which is defined in terms of taking increased responsibility for the consequences of one's behavior).

Hunt's (1978) model of conceptual development can be outlined as follows:

Substage I

He may react impulsively to situations in a negative, unsocialized manner by losing his temper or becoming aggressive. He is totally self-centered and does not consider other people's thoughts and/or feelings and is only concerned with what he wants, likes, feels, and believes. He resists being ruled or controlled by other people.

He may react defensively by withdrawing, ignoring the situation, or blaming others. It should be noted that hostility or anger may also be expressed at other levels, but this is not the only reaction to the situation.

Stage I

Concern with behaving in a socially acceptable way.

Polarized or dichotomous thinking or behavior. The person evaluates situations in a simple concrete fashion according to what is socially acceptable or correct (e.g., right–wrong, good–bad). He is sensitive to authority figures (teachers, parents) and how they would behave, or what they would expect of him in different situations. His concern with behaving correctly may be shown by feelings of anxiety or embarrassment when he has acted incorrectly. Once he has evaluated the situation, he is anxious for closure.

Transition Stage

He is open to other people's ideas and evaluates alternatives. But no attempt is made to integrate this evaluation with the solution or decision. He is very much concerned with his own thoughts and feelings and is striving for independence. In considering alternatives, he reveals an increased tolerance of uncertainty, ambiguity, and difference of opinion.

Stage II

The person considers and weighs alternatives, then decides upon the best possible solution to a particular problem. In doing so he shows concern for his own and others' ideas and feelings, and about the possible consequences of his decision. Where possible, he seeks a compromise which is suitable to all concerned. But he is secure in his independence and is aware of himself, of his relationship with others, and how they view him. He will not compromise his values, principles, or beliefs to please others or to conform. By the same token, he will accept full responsibility for the consequences of his decision.

The quest for independence, accompanied by taking responsibility, earmarks the direction of mature conceptual development. If the script goes according to Hunt's model, the ego-centered child grows into a confident and socially responsible person. The child with talent potential presumably will be ready sooner to enter a "higher" conceptual level than age-mates. In elementary school, this movement is frequently seen in a desire to pursue personal interests and reject instruction or direction from teachers and parents.

Using these theories as an organizing structure, the committee next generates appropriate program goals. These program goals are generated in accord with the guidelines presented in Chapter 7. Some sample program goals include:

1. Provide inservice programs to help teachers and parents utilize Klausmeier's and Hunt's models and understand their importance in meeting the special needs of talented students.
2. Identify talented students K-12 to include five percent of the school population.
3. Use Klausmeier's model to assess the conceptual development of talented students through Grade 5.
4. Use Hunt's model to assess the conceptual development of talented students in Grades 6 through 12.

5. Provide programming appropriate to needs identified in Goals 1 and 2, so that all students have achieved uppermost levels by the terminal grade indicated.
6. Evaluate the results of Goals 1 through 5.
7. Goal 1 is to be achieved during the first half of the next school year.
8. Goal 2 is to be achieved by February 15th of the next school year.
9. Goals 3 and 4 are to be achieved by the end of the next school year.
10. Goal 5 will be implemented on an individual basis beginning the following fall.
11. Goal 6 will be met by using goal attainment scaling to evaluate attainment of goals within specific timelines. Evaluation will be both formative and summational and will be complete by the end of the second year of program implementation.

Pupil Identification

After developing goals for their gifted and talented program the committee is faced with the task of pupil identification. The GIFTS Identification Instrument is one of many such instruments designed to assist in this process. The instrument allows users to address recognized identification issues and add their own significant criteria to the identification process. We have learned that the values of the persons who do the identification largely determine which students are selected into the program. To paraphrase an old adage, talent and talent potential are in the eye of the beholder. The GIFTS Identification Instrument was developed to incorporate local definitions and concerns for talent and at the same time provide structure and control over the process by including some universally accepted identification criteria.

The Initial Screening: Forming the Pool

Talent is a comparative behavior whereby an individual is considered exceptional in comparison to one or more referent groups. A referent group can be as limited as one's classmates and as inclusive as everyone in the world. A broad referent group increases the likelihood that identification will require standardized measures such as intelligence tests and expert judgment. An obvious limitation of standardized tests is their remoteness from actual classroom behavior; this may limit their usefulness as indicators of giftedness. More specific comparisons based on teacher and parental observations are usually more behaviorally oriented and lend themselves more directly to programmatic suggestions. However, identification performed solely by direct observation carries with it two flaws: observer bias and the inability to compare individuals with a wider universe of peers. Therefore, the most meaningful approach to identification and eventual programming is to include both observational and standardized measures.

The identification process is meant to be informative as well as functional. Persons involved in the identification of talented students often learn much about their own values and the values of the community. For example, consider a comparison of two ways to interpret nonconforming behavior in students. Each set of statements reflects a different value system.

Statements Describing Behaviors of Disruptive Students
and Behaviors of Talented Students

Disruptive Behavior	*Creative Thinking Behavior*
1. Does not plan ahead.	1. Uses ideas in new and different ways; avoids premature closure.
2. Challenges teacher's authority.	2. Takes risks to defend a position.
3. Talks when should be listening.	3. Asks a lot of questions; intellectually curious.
4. Gets other students to misbehave.	4. Questions authority.
5. Thinks everything is funny.	5. Has a keen sense of humor.
6. Bothers other students.	6. Expresses opinion freely.
7. Manipulates other students.	7. Takes leadership in getting things done.

It can be seen from the above example that a committee's values and perceptions can determine whether a student is identified as talented or a troublemaker.

As mentioned in Chapter 7, there are many screening techniques that can be used to form a pool of talented students. More definitive assessment measures are used to select the final program participants. Screening procedures should involve teachers, parents, *and* students when possible. Exhibit 8-2 shows a student nomination survey that was developed by the Milwaukee, Wisconsin School District to provide student input.

Screening devices for use by parents and teachers are available from various sources. Most are checklists where the person is asked to rate how much or how often a certain type of behavior has been observed by the rater when evaluating the student. These instruments, along with various nomination procedures and the use of some standardized test results, represent the usual means of forming an initial talent pool.

It is best to be as inclusive as possible in this first screening phase and to be aware of the characteristics of diverse subpopulations so as not to "overlook"

Exhibit 8-2 Student Nomination Survey

The purpose of this survey is to assist in the preliminary screening of potential candidates for the proposed School for the Gifted and Talented. Since this survey is only part of the total screening process, and since only a limited number of pupils will ultimately be selected for participation, you are asked NOT to share the pupil responses with your class.

Directions to Teacher
1. Read the following statements to your class:
   A. "Each of you has been asked to assist in an information gathering survey."
   B. "Please take out a sheet of paper and a pencil."
   C. "Number your paper from 1 to 5."
   D. "Please answer each question that I will read with the *complete* name of one student in our class."
   E. "Pick someone whom you think is the best choice and not just your friends."
   F. "You can pick the same person for more than one question if you think that person is your best choice."

QUESTIONS

_____ If a person from outer space wanted someone in your class to tell him about different things on earth, who do you think could tell the most?

_____ What student in class can complete his or her work and still have time to take part in other activities?

_____ Who says things in class that are most original, things that you never thought of before?

_____ If kids didn't have to go to school, what student in your class could talk you into going?

_____ Who do you think might invent or make something that no one ever made before? (This is the person you might ask to help you write a poem or play, or help you make something for a school fair.)

2. Complete the attached tally sheet.

Exhibit 8-2 continued

TALLY SHEET

Record the full name of each pupil identified by members of the class in response to the STUDENT NOMINATION SURVEY. In the columns numbered 1 to 5 (corresponding to the questions read to pupils from the STUDENT NOMINATION SURVEY) indicate the number of times that each pupil was selected by his peers. For example:

PUPIL NAME	1	2	3	4	5
John Doe	8	0	0	0	15

The tally noted above would indicate that John Doe was selected by eight (8) peers in response to Question #1, by no peers in response to Questions #2, 3, and 4, and by 15 peers in response to Question #5.

School _____   Teacher _____

Grade Level _____

PUPIL NAME	1	2	3	4	5

Source: Milwaukee, Wisconsin School District.

any talented or potentially talented persons. The definition of talent becomes operationalized through application of the screening techniques. Care must be taken that these techniques do not discriminate against *any* group or individual. In this instance ignorance of special student characteristics cannot be a valid excuse for prejudicial behavior. Be certain that *all* identification procedures are checked and developed in cooperation with all concerned groups.

Final Identification for Program Participation

Once the pool of talented students is formed, it is time to begin the task of selecting students to participate in the program. The screening process focuses on characteristics of a general, more easily observable type. Final identification for program participation should be based upon more specific criteria. The problem of identifying unrealized potential and unrecognized talent makes it necessary to include identification criteria that may only be observed outside the school or through criteria normally considered unrelated to academic achievement.

In seeking to identify talent it is essential to keep in mind the interrelationship between culture and talent. GIFTS Talent Identification Procedures (see Exhibit 8-3) permit identification across many types of talent. Given the educational goal of maximizing potential, a decision may have to be made whether to further development in a particular talent area, or program to develop talents across several areas.

In prescribing educational programs, a number of assumptions regarding the talent categories would be made. First, knowledge, represented by convergent thinking, is seen as the foundation for developing talent. We further assume that divergent and creative thinking and behavior will most frequently be manifested by pupils who are highly knowledgeable, who are personally secure, and who have experienced a wide variety of stimulating experiences to which they have responded in a personally and socially rewarding manner. Creativity suggests considerable self-initiative and self-maintenance in comparison to the "originality of response" that characterizes divergent thinking and behavior.

The affective, social, and physical behavior areas seem to be the most neglected for the talented population as a whole. Some students are "wise beyond their years." They might be the persons to whom peers turn in time of trouble and anguish. These "natural counselors" quite likely evidence levels of affective development far in advance of their peers. They are sensitive, vulnerable, and sometimes appear hostile when their values are attacked. Physical development usually has only organized athletics as an outlet, which restricts the definition of physical talent. The GIFTS Identification Instrument was designed with the aforementioned issues and concerns in mind.

The identification of talented and potentially talented persons is based on observed behavior. As noted in Chapter 1, all meaningful behavior stems from conscious thought and operations. It was also explained how convergent and divergent thought provides the basis for behavior. If a valued behavior is observed only occasionally, evidenced in fragments, or inferred from other behaviors, the individual is assumed to have talent potential. If a valued behavior is consistently demonstrated, the individual is assumed to be talented.

GIFTS Talent Identification Procedures incorporate the above considerations. Raters are asked to indicate whether a valued behavior is consistently demonstrated, inferred from fragmented or inconsistent behavior, or unobserved.

The listed behaviors are all relevant to the demonstration of talent across nearly all areas of performance. The rater considers to what extent the student has evidenced each behavior within the context of that rater's expertise and experience. For example, a mathematics teacher's rating would reflect the student's talent potential in mathematics. Parents' ratings would reflect more generalized talent or talent potential. A particular rater could rate a student on more than one dimension, depending on the rater's expertise and experience with the student. The particular area in which the student is being rated is noted on each Behavior Rating Sheet (see Exhibit 8-3).

Also, the Behavior Rating Sheets can be a valuable asset to increase self-awareness and understanding among talented persons. One can have the individual, his or her parents, and his or her teachers complete the rating sheets. Then the similarities and differences in perceptions can serve to enlighten the individual and others. They can also serve as a programmatic discussion starter. Goals can be established relative to areas in need of development, and the rating sheets can be completed a second time at some point in the future as a post-program evaluation measure.

It is important that we know with as much certainty as possible the underlying reasons for a student's behavior. The identification process simply begins our understanding and must be seen as only a part of the entire assessment process. The organization of the program depends on the type of information available on *each* student and the overall program goals.

The assessment program must correspond directly to the program goals. Individual assessment helps determine where each student is relative to the established program goals. Once this is known, objectives can be specified for each student. Just because students were initially identified using common criteria, one should not plan a common program for all the students. Each student is unique and requires individualized programming.

Both Klausmeier (1973) and Hunt (1975) have developed assessment materials that help determine a student's position along a developmental hierarchy. Once each student's developmental level is established, appropriate programming can be provided by both teachers and parents.

Many programming resources are available commercially; others can be developed by interested teachers and parents (see Section IV, Resources, for a compre-

Exhibit 8-3 GIFTS Talent Identification Procedures

Background

The GIFTS Talent Identification Procedures consist of one or more Behavior Rating Sheets, plus scoring and interpretation materials. Each rater is asked to consider those areas in which he or she has had the opportunity to observe the behavior of the individual being rated. The rater then selects the area(s) he or she feels competent to rate and completes a Behavior Rating Sheet for each area. If the individual's behavior is consistent across all areas, one rating sheet is sufficient. Separate rating sheets are required when there are differences in behavior.

Some sample areas of behavior that could be rated include:
- mathematics
- interpersonal relationships—peers, family, teachers
- English—literature, grammar, vocabulary, spelling, writing
- music
- speaking
- science
- reading
- art
- social studies
- physical activities
- special interest areas—hobbies, clubs, etc.
- foreign or second languages
- community activities
- others

BEHAVIOR RATING SHEET

Rater: _____

Relationship to person being rated: _____

Person whose behavior is being rated: _____

Area of behavior being rated: _____

BEHAVIORS	Unobserved in this person	Inferred from fragmented or inconsistent behavior	Consistently demonstrated by this person
1. takes calculated risks	_____	_____	_____

Exhibit 8-3 continued

BEHAVIORS	Unobserved in this person	Inferred from fragmented or inconsistent behavior	Consistently demonstrated by this person
2. adapts to unforeseen circumstances	_____	_____	_____
3. is a problem solver	_____	_____	_____
4. is a self-starter	_____	_____	_____
5. is self-evaluative	_____	_____	_____
6. accepts constructive feedback	_____	_____	_____
7. establishes relationships between previously unrelated ideas	_____	_____	_____
8. selects the most appropriate response given many alternatives	_____	_____	_____
9. withholds judgment in order to think through alternatives	_____	_____	_____
10. considers accepted standards when evaluating performance	_____	_____	_____
11. is a problem finder	_____	_____	_____
12. communicates effectively through language and behavior	_____	_____	_____
13. considers available resources (people, data, things) before taking action	_____	_____	_____
14. considers personal resources (abilities, limitations) before taking action	_____	_____	_____
15. effectively organizes resources toward a goal	_____	_____	_____
16. perseveres toward goals	_____	_____	_____
17. enjoys a challenge	_____	_____	_____
18. values the means of doing something as well as the outcome	_____	_____	_____
19. is willing to go beyond the usual or known	_____	_____	_____
20. utilizes information obtained through all primary senses (hearing, sight, sound)	_____	_____	_____

Exhibit 8-3 continued

BEHAVIORS	Unobserved in this person	Inferred from fragmented or inconsistent behavior	Consistently demonstrated by this person
21. utilizes extensive amounts of information and diverse information	_____	_____	_____
22. demonstrates behavior consistent with intent	_____	_____	_____
23. integrates newly acquired information with what previously is known	_____	_____	_____
24. is an effective leader	_____	_____	_____
25. is an effective teacher	_____	_____	_____
TOTALS:	_____	_____	_____

Are there other areas of behavior in which this individual demonstrates behavior *very* consistent with the ratings above? If so, what are they?

_____   _____   _____

In your experience with this person, are there any other areas of behavior that you believe may produce different ratings? If so, what are they?

_____   _____   _____

If you can, please rate this person's behavior in those areas where differences may exist with the above. Use a separate Behavior Rating Sheet for each area.

Scoring, Interpretation, and Use of Behavior Rating Sheets

To score the Behavior Rating Sheets, count each check as one and total each vertical column. This yields a score for unobserved, a score for inferred, and a score for consistently demonstrated behaviors. The score for inferred behaviors represents talent potential, and the score for consistently demonstrated behaviors represents talent in the areas rated. Selecting individuals to participate in a special program requires that you set cutoff points based on the number of individuals you wish to include. Individuals can be identified for specific talents, talent potential, or a combination of the two.

Exhibit 8-3 continued

If one wishes to focus on and identify a certain talent area, rating sheets can be given to those persons familiar with that area of expertise and with the individuals. Or rating sheets can be completed by those persons who have the most extensive contact with the individuals, and let each rater determine the areas to be rated. Either way, rating sheet totals can be combined across raters for a more comprehensive view of the rated individuals.

The Behavior Rating Sheets can also serve as indicators of needed programming. The rating sheets of selected individuals can be evaluated behavior by behavior. Unobserved behaviors would need to be developed, inferred behaviors need to be promoted, and consistently demonstrated behaviors need to be reinforced.

Source: Dr. Philip Perrone and Dr. Robert Male.

hensive listing of available resources). Goal attainment scaling is but one way to determine program content, sequence, and timelines, as well as provide the basis for evaluation.

The impact of programs for talented students often depends on the person with whom the student will work. Obviously counselors, teachers, and parents can each offer a certain type of expertise to any comprehensive program. Sometimes the team includes a mentor. It is easy to see that there must be a coordination of effort if such a program is to have maximal effect. Extensive communication is necessary between involved parties. Group planning and evaluation sessions are perhaps the best method of monitoring program content, sequence, and timelines.

At this point we present our model for the development of human talent. Remember that this approach to developing talent cannot be borrowed in its entirety and applied to any setting. It must be integrated with local program concerns in order to be effective.

A Model for the Development of Human Talent

This model is based on the understanding that knowledge about oneself and the physical and social environments is obtained daily through interpersonal relations, physical activity, and from the media. Individuals selectively respond to these inputs based on their collective experiences. The result is the formation of tastes, attitudes, and values.

Social, physical, and scholastic skills result from person-environment interactions. In some cases one's response potential combines with the richness of environmental support and stimulation, to produce behavior that is described as "potentially talented." When that behavior becomes more focused and productive, it merits the label "talented."

In presenting the scope and sequence of our human talent model, we make certain assumptions regarding individual development of children with talent potential. These are listed here:

1. The potentially gifted child progresses through the same stages and must master the same developmental tasks as other children.
2. The potentially gifted child can be pushed into manifesting talented behavior prior to late childhood, but more normal development would suggest a general level of exceptionality through the ages of 10 or 11. The child would develop a focus or outlet for this general exceptionality after developing a personal value system based upon a broad range of learning experiences.
3. Exceptional children will develop a time awareness of self-in-future in late childhood if given the opportunity to experience the consequences of their behavior. In effect, these children anticipate outcomes or consequences a few years before their peers.
4. The potentially talented child has a rich and vivid imagination that allows vicarious learning to be a prime source of learning and development.
5. The potentially gifted child will more readily accept responsibility in return for increased independence.
6. The traditional age-grade curriculum is two or three years below the talented student's cognitive level, and the instructional process is likely to be oriented toward children at least one conceptual level below that of the student with talent potential.

In the model there are five major phases (see Exhibit 8-4):

I. *Awareness of Self and Society*
   A. *Individual awareness objectives* stress knowing and being aware of aspects of self that are considered important for personal effectiveness.
   B. *Orientation of self toward societal objectives* which are enduring, learned predispositions to behave in a consistent way. The objectives specify attitudinal dimensions considered important for social effectiveness.

Self-awareness begins forming prior to language development. The knowledge gained in this first phase underlies and flows through the remaining four phases. The extent to which these objectives *are not* achieved is the extent to which they will need to be reexamined and developed in later life situations.

Exhibit 8-4 Model for Developing Human Talent

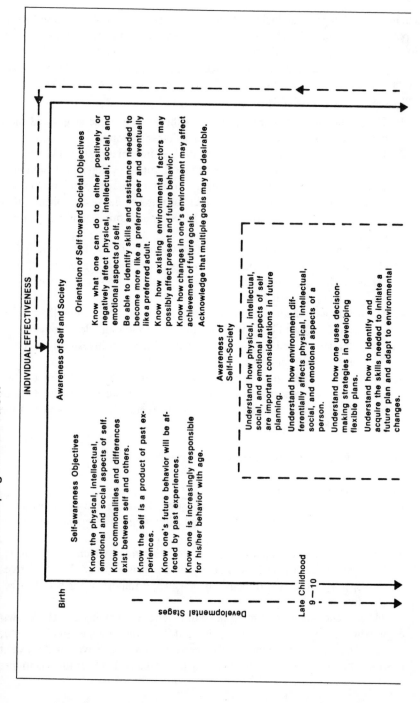

Exhibit 8-4 continued

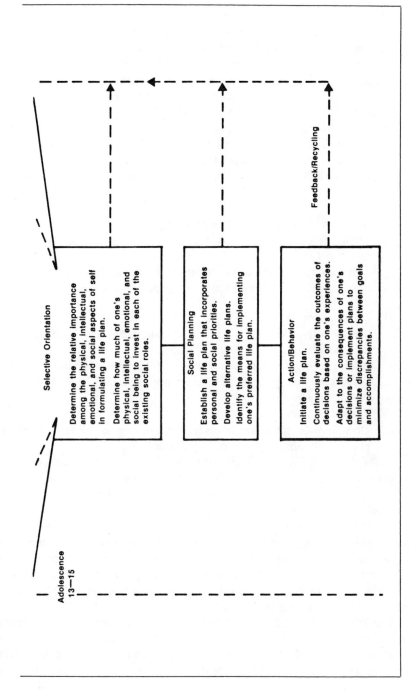

Adolescence
13—15

Selective Orientation

Determine the relative importance among the physical, intellectual, emotional, and social aspects of self in formulating a life plan.

Determine how much of one's physical, intellectual, emotional, and social being to invest in each of the existing social roles.

Social Planning

Establish a life plan that incorporates personal and social priorities.

Develop alternative life plans.

Identify the means for implementing one's preferred life plan.

Action/Behavior

Initiate a life plan.

Continuously evaluate the outcomes of decisions based on one's experiences.

Adapt to the consequences of one's decisions or implement plans to minimize discrepancies between goals and accomplishments.

Feedback/Recycling

II. *Awareness of Self-in-Society*

These objectives stress understanding how to relate what is known about self and society to future planning and decision making.

To achieve these objectives within the first two phases of development, and to achieve the objectives of the last three phases, the individual must be able to cognitively perceive abstractions. Developmentally this approximates Piaget's (1951) formal relation stage which begins around age 12 (possibly at age 9 or 10 among those with talent potential). The age continuum depicted on the left of the diagram (see Exhibit 8-4) indicates the *earliest* developmental age at which the competencies in Phase II are likely to be achieved. Some individuals may develop the necessary abstraction abilities earlier, and others later.

III. *Individual Selection Orientation/Valuing*

During this phase, worth (value) is ascribed to particular aspects of self and society.

As the individual develops the competencies in the first two phases, she or he begins to develop personal and social priorities or values.

IV. *Social Planning*

The objectives in this phase represent the integration of self-awareness and social awareness in future planning.

Choosing a plan for implementing one's future goals is a value judgment made after considering the range of alternatives and the likelihood of achieving the various alternatives.

V. *Action/Behavior*

Objectives in this phase represent the carrying out of the learning and planning that has taken place in the first four phases.

The first objective, initiating a life plan, would include several specific behaviors. The remaining objectives relate to evaluation and feedback. *An individual may have to repeat any phase more than once as personal, economic, and social conditions change.*

While the objectives are considered essential in order to implement a future career plan, the objectives also relate to effective behavior in the present. That is, whether one is an effective student, family member, and peer-group member also rests upon achieving these objectives. Educators can use the model to evaluate their teaching effectiveness; the model indicates how to better organize their approach and identifies needed inputs.

The intent of this model is to help ensure that talented pupils are offered an education that focuses on their total development. It is commonly assumed that if the area of gifted behavior receives special attention, other aspects of development will not require special attention. This is not true. Educators should develop a comprehensive set of human development objectives, as outlined in our model, in order to avoid such shortsightedness.

One technique that GIFTS has found to be particularly valuable is to develop questionnaires about a specific area of development and have the student, teachers, parents, and counselor respond. This way we are able to assess the information and provide "feedback" about the student from five or six different perspectives. We have used the behaviors in the Identification Procedures and the model for the Development of Human Talent in this fashion. We report the five or more different perspectives on the student's behavior. The results are often enlightening and promote useful discussions relative to both talent level and programming.

Another valuable approach to programming is to produce "learning modules" that deal with the many needs of talented students. The following exhibit (Exhibit 8-5) is one example of a learning module. This module was developed by Dr. Phyllis Post (1980), a research assistant with GIFTS. The module is used by GIFTS to foster the development of potentially gifted students. The module relates directly to Hunt's theories and to our model as well.

Exhibit 8-5 A Learning Module

ACHIEVEMENT MODULE GUIDELINES

Objectives:
1. Help students understand how they think about achievement and its meaning in their lives.
2. Help students understand the standards they use for achievement.
3. Help students understand their source of achievement.
4. Help students understand the basis of their expectations relative to personal achievement.

Introduce module by stating:
"The purpose of this module is to stimulate your thinking about achievement and rules. The questions to which you will respond are not difficult, but it is quite possible that you have not thought of them before. Please just write down whatever thoughts come to mind. There are no right or wrong answers."

"The first sheet is about your achievement in school." (Pass out sheet.)

"Please complete the information and read the instructions."

"Are there any questions?"

Exhibit 8-5 continued

"If not, then turn over the sheet. Questions 1–5 go together and questions 5–7 go together."
"Please begin."

(Allow approximately ten minutes. Watch to see when everyone is finished. Then discuss the questions.)

"The questionnaire focused on three aspects of achievement: (1) how you know when you have achieved; (2) the approval you receive for achievement; and (3) why you expect to achieve."
Ask students how they responded to these questions. Share the responses. Relate their expectations to being selected for GIFTS.

Hand out "What I Think."
"This activity will be timed. I will give you three minutes to answer each question. Please complete the heading and read the instructions. Are there any questions?"

Then discuss this questionnaire by asking:

1. Which questions were easiest for you to answer?
2. Which question was most difficult? Why?
3. Would anyone like to share her or his response? (Tell the students they can respond or not respond—and mean it. Comfort is the rule of the hour.)
4. How is this question related to achievement, rules, parents, and criticism?

ACHIEVEMENT MODULE

Name: _____

School: _____

Grade: _____ Sex: Male _____ Female _____

Father's Occupation: _____

Mother's Occupation: _____

Exhibit 8-5 continued

On the following page, you will be asked your thoughts about your schoolwork. Please think of school-related situations. There are no right or wrong answers. Give your own ideas and opinions about each question. Answer what you really think. Do not write what others may think. No one will see your answers unless you choose to show them.

1. Think of some schoolwork you did well. What was it?

   _____

   _____

2. How did you know you did well? (Do not write more than 3 sentences.) _____

   _____

   _____

   _____

   _____

3. Did you receive any approval because of your work?

   Yes____ No____

4. If "Yes," please describe the approval you received.

   _____

   _____

   _____

5. Can you think of some schoolwork you expect to do well in the future?

   Yes____ No____

6. If "Yes," what is it? _____

   _____

   _____

7. Why do you think you will do well? (Please do not write more than 3 sentences.) _____

   _____

Exhibit 8-5 continued

_____

_____

WHAT I THINK . . .

Name: _____ School: _____

ID#: _____ Sex: _____ Grade: _____ Date: _____

On the following pages you will be asked to give your ideas about several topics. Try to write at least three sentences on each topic.

There are no right or wrong answers, so give your own ideas and opinions about each topic. Indicate the way you _really_ feel about each topic, not the way others feel or the way you think you should feel.

You will have about three minutes for each page. Please wait for the signal to go to a new page.

1. What I think about rules . . .
   Try to write at least three sentences on this topic. WAIT FOR SIGNAL TO TURN PAGE (signal—turn page)

2. When I am criticized . . .
   Try to write at least three sentences on this topic. WAIT FOR SIGNAL TO TURN PAGE (signal—turn page)

3. What I think about parents . . .
   Try to write at least three sentences on this topic. WAIT FOR SIGNAL TO TURN PAGE (signal—turn page)

4. When someone does not agree with me. . .
   Try to write at least three sentences on this topic. WAIT FOR SIGNAL TO TURN PAGE (signal—turn page)

5. When I am not sure . . .
   Try to write at least three sentences on this topic. WAIT FOR SIGNAL TO TURN PAGE (signal—turn page)

6. When I am told what to do . . .
   Try to write at least three sentences on this topic.

Source: Hunt, Butler, Noy, and Rosser (1978), pp. 4, 5.

The Achievement Module in Exhibit 8-5 allows the collection of valuable data pertinent to individualized programming. Objectives can be selected for each student based on individual developmental levels. In addition, the self-awareness and self-understanding gained by students as they complete the forms increases the likelihood that they will be collaborators in their own development.

Evaluation is important in any program. Evaluation can be formative (ongoing) or summative (specified at the end). As noted in Chapter 7, techniques such as goal attainment scaling provide for both types of evaluation and are highly recommended. Evaluation data are useful only if the feedback is used to strengthen individual programs. Evaluation is always necessary but it is valuable only when results can be applied. An evaluation technique that considers goals and objectives along with timelines and levels of attainment makes evaluation fairly straightforward and is easy to use in program adaptation.

REFERENCES

Bloom, B.S., & Krathwohl, D.R. *Taxonomy of educational objectives—Cognitive and affective domains.* New York: David McKay Co., 1974.

Getzels, J.W., & Thelen, H.A. The classroom as a unique social system. In N.B. Henry (Ed.), *The dynamics of instructional groups. Yearbook of the National Society for the Study of Education,* 1969, *59,* Part II, 53–82.

Hunt, D.E. *Matching models in education.* Toronto: Institute for Studies in Education, 1971.

Hunt, D.E. The B-P-E paradigm for theory, research and practice. *Canadian Psychological Review,* 1975, *16,* 185–197.

Hunt, D.E., Butler, L.F., Noy, J.E., & Rosser, M.C. *Assessing by the paragraph completion method.* Toronto: Ontario Institute for Studies in Education, 1978.

Kagan, J. A developmental approach to conceptual growth. In H.J. Klausmeier & C.W. Harris (Eds.), *Analysis of concept learning.* New York: Academic Press, 1966, pp. 97–116.

Klausmeier, H. J., et al. *Development of conceptual learning and development assessment series III: Noun.* Madison, Wis.: Research and Development Center, 1973.

Klausmeier, H.J., Ghatala, E.S., & Frayer, D.A. *Conceptual learning and development: A cognitive view.* New York: Academic Press, 1974.

Lundy, R.A., Carey, R.W., & Moore, R.K. *Dimensions of learning for the highly gifted student.* Palo Alto, Ca.: Palo Alto Unified School District, 1977.

Page, E. B. In W.C. George, J.C. Standard, & J.C. Stanley (Eds.), *Educating the gifted: Acceleration and enrichment.* Baltimore: The John Hopkins University Press, 1979.

Piaget, J. *Psychology of intelligence.* London: Routledge & Kegan Paul, 1951.

Post, P.B. Relationship between students' perception of achievement and conceptual level, grade level, degree of talent, and sex. Doctoral Dissertation. University of Wisconsin. Madison, 1980.

Chapter 9

Looking Ahead

One argument advanced for providing special learning opportunities for talented persons is that we will need their insights to help solve the problems society faces now and in the future. A number of individuals and study groups have generated lists of future or potential crises. These lists only underscore the seriousness and complexity of current and potential world problems. No individual working alone can be expected to solve any of these problems, but thousands of talented persons working cooperatively have a greater chance of making major inroads.

We have chosen to discuss the implications for talent development posed by future crises identified by Schwartz, Teige, and Horman (1977). Their article identifies trends that give rise to various crises.

TRENDS

Some of these trends are primarily technical: depletion rate of nonrenewable resources, industrialization of nearly all human activities, and increasing isolation from nature as a result of attempts at environmental control. The majority of trends are social: the population explosion, the increasing gap between rich and poor, movement toward a single world economy, decrease in private property, decreasing cultural diversity, increasing demands for self-determination, increasing unemployment and underemployment, and declining productivity.

That these trends in turn lead to problems is all too apparent just three years after the article was published. A listing of just a few current crises will serve to underscore the enormity of the social and technical problems we face.

Social

- cultural exclusion of elderly
- conflict between central control and individual freedom

- urban violence
- famine
- teenage alcoholism
- impact of the changing role of women
- changing family forms
- stress
- loss of political and social cohesion
- chronic unemployment
- sociocultural effect of media

Technical

- global fuel shortages
- advances in biomedical technology, including life extension, genetic engineering, euthanasia
- famine
- weapons technology
- pollution
- catastrophic experiments
- vulnerability of water supplies
- waste disposal
- microcomputers and rights to privacy
- information explosion

The two lists suggest that smaller, regional problems have become large and global in nature. Increases in population, pollution, interdependence, and knowledge contrast with fewer resources, less space, less cooperation, and poorer management of knowledge.

IMPLICATIONS

We would like to speculate briefly on which behaviors society will come to value most during the next 25 to 30 years. It is important to focus on social needs, values, and priorities of the future because these will provide the basis for defining and developing talent.

The overlap and interdependence between social scientists and physical scientists should be apparent. Talent, to be meaningful at a global level, would require both technical and social knowledge and technical and social skills. The talented individual should have command of at least two, possibly three languages. That individual should be skilled in the use of computers, have excellent written and oral communication skills, and be able to facilitate group discussions, planning, and action. He or she should be able to cope with internal and external tension, maintain priorities, maintain a sense of humor, and experience a joy in living. This would help the individual counter the grim realities of global, regional, and local problems; it would also ensure the person's mental health and increase the individual's effectiveness. A commitment to bettering the lot of people in general would be essential.

As to the fine arts, one can only speculate as to whether society will continue to value, and thus pay the price to support, the vast diversity of music, painting, and sculpture that prevails in the 1980s. Will diminishing natural resources create an era of conservatism or escapism in the arts? Will the world economy continue to permit people to indulge their individual tastes?

We believe there will be a decided shift away from observing and appreciating the efforts of recognized masters, and a shift to performing and enjoying one's own performance. This shift implies that people who now pay others to produce will place a higher value on their own creative and productive processes. If this shift occurs, fewer artists and musicians are likely to be acclaimed as talented or geniuses, and those that are so acclaimed will likely be models for a generation of performance-oriented persons.

Already there is some evidence that more people are "into the arts." It is not possible to tell if the drastic decline in record sales and the drop in attendance at rock concerts is temporary or if we have moved into an era where people have to choose between food, energy, and the arts. Economics has also had an impact on many of the service industries. The trend toward gourmet cooking clubs, and even the do-it-yourself home redecorating indicates that more and more people are relying on their own talents and abilities for achieving personal enjoyment.

Artistic performers often require government subsidies. How long will the public support financial expenditure for the arts? It seems likely that artists will not flourish during the next 30 years, although there should be a great increase in involvement of people of all ages in the arts. Perhaps the performing arts will become a primary vehicle for self-expression and satisfaction during a time when the accomplishments and satisfaction normally found in career and family will diminish.

Of course, creative artists and musicians who can continue to challenge and excite people may continue to be appreciated. A nation of performers can be severe critics. Thus it may take even more talent and require greater risk to consider a career in the arts.

It is likely that the world population will experience considerable growth and that there will be a further increase in the elderly segment of the population. More people will mean less physical space per person. If cooperation is the byword for the new era, we may have to reconsider the meaning and value of personal space and individuality. The talented stand out, but even in 1980 we see that exceptionality, particularly in schools, is neither valued nor promoted by the masses. In the future children with talent potential may experience more pressure to conform to the prevailing norm.

It is possible that we will coin new terms and techniques such as "chemo-education," where intelligence can be increased with a pill. All children may be expert in the use of computers. There will be a decreased emphasis on memory, on retaining and regurgitating facts. Artificial aids to "intelligence" will render traditional intelligence and achievement testing obsolete.

If with the aid of computers, everyone can function as if they had a 1980-normed IQ of 200, what will distinguish the truly gifted person? Will the talented use their computers more efficiently? Just what is the value of calculating a few seconds faster than the norm? Einstein was 25 to 30 years ahead of his colleagues. Will anyone ever be that far out in front again?

Chemoeducation, biofeedback, and computer-assisted living may change the nature of education. Convergent thinking will be devalued while divergent, right-hemispheric processes will rise to the fore. It appears that curricula will be organized so that pupils would learn how to use memory banks and decision-making schemes. In effect, it will be like using a statistical formula without understanding, or needing to understand, how the formula was derived. One simply would trust the experts. Deductive problem solving therefore would be reduced to teaching all children how to recognize and codify a problem and choose the correct computer program. The emphasis would not be in evaluating the answers; it would be on defining the problems and accessing the system correctly.

As subjects that stress abstract, impersonal data (such as mathematics, science, foreign languages, and spelling) are relegated to a secondary place in the hierarchy of educational values, subjects that teach people about themselves and society (psychology, sociology, and physiology) and promote learning by doing should prevail. Until this era is accepted—it has already arrived technically—convergent thinking and behavior will likely be of prime importance when defining talent. Once education, and society, come of age, divergent and creative thinking and behavior will be the only area in which talent, as a manifestation of individual exceptionality, is likely to be recognized.

Returning to the definition of talent given in Chapter 1, we would like to share our thoughts on the functional, day-to-day meaning of the various components of that definition.

Effectiveness in school should be measured in terms of defining problems; accessing appropriate problem-solving systems; accepting, modifying, or rejecting proposed solutions; and applying and evaluating possible solutions. Communication, comprehension, application, and evaluation will be the foundation of special education programs for the talented.

Artistic and musical talent would require recognition and response from knowledgeable persons who can determine whether student products will be meaningful to and appreciated by a producing, rather than a consuming, public. Teachers will need to interpret and anticipate public tastes and hypothesize how budding artistic talent is manifested in the young.

Effectiveness in the physical realm may be less subject to change, although the value placed currently on professional athletes may change. Possibly those who can teach others will be more valued than those who entertain.

Socially, individuals who can facilitate communication and collaboration should be valued more than people who can direct the efforts of others.

More efficient use of perceptual systems suggests that individuals will need to be comfortable with a less dogmatic, less fixed perception of their environments. They will need to make a periodic assessment of biases and stereotypic perceptions so they can be aware when they begin relying on habitual and fixed perceptual patterns. Biofeedback should become well understood and self-applied so that individuals can regulate their own goal-oriented motivation and behavior.

More efficient use of conscious thought suggests to us the need to organize and present information and knowledge in a more concise, cogent, and integrated manner. Without exercising some quality control in the midst of the knowledge explosion, most individuals will be so overwhelmed by information that they will rely on distilled reports and "expert" conclusions. Moreover, in the interests of good communication, there should be some effort to minimize the jargon that presently marks and isolates each profession. It also seems necessary that most well-educated people have a speaking command of at least a few languages since it seems unlikely the peoples of the world will adopt a universal language.

More efficient transfer of data between the conscious and subconscious implies greater self-awareness. If data are derived from experiences rather than based on what is read, heard, or seen on television, it is likely that the individual's subconscious data will be more vivid and more accessible.

With more information, and a broader range of information available, the learner will need more time and resources for a breadth and depth of learning. Learning, of course, occurs everywhere. Talented students have enormous appetites for learning and are likely to exhaust rather quickly what the school typically makes available. Therefore, newly developed information and communication networks should become an integral part of the curriculum. Talented students should be given alternative learning opportunities (in lieu of the traditional curriculum) for which they can receive credit.

More efficient use of conscious and subconscious mental operations again implies the need to learn through application. Psychological operations function more efficiently when used and when evaluative feedback is provided. Application is also fundamental to developing more efficient overt behavior, a natural extension of more efficient operations.

In short, self-awareness, stimulating environments, learning by doing, self-regulation, alternatives, and evaluative feedback are all necessary elements of any educational program for talented students, both in the remaining years of the twentieth century and beyond.

REFERENCE

Schwartz, P., Teige, D. J., & Horman, W. W. In search of tomorrow's crises. *The Futurist,* 1977, *11*(5), 269–278.

Resources

In Section IV we present a comprehensive categorization and listing of resources that readers can utilize to plan and implement specific activities or curricula for talented and creative students. These resources can become a resource for an individual and serve as a curriculum resource as well.

Bibliography

This resource bibliography is organized so the reader can locate references pertinent to certain topical areas without relying on the article or book title. Certain selections overlapped categories and the rule of thumb was to place the publication under the category receiving primary emphasis. The reader will find that this is not an inclusive bibliography but only representative of publications we felt were worth considering after we read them. There were other publications that could have been included, but we chose only those we had read and believed would contribute to the readers' fund of knowledge. We excluded many references if their writers had more current articles we could include or if a particular writer treated a topic more inclusively or conclusively than others. This bibliography is arranged as follows:

I. General definitions and methods of identifying talented pupils.
II. General strategies for teaching the talented and those with talent potential.
III. Scholastic assessment and programming:
    A. Reading
    B. Mathematics and science
    C. Applied arts
    D. Social leadership
    E. Written and verbal communication
IV. Personal-social assessment and programming:
    A. Relations with parents and teachers
    B. Peer and sibling relations
    C. Affective development and motivation
    D. Creativity
    E. Planning and decision making

I. GENERAL DEFINITIONS OF TALENT AND METHODS OF IDENTIFYING TALENTED PERSONS

Baldwin, J. W. The relationship between teacher-judged giftedness, a group intelligence test, and an individual test with possible gifted kindergarten pupils. *Gifted Child Quarterly*, 1962, *6*(4), 153–165.

Barbe, W. B. Characteristics of gifted children. *Educational Administration and Supervision*, 1955, *41*, 207–217.

Bray, D. W. *Issues in the study of talent*. New York: Kings Crown Press, 1954.

Bruch, C. B. A proposed rationale for the identification and development of the gifted disadvantaged. *Gifted Children Newsletter*, 1970, *12*(2), 40–49.

Carroll, H. A. *Genius in the making*. New York: McGraw Hill, 1940.

Cornish, R. L. Parents', teachers' and pupils' perception of the gifted child's ability. *Gifted Child Quarterly*, 1968, *12*, 14–17.

Council for Exceptional Children. *Identification of the gifted: Tests and measurements: A selected bibliography*. (Exceptional Child Bibliography Series No. 668). Reston, Va.: Author, 1975.

DeHaan, R. F. Identifying gifted children. *School Review*, 1957, *65*, 41–48.

Dellas, M., & Gaier, E. L. Identification of creativity: The individual. *Psychological Bulletin*, 1970, *73*, 55–73.

Dennis, W., & Dennis, M. W. (Eds.). The intellectually gifted: An overview. New York: Grune and Stratton, 1976.

Frederickson, R. H., & Rothney, J. W. M. *Recognizing and assisting multipotential youth*. Columbus, Ohio: Charles Merrill, 1972.

Gallager, J. J. *Talent delayed—talent denied: The culturally gifted child*. Reston, Va.: The Foundation for Exceptional Children, 1974.

Gear, G. H. Accuracy of teacher judgment in identifying intellectually gifted children: A review of the literature. *Gifted Child Quarterly*, 1976, *20*, 478–487.

Gowan, J. C. *An annotated bibliography on the academically talented*. Washington, D.C.: National Education Association of the United States, 1961.

Grant, E., & Runzulli, J. S. *Sub-cultural indices of academic potential*. Storrs, Conn.: University of Connecticut Press, 1971.

Guilford, J. P. *Intelligence, creativity, and their educational implications*. San Diego: Robert R. Knapp, 1969.

Guilford, J. P. Intellect and the gifted. *Gifted Child Quarterly*, 1972, *16*(3), 175–184.

Guilford, J. P. *Way beyond the IQ*. Buffalo, N.Y.: Creative Education Foundation, 1977.

Hall, V. C., & Daye, D. B. Patterns of early cognitive development among boys in four subcultural groups. *Journal of Educational Psychology*, 1977, *69*(1), 66–87.

Hauch, B. B., & Freehill, M. F. *The gifted: Case studies*. Dubuque, Iowa: William C. Brown Co., 1972.

Hilliard, A. G. *Alternative to IQ testing: An approach to the identification of gifted "minority" children* (final report). Sacramento: California State Department of Education, Division of Special Education, June 1976.

Hollingworth, L. S. *Gifted children: Their nature and nurture*. New York: Macmillan Company, 1926.

Holt, E. E. *A selected and annotated bibliography on the gifted*. Columbus, Ohio: F. J. Heer Printing Company, 1960.

Issacs, A. F. The search for talent begins within. *Gifted Child Quarterly,* 1965, *9*(2), 89–96.

Jacobs, J. C. Effectiveness of teacher and parent identification of gifted children as a function of school level. *Psychology in the Schools,* 1971, *8*, 140–142.

Jensen, A. R. How much can we boost IQ and scholastic achievement? *Harvard Educational Review,* 1969, *39*, 1–23.

Karnes, M. B., & Bertschi, J. D. Identifying and educating gifted/talented nonhandicapped and handicapped pre-schoolers. *Teaching Exceptional Children,* 1978, *10*(4), 114–119.

Kincaid, D. A study of highly gifted elementary pupils. *Gifted Child Quarterly,* 1969, *13*, 261–267.

Landig, H. J., & Naumann, T. F. Aspects of intelligence in gifted pre-schoolers. *Gifted Child Quarterly,* 1978, *22*(1), 85–89.

Lazlow, A., & Nelson, P. A. Instant answers: Testing the gifted child in the elementary school. *Gifted Child Quarterly,* 1974, *18*(3), 152–162.

Lee, R. F., & Newland, T. E. A small community and its gifted school children. *The Educational Forum,* 1966, *30*, 363–368.

Levinson, B. M. Rethinking the selection of intellectually gifted children. *Psychological Reports,* 1956, *2*, 127–130.

Martinson, R., & Lessinger, L. M. Problems in the identification of intellectually gifted pupils. *Exceptional Child,* 1957, *23*, 199–201; 206.

McNemar, Q. Lost: Our intelligence? Why? *American Psychologist,* 1964, *19*(12), 871–882.

Moore, W. D., et al. Academic achievement of gifted children: A comparative approach. *Exceptional Children,* 1978, *44*(8), 618–619.

Newland, T. E. On defining the mentally superior in terms of social need. *Exceptional Children,* 1963, *29*, 237–240.

Oden, M. H. The fulfillment of promise: 40-year follow-up of the Terman gifted group. *Genetic Psychology Monographs,* 1968, *77*, 3–93.

Ogletree, E. J., & Ujlaki, W. Effects of social class status on tests of creative behavior. *The Journal of Educational Research,* 1973, *67*, 149–152.

Pressey, S. L. Concerning the nature and nurture of genius. *Science,* 1955, *68*, 123–129.

Pressey, S. L., & Pressey, A. Genius at 80, and other oldsters. *The Gerontologist,* 1967, *7*, 183–187.

Rader, J. R. Piagetian assessment of conservation skills in the gifted first grader. *Gifted Child Quarterly,* 1975, *19*(3), 226–229.

Shaw, M. C., & McCuen, J. T. The onset of academic under-achievement in bright children. *Journal of Educational Psychology,* 1960, *51*, 103–108.

Sisk, D. A. What if your child is gifted? *American Education,* 1977, *13*(8), 23–26.

Spearman, C. *The abilities of man.* New York: Macmillan Company, 1927.

Strang, R. Gifted adolescents' views of growing up. *Exceptional Children,* 1956, *23*, 10–15.

Sullivan, A. R. The identification of gifted and academically talented black students: A hidden exceptionality. *Journal of Special Education,* 1973, *7*(4), 373–379.

Sumption, M. R. *Three hundred gifted children.* Yonkers, N.Y.: World Book Co., 1941.

Thompson, M. Identifying the gifted. *National Elementary Principal,* 1972, *51*(5), 37–44.

Thorndike, R. L. Problems in identification, description, and development of the gifted. *Teachers College Record,* 1941, *42*, 402–406.

Torrance, E. P. Finding hidden talents among disadvantaged children. *Gifted Child Quarterly,* 1968, *12*, 131–137.

Torrance, E. P. Assessment of disadvantaged minority group children. *School Psychology Digest,* 1973, *2*(4), 3–10.

Torrance, E. P. *Discovery and nurturance of giftedness in the culturally different.* Reston, Va.: Council for Exceptional Children, 1977.

Wallach, M. A., & Wing, C. W. *The talented student: A validation of the creativity-intelligence distinction.* New York: Holt, Rinehart & Winston, 1969.

Willerman, L., & Fiedler, M. F. Intellectually precocious preschool children: Early development and later intellectual accomplishment. *Journal of Genetic Psychology,* 1977, *31*(1), 13–20.

Witty, P. A., & Bloom, S. W. The education of the superior high school student. *The Bulletin of the National Association of Secondary School Principals,* 1955, *39*, 14–22.

II. GENERAL STRATEGIES OF TEACHING THE TALENTED AND POTENTIALLY TALENTED

Adams, F., & Brown, W. *Teaching the bright child.* New York: Holt, 1930.

Arends, R., & Ford, P. M. *Acceleration and enrichment in the junior high school: A follow-up study.* Springfield: Illinois State Department of Education, July 1964.

Arn, W., & Fierson, E. An analysis of programs for the gifted. *Gifted Child Quarterly,* 1964, *8*, 4–8.

Axford, L. B. *A directory of educational programs for the gifted.* Metuchen, N.J.: Scarecrow Press, Inc., 1971.

Barbe, W. B. Evaluation of special classes for gifted children. *Exceptional Child,* 1955, *22*, 60–62.

Birch, F. W. Early school admission for mentally advanced children. *Exceptional Children,* 1954, *21*, 84–87.

Bishop, W. E. Successful teachers of the gifted. *Exceptional Children,* 1968, *34*, 317–325.

Boston, B. O. (Ed.). *Gifted and talented: Developing elementary and secondary school programs.* Reston, Va.: Counsel for Exceptional Children, 1975.

California State Department of Education. *Educating the gifted in California schools.* Sacramento: Author, 1975.

Cole, H. D., & Parson, D. E. The Williams total creativity program. *Journal of Creative Behavior,* 1974, *8*(3), 187–207.

Conant, J. B. Education of the academically talented. *School and Society,* 1958, *86*, 225–227.

Crow, A., & Crow, L. D. (Eds.). *Educating the academically able: A book of readings.* New York: David McKay, 1963.

Cureton, E. E. New developments in the education of abler students. *Proceedings, 1954 Invitational Conference on Testing Problems.* Princeton, N.J.: Educational Testing Service, 1954.

DeHaan, R. F., & Havighurst, R. J. *Educating gifted children.* Chicago: University of Chicago Press, 1961.

DeVito, A. Survival through creative education. *Journal of Creative Behavior,* 1976, *10*(1), 45–51.

Dunlap, J. M. Gifted children in an enriched program. *Exceptional Children,* 1955, *21*, 135–137.

Durrett, M. E., & Pirofski, F. Effects of heterogeneous and homogeneous grouping on Mexican-American and Anglo children. *Young Children,* 1976, *31*(4), 309–314.

Education of the gifted and talented. *Report to the Congress of the United States by the U.S. Commissioner of Education* (vol. 1), 1971.

Education of the gifted and talented. *Background papers submitted to the U.S. Office of Education* (vol. 2), 1971.

Educational Policies Commission. *Education of the gifted.* Washington, D.C.: The National Education Association, 1950.

Educational Policies Commission. *Research on the academically talented student.* Washington, D.C.: The National Education Association, 1961.

Elwood, C. Acceleration of the gifted. *Gifted Child Quarterly,* 1958, *2,* 21–23.

Feldhusen, J. F., & Treffinger, D. J. Design and evaluation of a workshop on creativity and problem-solving for teachers. *The Journal of Creative Behavior,* 1976, *10*(1), 12–14.

Feldhusen, J. F., Treffinger, D. J., & Elias, R. M. The right kind of programmed instruction for the gifted and talented. *National Society for Performance and Instruction Journal,* 1969, *8,* 6–11.

Fliegler, L. A. (Ed.). *Curriculum planning for the gifted.* Englewood Cliffs, N.J.: Prentice-Hall, 1961.

Fliegler, L. A., & Bish, C. E. The gifted and talented. *Review of Educational Research,* 1959, *29,* 408–450.

French, J. L. (Ed.). *Educating the gifted.* New York: Holt, Rinehart & Winston, 1964.

Gallager, J. J. *Teaching the gifted child.* Boston: Allyn & Bacon, 1975.

Gallagher, J. J., Aschner, M. J., & Jenne, W. *Productive thinking of gifted children.* Washington, D.C.: Council for Exceptional Children, 1967.

George, W. C. Discussion of barriers to education of the gifted: Attitudes and behaviors. *Talents and Gifts,* 1977, *19*(4), 2–4.

Goldberg, M. J., Passow, H., & Justman, J. *The effects of ability grouping.* New York: Teachers College Press, 1966.

Gowan, J. C., & Torrance, E. P. (Eds.). *Education of the ablest.* Itasca, Ill.: F. E. Peacock Publishers, 1971.

Halpin, G., Goldenberg, R., & Halpin, G. Are creative teachers more humanistic in their pupil control ideologies? *The Journal of Creative Behavior,* 1973, *7*(4), 282–286.

Khan, M. W., Iqbal, M., & Flodder, S. L. *Indiana study of educational needs and programs of the gifted and talented.* LaPorte, Ind.: Model Educational Research Center, 1976.

Khatena, J. Educating the gifted child: Challenge and response in the U.S.A. *Gifted Child Quarterly,* 1976, *20*(1), 76–90.

Klausmeier, H. J. Effects of accelerating bright older elementary pupils: A follow-up. *Journal of Educational Psychology,* 1968, *54,* 165–171.

Lazar, A. L., & Duncan, D. K. (Eds.). *The challenge of accountability in programs for the gifted.* Monterey, Ca.: California Association for the Gifted, 1971.

Lundy, R., et al. *Dimensions of learning for the highly gifted student.* Palo Alto, Ca.: Palo Alto Unified School District, 1977.

Maltzman, I. On the training of originality. *Psychological Review,* 1960, *67,* 229–242.

Martinson, A. *A guide toward better teaching for the gifted.* Ventura, Ca.: Ltd. Publications, 1976.

Martinson, R. A. *Curriculum enrichment for the gifted in primary grades.* Englewood Cliffs, N.J.: Prentice-Hall, 1968.

Martinson, R. A., Hermanson, D., & Banks, G. An independent study-seminar program for the gifted. *Exceptional Children,* 1972, *38,* 421–426.

Massalas, B. G., & Zevin, J. *Creative encounters in the classroom: Teaching and learning through discovery.* New York: Wiley & Sons, 1967.

216 DEVELOPMENTAL EDUCATION AND GUIDANCE OF TALENTED LEARNERS

Meredeth, P., & Landen, L. *100 activities for gifted children*. San Francisco: Fearon Publishers, 1957.

Mohan, M. Is there a need for a course in creativity in teacher education? *Journal of Creative Behavior*, 1973, *7*(3), 175–186.

Morrison, H. B. The creative classroom. *Journal of Creative Behavior*, 1973, *7*(3), 196–200.

National Society for the Study of Education. *The education of gifted children*. 23rd Yearbook, National Society for the Study of Education, Part I. Chicago: University of Chicago Press, 1924.

National Society for the Study of Education. *The education of gifted children*. 57th Yearbook, National Society for the Study of Education, Part II. Chicago: University of Chicago Press, 1958.

Newland, T. E. Some observations on essential qualifications of teachers of the mentally superior. *Exceptional Children*, 1962, *29*, 111–114.

Otto, J. J. (Ed.). *Enriching the curriculum for the gifted elementary school children in regular classes*. Austin: University of Texas Press, 1955.

Parnes, S. J., Noller, R., & Biondi, A. *Guide to creative action: Creative actionbook*. New York: Scribner, 1977.

Perrone, P. A., and Pulvino, C. J. New directions in the guidance of the gifted and talented. *The Gifted Child Quarterly*, 1977, *21*(3), 326–335.

Plowman, D. D., et al. *Gifted and talented education management team*. Sacramento: Bureau of Publications, 1976.

56 practices for the gifted. Albany, N.Y.: University of the State of New York, 1958.

Pressey, S. L. *Educational acceleration: Appraisals and basic problems*. Columbus: Ohio University Press, 1949.

Promising practices: Teaching the disadvantaged gifted. Washington, D.C.: Office of Education, 1975.

Raspberry, W. What about elitist high schools? *Today's Education*, 1976, *65*, 36–39.

Renzulli, J. S. Identifying key factors in programs for the gifted. *Exceptional Children*, 1968, *35*, 217–221.

Renzulli, J. S. *The enrichment triad model: A guide for developing defensible programs for the gifted and talented*. Weathersfield, Conn.: Creative Learning Press, 1977.

Rice, J. P. *The gifted, developing total talent*. Springfield, Ill.: Charles C Thomas, 1970.

Ripple, R. E. A controlled experiment in acceleration from the second to the fourth grade. *Gifted Child Quarterly*, 1965, *5*, 119–120.

Rockefeller Panel Reports. *The pursuit of excellence: Education and the future of America*. Special studies project. Garden City, N.Y.: Doubleday, 1958.

Sato, I. S. The culturally different gifted child—the dawning of his day. *Exceptional Children*, 1974, *40*(8), 572–576.

Shertzer, B. (Ed.). *Working with superior students*. Chicago: Science Research Associates, 1960.

Sisk, D. A. Teaching the gifted and talented teacher: A training model. *Gifted Child Quarterly*, 1975, *19*(2), 81–88.

Sisk, D. A. Centering activities for gifted/talented children. *Gifted Child Quarterly*, 1978, *22*(1), 135–139.

Stanley, J. C. Accelerating the educational progress of intellectually gifted youths. *Educational Psychologist*, 1973, *10*, 133–146.

Tan, E., Piwnica, P., & Parker, S. *Bright ideas: Complete enrichment units from a gifted resource room*. Monterey Park: Creative Teaching Press, Inc., 1976.

Taylor, C. W., & Williams, F. E. (Eds.). Instructional media and creativity. *Proceedings of the Sixth Utah Creativity Research Conference.* New York: Wiley, 1966.

Terman, L. M., & Oden, M. H. Major issues in the education of gifted children. *Journal of Teacher Education,* 1954, *5*, 230–232.

Torrance, E. P. Readiness of teachers of gifted to learn from culturally different gifted children. *Gifted Child Quarterly,* 1974, *18*(2), 137–142.

Torrance, E. P., & Meyers, R. E. *Creative learning and teaching.* New York: Dodd, Mead and Company, 1970.

Toynbee, A. Is America neglecting her creative minority? In C. W. Taylor (Ed.), *Widening horizons in creativity.* New York: Wiley, 1964.

Treffinger, D. J. Teaching for self-directed learning: A priority for the talented and gifted. *Gifted Child Quarterly,* 1975, *19*(1), 46–59.

Ward, V. S. *Educating the gifted: An axiomatic approach.* Columbus, Ohio: Charles E. Merrill, 1961.

Witty, P. A. The education of the gifted and creative. *Gifted Child Quarterly,* 1971, *15*(2), 109–116.

Wodke, K. H., & Wallen, N. E. The effects of teacher control in the classroom on pupils' creativity test gains. *American Educational Research Journal,* 1965, *2*, 75–82.

Worcester, D. A. *The education of children of above average ability.* Lincoln: University of Nebraska, 1956.

III. SCHOLASTIC ASSESSMENT AND PROGRAMMING

Reading

Labuda, M. (Ed.). *Creative reading for gifted learners: A design for excellence.* Newark, Del.: International Reading Association, 1974.

Nash, W. R., & Torrance, E. P. Creative reading and the questioning abilities of young children. *Journal of Creative Behavior,* 1974, *8*(1), 15–19.

Nauman, T. F. A first report on a longitudinal study of gifted preschool children. *Gifted Child Quarterly,* 1974, *18*(3), 171–172.

Robinson, H. M. (Ed.) Promoting maximal reading growth among able learners. *University of Chicago Supplementary Educational Monograph,* 1954, 81.

Trezise, R. L. Teaching reading to the gifted. *Language Arts,* 1977, *54*(8), 920–924.

Ushenberg, D. C., & Howell, H. *Reading and the gifted child: A guide for teachers.* Springfield, Ill.: Charles C. Thomas, 1974.

Mathematics and Science

Aiken, L. R. Ability and creativity in mathematics. *Review of Educational Research,* 1973, *43*(4), 405–432.

Albers, M. E., & Seagoe, M. V. Enrichment for superior students in algebra classes. *Journal of Educational Research,* 1947, *40*, 487–495.

Ashbrook, A. Teaching mathematics to gifted children. *Trends in Education,* Summer 1977, 3–5.

Brandwein, P. F. *The gifted student as future scientist.* New York: Harcourt Brace, 1955.

Clark, R. W. *Einstein: The life and times.* New York: World Publishing Co., 1971.

Cole, C. C. *Encouraging scientific talent.* New York: College Entrance Examination Board, 1956.

Edgerton, H. A., & Britt, S. H. The first annual science talent search. *The American Scientist,* 1943, *31*, 55–68.

Goodrich, H. B., & Knapp, R. H. *Origins of American scientists.* Chicago: University of Chicago Press, 1952.

Gordon, G. G. *Providing for outstanding science and mathematics students.* Los Angeles: University of Southern California Press, 1955.

Hansen, R. A., & Neujahr, J. Career development of high school students talented in science. *Science Education,* October/December 1976, 6–9.

Helson, R., & Crutchfield, R. S. Mathematicians: The creative researcher and the average Ph.D. *Journal of Consulting and Clinical Psychology,* 1970, *34*, 250–257.

National Council of Teachers of Mathematics. *Program provisions for the mathematically gifted student in the secondary school.* Washington, D.C.: National Education Association, 1957.

National Education Association. *Mathematics for the academically talented student.* Washington, D.C.: Author, 1959(a).

National Education Association. *Science for the academically talented student.* Washington, D.C.: Author, 1959(b).

Roe, A. *The making of a scientist.* New York: Dodd and Mead, 1953.

Snow, A. J. Ethno science and the gifted in American Indian education. *Gifted Child Quarterly,* 1977, *21*(1), 53–57.

Stanley, J. C., Keating, D. F., & Cox, L. H. *Mathematical talents.* Baltimore: The Johns Hopkins University, 1974.

Taylor, C. W. (Ed.) *Research conference on the identification of creative scientific talent.* Salt Lake City: University of Utah Press, 1956, 1958, 1959.

Taylor, C. W., & Barron, F. (Eds.). *Scientific creativity: Its recognition and development.* New York: Wiley, 1963.

Terman, L. M. Scientists and non-scientists in a group of 800 gifted men. *Psychological Monographs: General and Applied,* 1954, *68*(7).

Thomas Alva Edison Foundation Institute. *Strengthening science education for youth and industry.* New York: New York University Press, 1957.

Applied Arts

Barron, F., & Welsh, G. Artistic perceptions as a possible factor in personality style: Its measurement by a figure preference test. *Journal of Psychology,* 1952, *33*, 199–203.

Behrens, R. R. Beyond caricature: On types of humor in art. *Journal of Creative Behavior,* 1977, *11*(3), 165–175.

Beittel, K. R. Creativity in the visual arts in higher education. In C. W. Taylor (Ed.), *Widening horizons in creativity.* New York: Wiley, 1964.

Brown, C. *Creative drama in the lower school.* New York: Appleton-Century-Crofts, 1929.

Brown, D. S. *Teaching gifted students art in grades seven through nine.* Sacramento: California State Department of Education, 1973.

Cross, P. G., Cattell, R. B., & Butcher, H. J. The personality patterns of creative artists. *British Journal of Educational Psychology,* 1967, *37*, 292–299.

Davis, G. A., Helfert, C. J., & Shapiro, G. R. Let's be an ice cream machine! Creative Dramatics. *Journal of Creative Behavior*, 1973, *7*(1), 37–48.

Drevdahl, J. E., & Cattell, R. B. Personality and creativity in artists and writers. Journal of Clinical Psychology, 1958, *14*, 107–111.

Eberle, B. Does creative dramatics really square with research evidence? *Journal of Creative Behavior*, 1974, *8*(3), 177–182.

Feinberg, S. Creative problem-solving and the music listening experience. *Journal of Creative Behavior*, 1977, *11*(3), 158–164.

Getzels, J. W., & Csikszentimihalyi, M. *The creative vision: A longitudinal study of problem finding in art.* New York: Wiley, 1976.

Gowan, J. C. Creative inspiration in composers. *Journal of Creative Behavior*, 1977, *11*(4), 249–255.

Graham, R. M. *Music for the exceptional child.* Reston, Va.: Music Educators National Conference, 1975.

Grove, R. *The arts and the gifted.* Reston, Va.: Eric Clearinghouse on Handicapped and Gifted Children, 1975.

Hammer, E. F. Artistic creativity: Giftedness or sickness. *Art Psychotherapy,* 1975, *2*(2), 173–175.

Hammer, E. G. Creativity and feminine ingredients in young male artists. *Perceptual and Motor Skills,* 1964, *19*, 414.

Helson, R. Personality of women with imaginative and artistic interests: The role of masculinity, originality, and other characteristics in their creativity. *Journal of Personality*, 1966, *34*, 1–25.

Luca, M. C., & Allen, B. *Teaching gifted children art in grades four through six.* Sacramento: California State Department of Education, 1973.

National Education Association. *Music for the academically talented student in the secondary school.* Washington, D.C.: Author, 1960.

Rosen, J. C. The Barron-Welsh art scale as a predictor of originality and level of ability among artists. *Journal of Applied Psychology,* 1955, *39*, 366–367.

Rossman, B. B. Art, creativity and the elephant: Some clues to artistic creativity among the gifted. *Gifted Child Quarterly,* 1976, *20*(4), 392–401.

Taylor, F. D., et al. *Creative art tasks for children.* Denver: Love Publishing Co., 1970.

Torrance, E. P. Originality of imagery in identifying creative talent in music. *Gifted Child Quarterly,* 1969, *13*(1), 3–8.

Social Leadership

Berry, C. S. *The education of gifted children for leadership.* Columbus: The Ohio State University Press, 1945.

Bleedorn, B. D. Future studies for the gifted. *Gifted Child Quarterly,* 1976, *20*(4), 490–496.

Guilford, J. P., Hendricks, M., & Hoepfner, R. Solving social problems creatively. *Journal of Creative Behavior,* 1968, *2*(2), 155–164.

Jarecky, R. K. Identification of the socially gifted. *Exceptional Children,* 1959, *25*, 415–419.

Oliver, A. Identifying the academically talented pupil. In R. W. Gavin (Ed.), *The social education of the academicaliy talented.* Washington, D.C.: National Council for Social Studies, 1958.

Rivlin, L. Creativity and self-attitudes and sociability of high school students. *Journal of Educational Psychology,* 1959, *50*, 147–152.

Torrance, E. P. Students of the future: Their abilities, achievements and images of the future. *Creative Child and Adult Quarterly*, 1976, *1*(2), 76–90(a).

Torrance, E. P. Give the gifted children of the world a chance to solve future problems. *Talents and Gifts*, 1976, *18*(3), 22–24(b).

Torrance, E. P., Bruch, C. B., & Torrance, J. P. Interscholastic futuristic creative problem-solving. *Journal of Creative Behavior*, 1976, *10*(2), 117–125.

Yakima School District No. 7, Washington. *Developing leaders through future-aimed curriculum: An instructional future-aimed curriculum model*, USOE Programs for the Education of the Gifted and Talented. Office of Education, 1977.

Written and Verbal Communication

Adams, A. H., et al. *Mainstreaming language arts and social studies: Special ideas and activities for the whole class*. Santa Monica, Ca.: Goodyear Publishing Co., Inc., 1976.

Alexakas, C. E., Stankowski, W. M., & Sanborn, M. P. Superior high school students' thoughts about the future and their later college achievements. *Vocational Guidance Quarterly*, 1967, *15*, 273–280.

Bachtold, L. M. Effects of learning environments on verbal creativity of gifted students. *Psychology in the Schools*, 1974, *11*(2), 226–228.

Drews, E. M. (Ed.). *Guidance for the academically talented student*. Washington, D.C.: National Education Association, 1961.

Hogan, R., & Garvey, C. Study of verbally gifted youth. *Fourth annual report to the Spencer Foundation*. Baltimore: Johns Hopkins University, Department of Psychology, 1976.

Knight, L. N. *Language arts for the exceptional: The gifted and the linguistically different*. Itasca, Ill.: F. E. Peacock, 1974.

Love, H. D., et al. *Language development of exceptional children*. Springfield, Ill.: Charles C. Thomas, 1976.

Lowe, B. Individualized creative writing in the open classroom. *Elementary English*, 1975, *52*(2), 167–169.

Meyers, R. E., & Torrance, E. P. *Invitations to speaking and writing creatively*. Lexington, Mass.: Ginn and Co., 1965.

National Council of Teachers of English. *English for the academically talented student*. Washington, D.C.: National Education Association, 1960.

Taylor, C. W. A factorial study of fluency in writing. *Psychometrika*, 1947, *12*, 239–262.

Yamamoto, K. Creative writing and school environment. *School and Society*, 1963, *91*, 307–308.

IV. PERSONAL-SOCIAL ASSESSMENT AND PROGRAMMING

Relations with Parents and Teachers

Barbe, W. B. A study of the family background of the gifted. *Journal of Educational Psychology*, 1956, *47*, 302–309.

Brumbaugh, F. N., & Rosho, B. *Your gifted child: A guide for parents*. New York: Holt, 1959.

Cornish, R. L. Parents', teachers' and pupils' perceptions of the gifted child's ability. *Gifted Child Quarterly*, 1968, *12*(1), 114–117.

Cutts, N. E., & Moseley, N. *Bright children—A guide for parents.* New York: Putnam, 1953.

Drews, E., & Teahan, J. E. Parental attitudes and academic achievement. *Journal of Clinical Psychology,* 1957, *13*, 328–332.

Ginsberg, G., & Harrison, C. H. *How to help your gifted child: A handbook for parents and teachers.* New York: Monarch Press, 1977.

Laycock, S. R. Counseling parents of gifted children. *Exceptional Children,* 1956, *23*, 108–110.

Martinson, R. A., & Delp, J. *The gifted and talented: A handbook for parents.* Ventura, Ca.: Office of County Superintendent, Ventura County Schools.

Milgram, R. M. Perception of teacher behavior in gifted and non-gifted children. *Journal of Educational Psychology,* 1978, *70*, 988–991.

Peterson, D. C. The heterogeneously gifted family. *Gifted Child Quarterly,* 1977, *21*(3), 396–398.

Solano, C. H. Teacher and pupil stereotypes of gifted boys and girls. *Talents and Gifts,* 1977, *19*(4), 4–8.

Stewart, J. C. *Counseling parents of exceptional children.* Columbus, Ohio: Charles E. Merrill, 1978.

Strang, R. *Helping your gifted child.* New York: Dutton, 1960.

Strickland, M. I was a 'wrong answer' kid. *Journal of Creative Behavior,* 1974, *8*(3), 153–156.

Thorne, A. Mothering the gifted to encourage curiosity, learning, and creativity. *Gifted Child Quarterly,* 1963, *7*(1), 47–50.

Peer and Sibling Relations

Bachtold, L. M. Interpersonal values of gifted junior high school students. *Psychology in the Schools,* 1968, *5*, 368–370.

Foster, F. P. The human relationships of creative individuals. *Journal of Creative Behavior,* 1963, *2*(2), 111–118.

Friedenberg, E. Z. The gifted student and his enemies. *Commentary,* 1962, *33*, 410–419.

Gallaher, J. J. Peer acceptance of highly gifted children in elementary school. *Elementary School Journal,* 1958, *58*, 465–470.

Gallaher, J. J., & Crowder, T. The adjustment of gifted children in the regular classroom. *Exceptional Children,* 1957, *23*, 306–312; 317–319.

Gallaher, J. J., et al. Individual classroom adjustments for gifted children in elementary schools. *Exceptional Child,* 1960, *23*, 409–422; 432.

Gavin, R. (Ed.). *The social education of the academically talented* (Curriculum Series No. 10). Washington, D.C.: National Council for the Social Studies, 1958.

Haggard, E. A. Socialization, personality and academic achievement in gifted children. *School Review,* 1957, *65*, 388–414.

Hallman, R. J. Human relations and creativity. *Journal of Creative Behavior,* 1974, *8*(3), 157–165.

Justman, J. Personal and social adjustment of intellectually gifted accelerants and non-accelerants in junior high school. *The School Review,* 1953, *62*, 142–145.

Kurtzman, K. A. A study of school attitudes, peer acceptance, and personality of creative adolescents. *Exceptional Children,* 1967, *34*(3), 157–162.

Mann, H. How real are friendships of gifted and typical children in a program of partial segregation? *Exceptional Children,* 1957, *23*, 199–201; 206.

Mirman, N. Are accelerated students socially maladjusted? *Elementary School Journal*, 1962, *62*, 273–276.

Morgan, A. B. Critical factors in the academic acceleration of gifted children: A follow-up study. *Psychological Reports*, 1959, *5*, 619–653.

Moustakas, C. E. *Creativity and conformity*. Princeton, N.J.: Van Norstrand, 1967.

Pielstick, N. L. Perception of mentally superior children by their classmates in fourth, fifth, and sixth grades. *Perceptual and Motor Skills*, 1963, *77*, 47–53.

Scheifele, M. *The gifted child in the regular classroom*. New York: Bureau of Publications, Teachers College, Columbia University, 1953.

Shaerstein, S. How snobbish are the gifted in regular class? *Exceptional Children*, 1962, *28*, 323–324.

Affective Development and Motivation

Ashley, R. M. *Activities for motivating and teaching bright children*. West Nyack, N.Y.: Parker Publishing, 1973.

Bachtold, L. M. Reflections of gifted learners. *Gifted Child Quarterly*, 1978, *22*(1), 116–124.

Bem, S. L. Sex role adaptability: One consequence of psychological androgyny. *Journal of Personality and Social Psychology*, 1975, *31*, 634–643.

Bonsall, M., & Stellfre, B. The temperament of gifted children. *California Journal of Educational Research*, 1955, *6*, 195–199.

Bridges, S. *Problems of the gifted child: IQ-150*. New York: Crane-Russak & Co., Inc., 1973.

Cohn, S. J. Myth no. 2: Educational acceleration leads to the social maladjustment of intellectually talented youth. *Gifted Child Quarterly*, 1978, *22*(1), 125–128.

Denko, J. D. *Through the keyhole of gifted men and women*. Brooklyn, N.Y.: American Mensa Society, 1977.

Department of Health, Education and Welfare, Office of Education. *Guidance for the underachiever with superior ability*. Author, 1961.

Elkind, D., Deblinger, J., & Adler, D. Motivation and creativity: The context effect. *American Educational Research Journal*, 1970, *7*, 351–357.

Flescher, I. Anxiety and achievement of intellectually gifted and creatively gifted children. *Journal of Psychology*, 1963, *56*, 251–268.

Gensley, J. The gifted child in the affective domain. *Gifted Child Quarterly*, 1975, *19*(3), 307–309.

Gowan, J. C. The gifted underachiever—A problem for everyone. *Exceptional Children*, 1955, *21*(7), 247–249; 270–271.

Gowan, J. C. Dynamics of the underachievement of gifted students. *Exceptional Child*, 1957, *24*, 98–101; 122.

Green, D. A. A study of talented high school drop-outs. *Vocational Guidance Quarterly*, 1963, *10*, 171–172.

Groth, J. J., & Holbert, P. Hierarchical needs of gifted boys and girls in the affective domain. *Gifted Child Quarterly*, 1969, *13*(1), 129–133.

Haggard, E. A. Socialization, personality and academic achievement in gifted children. *School Review*, 1957, *55*, 388–414.

Halpin, G., & Halpin, G. The effect of motivation on creative thinking abilities. *Journal of Creative Behavior*, 1973, *7*(1), 51–53.

Holland, J. L. Creative and academic performance among talented adolescents. *Journal of Educational Psychology*, 1961, *52*, 136–147.

Holland J. L., & Austin, A. W. The prediction of the academic, artistic, scientific and social achievement of undergraduates of superior scholastic aptitude. *Journal of Educational Psychology*, 1962, *53*, 132–143.

Hollingsworth, L. S. The development of personality in highly intelligent children. *National Elementary Principal*, 1936, *15*, 272–281.

Horrall, B. M. Academic performance and personality adjustment of highly selected college students. *Genetic Psychology Monographs*, 1957, *55*, 3–83.

Jenkins, M. D. Intellectually superior Negro youth: Problems and needs. *Journal of Negro Education*, 1950, *19*, 322–332.

John, V. P. The intellectual development of slum children: Some preliminary findings. *American Journal of Orthopsychiatry*, 1963, *33*, 813–822.

Justman, J. Academic achievement of intellectually gifted accelerants and non-accelerants in junior high school. *School Review*, 1954, *62*, 142–150.

Kogan, N., & Morgan, F. T. Task and motivational influences on the assessment of creative and intellectual ability in children. *Genetic Psychology Monographs*, 1969, *80*, 91–127.

Krugman, M., & Impellizzeri, I. H. Identification and guidance of underachieving gifted students. *Exceptional Children*, 1960, *26*, 283–286.

Lazer, A. L., Gensley, J., & Gowan, J. Developing positive attitudes through curriculum planning for young children. *Gifted Child Quarterly*, 1970, *16*(1), 27–31.

Liddle, G. Overlap among desirable and undesirable characteristics in gifted children. *Journal of Educational Psychology*, 1958, *49*, 219–223.

McClellend, D. D. *Talent and society*. Princeton, N.J.: Princeton University Press, 1953.

Milgram, N. A., & Milgram, R. M. Dimensions of locus of control in children. *Psychological Reports*, 1975, *37*, 523–538.

Montour, K. The marvelous boys: Thomas Chatterton, Evariste Galois and the modern counterparts. *Gifted Child Quarterly*, 1978, *22*(1), 68–78.

Morse, J. A., & Bruch, C. Gifted women: More issues than answers. *Educational Horizons*, 1970, Fall, 25–32.

Neuber, M. A. When a child has high potential. *The School Executive*, 1957, *76*, 70–74.

Nichols, R. C., & Davis, J. A. Characteristics of students of high academic aptitude. *Personnel and Guidance Journal*, 1964, *42*(8), 794–800.

Oden, M. The fulfillment of promise: 40-year follow-up of the Terman gifted group. *Genetic Psychology Monographs*, 1968, *77*, 3–93.

Painter, E. *Thesis on a comparison of achievement and ability in children of high intellectual potential*. London: London Institute of Education, 1976.

Sanborn, M. P., & Wasson, R. Guidance of students with special characteristics. *Review of Educational Research*, 1966, *36*, 308–326.

Schaefer, C. E. The self-concept of creative adolescents. *Journal of Psychology*, 1969, *72*, 233–242.

Schauer, G. H. Emotional disturbance and giftedness. *Gifted Child Quarterly*, 1976, *20*(4), 470–477.

Sears, R. S. Sources of life satisfactions of the Terman gifted men. *American Psychologist*, 1977, *32*(2), 119–128.

Sewell, W. H., & Shah, V. P. Socioeconomic status, intelligence, and the attainment of higher education. *Sociology of Education*, 1967, *40*, 1–23.

Shaw, M. C., & Alves, G. J. The self-concept of bright academic under-achievers. *Personnel and Guidance Journal,* 1963, *42*(4), 401–403.

Stanley, J. C. Radical acceleration: Recent educational innovation at Johns Hopkins University. *Gifted Child Quarterly,* 1978, *22*(1), 62–67.

Stewart, L. H. Interest patterns of a group of high-ability, high-achieving students. *Journal of Counseling Psychology,* 1959, *6*(2), 132–139.

Strang, R. Gifted adolescent views of growing up. *Exceptional Children,* 1956, *23*, 10–15; 20.

Torrance, E. P. Prediction of adult creative achievement among high school seniors. *Gifted Child Quarterly,* 1969, *13*, 223–229.

Torrance, E. P., & Dauw, D. C. Aspirations and dreams of three groups of creatively gifted high school seniors and comparable unselected groups. *Gifted Child Quarterly,* 1965, *9*, 177–182.

Walker, J. J. Developing values in gifted children. *Teaching Exceptional Children,* 1975, *7*(3), 98–100.

Weisber, P. S., & Springer, K. J. Environmental factors in creative function: A study of gifted children. *Archives of General Psychiatry,* 1961, *5*, 554; 564.

Werner, E. E., & Bachtold, L. M. Personality factors of gifted boys and girls in middle childhood and adolescence. *Psychology in the Schools,* 1969, *6*(2), 177–182.

Williams, R. E. Rediscovering the 4th-grade slump in a study of children's self-concept. *Journal of Creative Behavior,* 1976, *10*(1), 15–28.

Witkins, H. A., et al. Educational implications of cognitive style. *Review of Educational Research,* 1977, *47*(1), 1–64.

Yamamoto, K. Role of creative thinking and intelligence in high school achievement. *Psychological Reports,* 1964, *14*, 783–789.

Creativity

Alamshak, W. H. Blockages to creativity. *Journal of Creative Behavior,* 1972, *6*(2), 105–113.

Anderson, H. H. (Ed.). *Creativity and its cultivation.* New York: Harper and Row, 1959.

Anderson, H. H. (Ed.). *Creativity in childhood and adolescence: A variety of approaches.* Palo Alto, Ca.: Science and Behavior Books, 1965.

Bachtold, L. M., & Werner, E. E. An evaluation of teaching creative skills to gifted students in grades five and six. *Journal of Educational Research,* 1970, *63*, 253–256.

Barron, G. *Creativity and personal freedom.* New York: Van Nostrand, 1968.

Biber, B. Premature structuring as a deterrent to creativity. *American Journal of Orthopsychiatry,* 1959, *29*, 280–290.

Biondi, A. *The creative process.* Buffalo: D. O. K. Publishers, 1972.

Buel, W. D. The validity of behavioral rating scale items for the assessment of individual creativity. *Journal of Applied Psychology,* 1960, *44*, 407–412.

Bruch, C. B. Assessment of creativity in culturally different children. *Gifted Child Quarterly,* 1975, *19*(2), 164–174.

Cartledge, C. J., & Krauser, E. L. Training first-grade children in creative thinking under quantitative and qualitative motivation. *Journal of Educational Psychology,* 1963, *54*(3), 295–299.

Cashdon, S., & Welsh, G. S. Personality correlates of creative potential in talented high school students. *Journal of Personality,* 1966, *34*(3), 445–455.

Crockenberg, S. B. Creativity tests: A boon or boondoggle for education? *Review of Educational Research,* 1972, *42*(1), 27–45.

Cropley, A. J. A five-year longitudinal study of the validity of creativity tests. *Development Psychology*, 1972, *6*, 119–124.

Darrow, H. F., & Roach, V. A. *Independent activities for creative learning*. New York: Teachers College Press, 1961.

Davis, G. A. Instruments useful in studying creative behavior and creative talent. *Journal of Creative Behavior*, 1971, *5*, 162–165.

Davis, G. A., & Scott, J. A. (Eds.). *Training creative thinking*. New York: Holt, Rinehart and Winston, 1971.

Drews, E., & Montgomery, S. Creative and academic performance in gifted adolescents. *High School Journal*, 1964, *48*, 94–101.

Dudek, S. Z. Creativity in young children—Attitude or ability? *Journal of Creative Behavior*, 1974, *8*(4), 282–292.

Durio, H. F. Mental imagery and creativity. *Journal of Creative Behavior*, 1975, *9*(4), 233–244.

Eberle, R. F. *Scamper: Games for imagination development*. Buffalo: D. O. K. Publishers, 1971.

Fearn, L. Individual development: A process model in creativity. *Journal of Creative Behavior*, 1976, *10*(1), 55–64.

Feldhusen, J. F., & Treffinger, D. J. *Teaching creative thinking and problem solving*. Dubuque, Iowa: Kendall Hunt, 1977.

Feldhusen, J. F., Treffinger, D. J., & Bahlke, S. J. Developing creative thinking: The Purdue creativity program. *Journal of Creative Behavior*, 1970, *4*, 85–90.

Ferris, D. R. Humor and creativity: Research and theory. *Journal of Creative Behavior*, 1972, *6*(2), 75–79.

Getzels, J. W., & Jackson, P. W. *Creativity and intelligence*. New York: Wiley, 1962.

Gordon, W. J. *Synetics: The development of creative capability*. New York: Harper, 1961.

Guilford, J. P. Creativity: Yesterday, today, and tomorrow. *Journal of Creative Behavior*, 1967, *1*, 3–14.

Guilford, J. P. Varieties of creative giftedness, their measurement and development. *Gifted Child Quarterly*, 1975, *19*(2), 107–121.

Hudson, L. *Contrary imaginations: A psychological study of the young student*. New York: Schocken Books, 1966.

Jackson, P. W., & Messick, S. The person, the product, and the response: Conceptual problems in the assessment of creativity. *Journal of Personality*, 1965, *33*, 309–329.

Jensen, L. R. Diagnosis and evaluation of creativity, research and thinking skills of academically talented elementary students. *Gifted Child Quarterly*, 1978, *22*(1), 98–110.

Kagan, J. (Ed.). *Creativity and learning*. Boston: Beacon Press, 1967.

Kogan, N., & Pankove, E. Creative ability over a five-year span. *Child Development*, 1972, *43*, 427–441.

MacKinnon, D. E. (Ed.). *The creative person*. Berkeley: University of California Press, 1962.

Maddi, S. R. Motivational aspects of creativity. *Journal of Personality*, 1963, *33*, 330–347.

Mar'i, S. K. Toward a cross-cultural theory of creativity. *Journal of Creative Behavior*, 1976, *10*(2), 108–116.

Mednick, S. A. The associative basis of the creative process. *Psychological Review*, 1962, *69*, 220–232.

Miligram, R. M., Yitzhak, U., & Milaram, N. A. Creative activity and sex role identity in elementary school children. *Perceptual and Motor Skills*, 1977, *45*, 371–376.

Naumann, T. F. A first report on a longitudinal study of gifted pre-school children. *Gifted Child Quarterly,* 1974, *18,* 171–172.

Nicholls, J. G. Creativity in the person who will never produce anything original and useful: The concept of creativity as a normally distributed trait. *American Psychologist,* 1972, *27,* 717–727.

Noller, R. B., & Parnes, S. J. Applied creativity: The creative studies project, Part III—The curriculum. *Journal of Creative Behavior,* 1972, *6*(4), 275–294.

Pankove, E., & Kogan, N. Creative ability and risk taking in elementary school children. *Journal of Personality,* 1968, *36,* 420–430.

Parnes, S. J. *Creative Behavior Guidebook.* New York: Charles Scribner's Sons, 1967.

Parnes, S. J. *Creativity: Unlocking human potential.* Buffalo: D. O. K. Publishers, 1972.

Parnes, S. J., & Biondi, A. M. Creative behavior: A delicate balance. *Journal of Creative Behavior,* 1975, *9*(3), 149–158.

Parnes, S. J., & Harding, H. F. (Eds.). *A source book for creative thinking.* New York: Charles Scribner's Sons, 1962.

Parnes, S. J., & Noller, R. B. Applied creativity: The creative studies project, Part II—Results of the two-year program. *Journal of Creative Behavior,* 1972, *6*(1), 164–186.

Rusch, R. R., Denny, D. A., & Ives, S. Fostering creativity in sixth grade. *Elementary School Journal,* 1965, *65,* 262–268.

Schaefer, C. E., & Anastasi, A. A bibliographic inventory for identifying creativity in adolescent boys. *Journal of Applied Psychology,* 1968, *52,* 42–48.

Schubert, D. S., & Bioni, A. M. Creativity and mental health, Part II—Types of creativity. *Journal of Creative Behavior,* 1976, *10*(1), 67–70.

Singer, D. L., & Berkowitz, L. Different "creativities" in the wit and the clown. *Perceptual and Motor Skills,* 1972, *35,* 3–6.

Singer, D. L., & Rummo, J. Ideational creativity and behavioral style in kindergarten-age children. *Developmental Psychology,* 1973, *8,* 154–161.

Smith, M. M. Creative thinking abilities of educable mentally handicapped children in the regular grades. *American Journal of Mental Deficiency,* 1967, *71,* 571–575.

Solomon, A. O. Analysis of creative thinking of disadvantaged children. *Journal of Creative Behavior,* 1974, *8*(4), 293–295.

Spearman, C. T. *The creative mind.* New York: Cambridge University Press, 1931.

Stein, M. I., & Heinze, S. J. *Creativity and the individual.* Glencoe, Ill.: Free Press, 1960.

Taylor, I. A. Psychological sources of creativity. *Journal of Creative Behavior,* 1976, *10*(3), 193–202.

Taylor, I. A., & Getzels, J. W. (Eds.). *Perspectives in creativity.* Chicago: Aldine Publishing Co., 1975.

Thorndike, R. L. Measurement of creativity. *Teachers College Record,* 1963, *64,* 422–424.

Torrance, E. P. A longitudinal examination of the 4th grade slump in creativity. *Gifted Child Quarterly,* 1968, *2*(2), 165–178.

Torrance, E. P. Interscholastic brainstorming for gifted disadvantaged children. *Gifted Child Quarterly,* 1974, *18*(1), 3–6.

Treffinger, D. J., et al. Encouraging affective development: A compendium of techniques and resources. *Gifted Child Quarterly,* 1976, *20*(1), 47–65.

Treffinger, D. J., and Gowan, F. C. An updated representative list of methods and educational programs for stimulating creativity. *Journal of Creative Behavior,* 1971, *5,* 127–139.

Treffinger, D. J., Speedie, S. M., & Brunner, W. D. Improving children's creative problem-solving ability: The Purdue creativity project. *Journal of Creative Behavior,* 1974, *8*(1), 20–30.

Wallach, M. A., & Kogan, N. *Modes of thinking in young children: A study of the creativity-intelligence distinction.* New York: Holt, Rinehart and Winston, 1965.

Welsh, G. S. Perspectives in the study of creativity. *Journal of Creative Behavior,* 1973, *7*(4), 231–246.

Whiting, B. G. How to predict creativity from biographical data. *Journal of Creative Behavior,* 1973, *7*(3), 201–207.

Williams, F. E. *Classroom ideas for encouraging thinking and feelings.* Buffalo: D. O. K. Publishers, 1970.

Williams, F. E. *Classroom ideas for developing productive divergent thinking.* Buffalo: D. O. K. Publishers, 1966.

Williams, F. E. Models for encouraging creativity in the classroom by integrating cognitive and affective behaviors. *Educational Technology,* 1969, *2*, 7–13.

Wright, F. J., Fox, M., & Noppe, L. The interrelationship of creativity, self-esteem, and creative self-support. *Psychology,* 1975, *12*(2), 11–15.

Planning and Decision Making

Barbour, E. Counseling gifted high school students. *California Journal of Secondary Education,* 1954, *29*, 476–479.

Bennis, W. G. A funny thing happened to me on the way to the future. *American Psychologist,* 1970, *25*, 595–608.

Getzels, J. W., & Jackson, P. W. Occupational choice and cognitive functioning: Career aspirations of highly intelligent and highly creative adolescents. *Journal of Abnormal and Social Psychology,* 1970, *61*, 119–123.

Gifted and talented students, laboratory research: Theses, abstracts, and 12-year follow-up study. *Gifted Child Quarterly,* 1977, *21*(3), 347–358.

Gowan, J. C. Organization of guidance for gifted children. *Personnel and Guidance Journal,* 1960, *39*, 275–279.

Gowan, J. C., & Demos, G. D. *The education and guidance of the ablest.* Springfield, Ill.: Charles C. Thomas, 1964.

Hays, D. G., & Rothney, J. W. M. Educational decision-making by superior secondary-school students and their parents. *Personnel and Guidance Journal,* 1961, *40*(1), 26–30.

Krippner, S. Sex, ability and interest: A test of Tyler's hypothesis. *Gifted Child Quarterly,* 1962, *6*(1), 105–110.

Perrone, P. A., Male, R. A., & Karshner, W. W. Career development needs of talented students: A perspective for counselors. *School Counselor,* 1979, *27*(1), 16–23.

Rodenstein, J., Pfleger, L. R., & Colangelo, N. Career development of gifted women. *Gifted Child Quarterly,* 1977, *21*(3), 340–347.

Sanborn, M. P. Vocational choice, college choice, and scholastic success of superior students. *Vocational Guidance Quarterly,* 1965, *13*, 161–169.

Sanborn, M. P. Career development problems of gifted and talented students. In K. B. Hoyt & J. R. Hebeler (Eds.), *Career education for gifted and talented students.* Salt Lake City: Olympus Publishing Co., 1974.

Terman, L. A. The vocational successes of intellectually gifted students. *Occupations,* 1942, *20,* 493–498.

Thomas, G. E., & Crescimbeni, J. *Guiding the gifted child.* New York: Random House, 1966.

Torrance, E. P. Future careers for gifted and talented students. *Gifted Child Quarterly,* 1976, *20,* 142–156.

Welsh, G. S. Vocational interests and intelligence in gifted adolescents. *Educational and Psychological Measurement,* 1971, *31*(1), 155–164.

Wilson, S. H., et al. Synectics, a creative problem-solving technique for the gifted. *Gifted Child Quarterly,* 1973, *17*(4), 260–267.

Index

A

Ability, 68, 69, 174
Abstract learning, 53
Abstract perception, 196
Academic achievement, 43, 174, 177
  See also Scholastic achievement
Acceleration, 22
Acceptance, 5, 53, 56
Accessibility of data, 18, 27, 28, 29
Accumulation of information, 53
Achievement, 45, 53
  scholastic (academic), 41, 43, 44, 174,
    177, 192, 206, 217-220
Achievement module, 197-200, 201
Achievement motivation, 65-70
Achievement-oriented society, 53
Acquisition of information, 52
  vs. presentation rates, 51
Activities
  conscious, 11, 15, 27, 29
  covert, 13, 14
  goal-directed, 15
  gross motor, 12
  habitual patterns of, 27
  overt, 13, 14
  physiological, 15

subconscious, 12, 27, 29
Adaptability of teachers, 170
Adjustments, 26
Adult approval, 56
Advantageous environment. See
  Supportive environment
Affective development, 56, 173, 176, 187
  books on, 222-224
Affiliation needs, 22, 24, 33
Aloneness, 50
American Indians, 44, 161, 163-164
American Journal of Psychology, 111
Androgyny, 168
Anthony, Susan B., 107, 108
Approval, 53, 56
Architecture, 71
Art, 71, 176, 205
Artificial aids to intelligence, 206
Artistic talent, 207
Artists, 205
Aspirations, 53
Assertiveness, 50
Assessment, 188
  of conceptual level, 175
  individualized, 165-166
Assimilation, 38
Atkinson, J.W., 66

Attention-seeking behaviors, 52
Attention span, 27, 50
Attitudes, 5
Attribution, 65, 68
Auditory system, 10
Authoritarian individuals, 51
Autocratic parents, 169, 170
Avoidance of failure, 65, 66
Avoidance of punishment, 65
Awareness, 11, 12, 26, 27, 193
   of death, 53
   of future, 53
   of three time dimensions, 54

B

Background, importance of, 45
Baker, C., 85
Bandler, R., 27
Banks, W.C., 43, 44
Baruch, Bernard M., 120, 123-124
Behavior, 4, 7, 10-11, 14, 18, 21, 26,
   27, 33, 65, 174
   attention-seeking, 52
   covert, 10, 12, 15
   daily-life, 34
   effective, 17, 18
   evaluation of, 56
   framework for, 8-13
   and motivation, 24
   organized, 31
   overt, 10, 12, 15
   symptomatic. See Symptomatic
   behaviors
   withdrawal, 52
Behavior delivery systems, 17, 18, 27,
   29, 30, 31
Behavior Rating Sheet, 188
Bell, Alexander Graham, 35, 37, 38, 68,
   69, 101-103
Belongingness, 22, 24, 33
Binet Test, 177
Biofeedback, 15, 206, 207
Biological coping, 24
Blacks, 44, 161
Bloom, B.S., 57, 176

Book learning, 53
Books, 3, 4, 53
Boredom, 29, 49, 51
Boston Conservatory of Music, 106
Broad range of experiences, 46
Brothers Karamazov, 82
Buck, Pearl S., 84-85
Bunche, Ralph, 104, 109
Burbank, Luther, 104, 107

C

Capability and efficiency, 28
Career counseling, 67
Career planning 67
Carnegie, Andrew, 108, 120-121
Carver, George Washington, 25, 35, 38,
   39, 40, 104-107, 109
Case studies, 129-142
Case study approach, 165-166
Champigneulle, B., 72
Chance. *See* Luck
Change, principles of, 148-149
Chemoeducation, 206
Christ, 39
Christianity and the Social Class, 110
Chryst, Bill, 103
Cigarette smoking, 15
Clark, B.H., 94
Classificatory level of conceptual
   development, 180
CLD. *See* Conceptual Learning and
   Development
Cognitive functioning 173, 176
Colangelo, Nicholas, 129
Collective decision making, 164
Communication skills, 41, 46, 52, 175,
   204
   assessment of, 220
   written, 175, 204
Community values, 45
Comparative recognition, 5
Competition, 53, 69
"Computer personality," 53
Computers, 204, 206
Concepts, defined, 174

Conceptual development, 50, 52, 53, 54, 57, 173-177
  levels of, 180-181
  model program for, 178-201
Conceptual Learning and Development (CLD), 180
Concrete level of conceptual development, 180
Conformity, 40
Conscientious level, 60
Conscious, 10, 12, 27, 31
Conscious activities, 11, 15, 27, 29
Conscious drives, 22
Consciousness, 11, 13
Conscious operations, 12, 13, 17, 27
Conscious thought, 11, 15, 17, 28, 30, 207
Continual flow of information, 26
Continuous operations 12, 13, 14
Continuous thought, 12
Control, 46, 67
  by others, 53
Convergent thought, 11, 14, 15, 16, 17, 18, 27, 176, 187, 188, 206
Cooperation, 41, 46
Coopersmith, S., 170
Coordination, 50
Coping, 24, 35, 37, 175
Covert activities, 13, 14
Covert behavior, 10, 12, 15
Covington, M.W., 69
Creative Mind and Method, The, 71
Creative writing, 176
Creativity, 42, 71, 77, 78, 170, 187
  books on, 224-227
  and divergent thought, 17
  ingredients of, 56
Cultural mainstream, 46
Cultural values, 45
Curie, Marie, 4, 39
Curiosity, 3, 50
Curtis, 44

D

Daily-life behavior, 34

Data
  See also Information
  accessibility of, 18, 27, 28, 29
  exteroceptive, 10
  proprioceptive, 10
  storage of, 13, 18, 27, 29, 30,
  transfer of, 17, 18, 27, 30, 31, 207
Death awareness, 53
Death of a Salesman, 83
Decision making, 11, 12, 14, 15, 17, 26, 39, 178
  books on, 227-228
  collective, 164
  effective, 175
  participatory, 170
Deductive problem solving, 206
Deductive thought, 11
Deficiency needs, 22
Delivery systems. *See* Behavior delivery systems
Democratic parents, 169, 170
Dependence, 174
Depression, 54
Deprivation needs, 25
Detection, 26
Developmental consistencies, 42-43
Developmental differences in talented, 1
Developmental gap, 55
Developmental theory, 57, 173, 179, 180
  stage approach, 1, 56, 58, 173
Dewey, John, 111-112
Dictatorial parents, 169
Dictionary of Science, 98
Difference, 4, 7-8, 32, 53, 54, 174
Differentiation, 26, 181
Direct experience, 53
Direction, 36, 38, 45, 51, 52, 56, 65, 168
Direct perception, 13
Discrimination, 181
Discursive type individuals, 42
Disrespect, 51
Divergent thought, 11, 15, 16, 17, 18, 27, 176, 188, 206
Dominance, 27
Dostoevsky, F.M., 82

"Dungeons and Dragons" game, 70
Dvorak, Anton, 90
Dynamic process, 22, 26

E

Edison, Thomas A., 4, 35, 37, 38,
    40, 43, 68, 69, 98-101
Education, 42, 43
    function of, 45
    objectives of, 57, 68
Effective, defined, 17
Effective behavior, 17, 18
Effective decision making, 175
Effective orientation, 26
Effective school performance, 206
Efficiency
    and capability, 28
    defined, 18
Effort, 68, 69
    and interest, 44
"Egghead," 53
Ego development, 57, 60
Einstein, Albert, 5-6, 35, 37, 39,
    40, 67, 94-95
Eisenhower, Dwight D., 35, 112, 117
Elder, G.H., 169
Elderly, 205
Elements of talent, 7
Ellington, Duke, 92
Eminence, 42, 45, 65
Emotional development, 4, 39, 53, 56
Emotional support from family, 52
Encoding, 12
    efficiency of, 29
Enrichment, 22
Environment, 1, 4
    advantageous. See supportive
    vs. heredity, 26
    and individual, 26
    intellectual, 21, 26, 45
    interaction with, 3, 56
    learning, 60
    nonsupportive, 36, 38
    physical, 21-32, 45, 57
    psychosocial, 33-46

    relating to, 3, 56
    social, 21, 26, 45
    supportive, 36, 38, 46, 57
    types of, 8-10
Equilibrium, 25
Esteem. See Self-esteem
Ethnic mainstream, 46
Ethnic values, 45
Evaluation
    of behavior, 56
    of product, 18
    of programs, 201
"Exciting life" as a value, 34
Exclusivistic thought, 11
Expectations, 53, 65
Experiences, 46
    direct, 53
Expression of feelings, 4
External rewards, 65
Exteroceptive information, 10, 18, 27
Exteroceptive stimuli, 12, 13, 15, 26
Extremists, 37

F

Factor analysis, 42
Failure avoidance, 65, 66, 67
Family
    emotional support from, 52. See also
    Supportive environment security of,
      34
Faulkner, William, 4, 83-84
"Fear of success" syndrome, 68
Feedback, 39, 51, 52, 208
Feelings, 39, 53, 56
    expression of, 4
Females
    attribution in, 44, 68
    successful use of intellect in, 168
Femininity, 68, 168, 169
Flexibility of teachers, 170
Focus, 38
Force-field analysis, 147, 148-151, 179
Ford, Henry, 4, 120, 122
Formal education, 42

Formal level of conceptual
    development, 181
Formal operational thought, 167
Formal relation stage of development,
    196
Formative evaluation, 201
Foundation for Exceptional Children,
    161
Freedom, 34
Friedman, Ella, 95
Froebel, Fredrich, 74
Frost, Robert, 67, 69, 80
Frustration, 50
Fuller, Buckminster, 76-77
Future awareness, 53

G

Generalizing, 180
General Motors, 103
Generativity, 60
Genetic functioning, 45
Genetic inheritance, 13
    See also Heredity
Gershwin, George, 90-91
Getzels, J.W., 175, 176
"Gifted" label, 4
GIFTS. *See* Guidance Institute for
    Talented Students
Glass Menagerie, The, 81
Goal attainment, 18
    follow-up guide for, 156
Goal attainment scaling, 147, 148,
    152-155, 179, 192, 201
Goal-directed activity, 15
Goals, 38, 168, 201
    attainment of. *See* Goal attainment
    in behavioral terms, 152
    direction of, 168
    of education, 57
    long-range, 33
    of program for talented, 145, 146-147,
        182
    redefining of, 66
    setting of, 67
    statements of, 153

for teachers, 168-169
Grades, 54, 70
    distribution of, 69
Grinder, J., 27
Gropius, Walter, 77-78
Gross motor activity, 12
Growth, 22, 57, 60, 174
Guess Who's Coming to Dinner, 36
Guidance Institute for Talented
    Students (GIFTS), 36, 44, 52, 129,
        130, 132, 138-139, 145, 161, 166
        167, 170, 183, 187, 188, 189, 197

H

Habit acquisition, 14
Habitual patterns of activity, 27
Hall, G. Stanley, 110-111, 111
Hart, Moss, 87
Heider, 67
Hellman, Lillian, 86
Hemingway, Ernest, 37, 85-86
Heredity, 4, 13, 26, 45
    vs. environment, 26
Heroes, 39
*Hierarchical Description of the
    Metaphoric Mind*, 57
Hierarchy of needs, 22-26, 28, 32,
    33, 65
High achievers, 53
History courses, 176
Home life, 34, 52
    and motivation, 45
Homeostasis, 25
Honesty, 35
Hoover, Herbert, 115
Horman, W.W., 203
Howard University, 109
Hubbard, J.L., 43
Humphrey, Hubert, 118, 119-120
Hunt, D.E., 181, 182, 188
Hyperactivity, 52

I

Identification of talent, 4, 6, 7, 145,
    159-164, 183-184, 187-188

books on, 212-214
Identity level of conceptual
  development, 180
Imagination, 35, 76
Imbalance, 28-32, 167
Impatience, 50
Impoliteness, 51
Inclusivistic thought, 12
Independence, 6, 35, 36, 56, 170, 174,
  178, 182
Individual
  defined, 8
  and environment, 26
  performance standards for, 70
Individualized programming, 165-166, 201
Inductive thought, 12
Information
  See also Data
  accumulation of, 53
  acquisition of, 51, 52
  continual flow of, 26
  exteroceptive, 18, 27
  linear, 51
  overload of, 28, 50
  processing of, 51, 56
  proprioceptive, 18, 27
  seekers of, 51
  transfer of, 12
  types of, 10
Inquisitiveness, 50
Inspiration, 43
Instinct, 76
Instruction, 55, 166-168
  methods of, 43
Instructional mode of learning, 176
Instrumental values, 34
Integration, 42, 168, 181
Intellectual assertiveness, 50
Intellectual curiosity, 50
Intellectual development, 52, 55, 173
Intellectual dimensions, 49
Intellectual environment, 3, 10, 21,
  26, 45
Intellectual understanding, 41
Intelligence tests, 52, 183
Intelligent acting, 39

Intended action, 12
Intent, 31
Interaction with environment, 3, 56
Interdependence, 28
Interest, 44
Internal frame of reference, 56
Internal locus of control, 36, 46
Interpersonal maturity, 181
Intuition, 76
Inventors, 98
Iowa State University, 106
IQ, 177, 206
  tests of, 52, 183
Isolation, 54, 70

J

Johnson, Lyndon B., 112, 118-119
Judgment, 11, 12, 14, 17, 26

K

Kagan, J.A., 174
Kaplan, S.N., 147
Kaufman, George S., 87
Keller, Helen, 4
Kennedy, John F., 35, 112, 117-118
Kennedy, Joseph, 118
Kern, Jerome, 91-92
Kettering, Charles Franklin, 103
King, Martin Luther, Jr., 4, 104, 110
Kirsuk, Thomas J., 152, 154
Klausmeier, H.J., 174, 180, 182, 188
Knowledge, 43, 56, 187
  and creativity, 77
  levels of, 46
  vs. wisdom, 41
Kohlberg, L., 57, 60
Kruglanski, A.W., 69

L

Land, G.T., 57
Languages, 176, 204
Leadership for programs, 147
Learning, 4, 7, 18, 26, 174

abstract, 53
book, 53
efficiency of, 43
elements of, 38-40
enjoyment of, 69, 70
framework for, 8-13
one-trial, 51
processes of, 7
styles of, 181
Learning environment, 60
Learning modules, 197
Left hemispheric functioning, 51, 176
Legacy, 39
Life as a dynamic process, 22
Life goal values. *See* Terminal values
Limitations, testing of, 51, 52
Lindbergh, Charles A., 120, 124
Linear information, 51
Listening, 3, 4
Literature, 79
Loevinger, J., 57
Logic, 35, 53, 76
Longfellow, William Wadsworth, 39
Long-range goals, 33
Looking, 3
Love, 22, 24, 35
Luck, 44, 65, 67, 68

M

Macalester College, 120
Males
attribution in, 44, 68
successful use of intellect in, 168
Manifestation of talent, 5
Manipulation of things, 4
Marshall, George, 112, 116, 117
Masculinity, 168, 169
Maslow, Abraham, 21, 22-26, 28, 32, 33-35, 38, 57, 60, 65
Mastery, 22, 38-40, 45, 51, 53, 65, 67, 68, 70, 71
Mathematics, 176, 217-218
McClelland, D.C., 65
McQuater, G.V., 43, 44

Mead, Margaret, 35, 108-109
Memorization, 53
Memory, 12, 13, 28, 30, 31, 50, 54
Mental imagery, 51
Mexican-Americans, 44, 161, 162-163
Miller, Arthur, 82-83
Mind and body, 7
Minorities, 44, 161-164
Mismatching of skills, 28-32, 167
Moore, George, 32
Morality, 40
Moral Stages, 57
Morris, George, 111
Motivation, 53, 70, 71
achievement, 65-70
books on, 222-224
and home life, 45
vs. stimulation, 56
theories of, 1, 21, 22-26
Motor coordination, 50
Movement, 12
Mozart, Wolfgang, 88, 89
Muir, John, 104, 108
Multicultural talent, 44, 161-162
Music, 88-89, 176, 207
Mutuality, 60

N

Nature
vs. nurture, 35
understanding of, 37, 46
Needs, 46
hierarchy of, 22-26, 28, 32, 33, 65
satisfaction of, 24
understanding of, 39
Negative self-concept, 53
Nelson, B., 82
Neutra, Richard, 77
Newton, Isaac, 37
Newton's Principles, 99
Nicholls, J.G., 69
Nobel prize winners, 42, 43
Nonexplaining parents, 170
Nonsupportive environment, 36, 38
Nonsystematic thought, 12

O

Ohio State University, 103
Omelich, C.L., 69
O'Neill, Eugene, 86-87
One-trial learning, 51
Operational definition of talent, 5,
  17-19
Operations, 11
  conscious, 12, 13, 17, 27
  continuous, 13, 14
  physiological, 26
  psychological, 26, 207
  situational, 13
  subconscious, 13, 17
  and thought, 30
Oppenheimer, Robert, 35, 95-96
Organized behavior, 31
Outer world, 8
Output, 27
Overload of information, 28, 50
Overt activities, 13, 14
Overt behavior, 10, 12, 15
Ownership
  of accomplishments and failures, 65
  of behavior, 69

P

Page, E.B., 175
Parents
  autocratic, 169, 170
  democratic, 169, 170
  dictatorial, 169
  participatory, 169
  permissive, 169, 170
  relationship with, 169, 220-221
  types of, 169, 170
Parker, R.G., 98
Participatory decision making, 170
Participatory style of parenting, 169
Path analysis, 42
Peace as value, 34
Peer context in class, 178
Peer relationships, 53, 54, 56
  books on, 221-222

Penrose, R., 73
Perception, 26
  of abstractions, 196
  direct, 13
Perceptual orientation, 26-27
Perceptual systems, 10, 12, 13, 14, 17,
  18, 26, 27, 207
Performance, 18, 19, 27
  standards of, 70
Permissive parents, 169, 170
Personal experience of existence, 11
Personality, 26, 49, 176
Perspective, 38
Philosophers, 104
Physical behavior, 187
Physical development, 173
Physical environment, 1, 3, 8, 21-32,
  45, 57
Physical restlessness, 50
Physical skills, 192
Physiological activities, 15
Physiological elements, 7
Physiological needs, 22, 24, 40
Physiological operations, 26
Physiological self, 8, 10-11, 12
Piaget, J., 196
Picasso, Pablo, 73-74
Planning, 147
  books on, 227-228
Planning committee, 147, 179
Pleasure, 34
Pluralistic society, 43-44
Politeness, 35
Politics, 112
Population of the world, 205
Post, Phyllis, 197
Potentially talented. See Talent potential
Preparation for program, 147
Presentation vs. acquisition rates, 51
Presentational type individuals, 42
Presley, Elvis, 4
Primary perceptual systems, 10, 18, 27
Problem resolution, 11
Problem solving, 41, 206
Process evaluation, 18
Processing of information, 51, 56

Product evaluation, 18
Proprioceptive information, 10, 18, 27
Proprioceptive stimuli, 12, 15, 26
Pseudotalented, 176
Psychological autonomy, 56
Psychological elements, 7
Psychological growth, 173
Psychological needs, 22
Psychological operations, 26, 207
Psychological self, 8, 11-13
Psycho-physiological security, 24
Psychosocial development, 1
Psychosocial dimensions, 57
Psychosocial environment, 33-46
Puerto Ricans, 44, 161, 162
Punishment avoidance, 65

Q

Questioning, 50

R

Range of experiences, 46
Rauschenbusch, Walter, 110
Reading, 4
Reading assessment, 217
Reasoning, 41, 53, 76
Recall, 12, 50
  efficiency of, 29
Recognition, 5, 14, 33, 34, 56
"Red Power," 164
Relations with people, 3. *See also* Social
Religious values, 33
Reporting, 39
Research centers, 41
Resources, 5
Responsibility, 40, 46, 65, 173, 181, 182
Restlessness, 50, 51
Rewards, 65
Right hemispheric functioning, 51, 176, 206
Risk taking, 51, 60, 66, 67
Rockefeller, John D., 120, 123
Rodin, Auguste, 72-73
Roe, Anne, 45

Rokeach, Milton, 33, 34, 35
Role models, 39
Roosevelt, Franklin D., 35, 112, 113-114, 118
Roosevelt, Theodore, 4, 112-113
Rosenzweig, Max, 90
Routine satisfaction, 24
Rubinstein, Artur, 89-90
Runyon, Damon, 35, 38, 87-88
Ruth, Babe, 4, 5

S

Saarinen, Elliel, 76
Sacred values, 33
Safety, 24
Salvation, 34
Samples, B., 57, 60
Satisfaction of needs, 24
Schafer, M., 88
Scholastic achievement, 41, 44, 192, 206
  See also Academic achievement
  assessment of, 217-220
School, 54
  effective performance in, 206
  subjects in, 176-177
  variety in, 178
School of Natural Philosophy, 98
Schwartz, P., 203
Science, 41, 43, 94, 176, 217-218
Scott, Thomas, 121
Security, 22, 24, 33, 34
Seeing, 4
Selection criteria for programs for talented, 145, 159, 164-165
Self-acceptance, 25
Self-actualization, 7, 22, 24, 25, 33, 51, 60
Self-awareness, 21, 24, 188, 193, 207, 208
Self-centeredness, 173
Self-competence, 22, 38-40
Self-concept, 53, 68, 69, 168
Self-confidence, 168, 170
Self-control, 35

Self-direction, 36-37, 40, 41, 45, 51, 56, 65
Self-esteem, 22, 25, 33, 169, 170
Self-improvement, 22
Self-initiative, 187
Self-maintenance, 187
Self-motivation, 53, 65
Self-realization, 22, 51
Self-respect, 60
Self-reward, 53
Self-worth, 54
Sense organs, 10
Sensitivity, 42
Serendipity, 65
Shahn, Ben, 71
Sherman, Robert E., 152, 154
Sibling relationships, 221-222
Simonton, D.K., 42
Situational operations, 13
Social awareness, 174
Social behavior, 187
Social comparison, 69
Social concern, 174
Social conformity, 40
Social development, 173
Social environment, 3, 4, 8, 21, 26, 45
Socialization process, 33
Social planning, 196
Social pressures, 41
Social responsibility, 40, 46, 182
Social skills, 192, 204
Societal objectives, 193, 196
Sohn, D., 69
Southwest Texas State Teachers College, 119
Special instruction, 55
Staff involvement in program, 155, 158-159
Stages of Growth Processes Based on Systems Theory), 57
Stage theory of development, 1, 56, 58, 173
Stereotypes, 53, 68
Stimulation
    defined, 56
    vs. motivation, 56

Stimuli
    external, 65
    exteroceptive, 12, 13, 15, 26
    proprioceptive, 12, 15, 26
Stitle, 44
Storage of data, 18, 27, 29, 30
Study habits, 175
Subconscious, 10, 12, 13, 14, 27, 31
Subconscious activities, 12, 27, 29
Subconscious operations, 13, 17
Subconscious thought, 13
Subcultures, 43
Success, 65, 66, 67
Sullivan, Louis, 74, 75-76
Summative evaluation, 201
Summerfield, J.D., 71
Supportive environment, 36, 38, 46, 57
Survival needs, 25
Symbolic mode, 60
Symptomatic behaviors, 1, 49
    chronology of, 55-57
Symptoms
    defined, 49
    of talent potential, 50-55
Synergy, 76
Systematic thought, 11

T

Tactile system, 10
Taft, Robert A., 36, 115
Talent
    acceptance of, 5
    definitions of, 17-19, 212-214
    elements of, 7
    identification of, 145
    instructional concerns for
        development of, 166-168
    manifestation of, 5
    multicultural, 44
    operational definition of, 17-19
    potential for. *See* Talent potential
    recognition of, 5
Talent potential
    definition of, 5
    dimensions of, 22

identification of, 4, 6, 7, 145
symptoms of, 50-55
Talmey, Max, 94
Task difficulty, 68, 69
Task persistence, 168
Taxomony of Cognitive and Affected Educational Objectives, 57
Teachers
communications with, 52
flexibility and adaptability of, 170
goals for, 168-169
relationships with, 220-221
resentment of, 41
Teaching strategies, 213-217
Teaching styles, 169-170, 177-178
Team efforts, 41, 46
Technical skills, 204
Teenagers, 56
Teige, D.J., 203
Television, 3
Ten Commandments of Goal Attainment Follow-up Guide Construction, The, 154
Terman, L.A., 52, 168
Terminal values, 33-34
Testing of limitations, 51, 52
Thatcher, L., 71
Thelen, H.A., 175, 176
Theory of Ego Development, 57
Theory of Human Motivation, 57
Think tanks, 41
Thought
conscious, 15, 17, 28, 30, 207
convergent, 11, 14, 15, 16, 17, 18, 27, 176, 187, 188, 206
divergent, 11, 15, 16, 17, 18, 27, 188, 206
efficiency of, 30
formal operational, 167
and operations, 30
processes for, 7
subconscious, 13
types of, 11
Time dimension awareness, 54
Time perspective, 53
Touching, 3, 4

Transfer of data, 12, 17, 18, 27, 30, 31, 207
efficiency in, 30
Transformation, 60
Trends, 203-204
Truman, Harry S., 35, 114-115
Tuskegee Institute, 106

U

Ultimate goals, 33
Unconscious drives, 22, 24
Understanding, 14, 41, 45, 188
desire for, 3
of feelings, 53
growth in, 173
of nature, 37, 46
University of California, LA, 109
University of Chicago, 112
University of Michigan, 111
University of Wisconsin, 66, 93

V

Values, 5, 18, 28, 33, 46, 184, 196
clarification of, 179
community, 45
conflict between, 35
cultural, 45
ethnic, 45
instrumental, 34
religious, 33
terminal, 33-34
Valuing, 39
Variety in school, 178
Visual system, 10

W

Walters, Barbara, 93
Weiner, B., 67, 68
Weschler Intelligence Test, 177
Westinghouse, George, 104
Whites, 44
Whitman, Walt, 37, 79-80
Why England Slept, 118

Wiener, Norbert, 96-97
Williams, Tennessee, 81-82
Wilson, James, 106
Wisdom, 41
Withdrawal behaviors, 52
Wonder, Stevie, 92-93

"World at peace" as a value, 34
World population, 205
Wright, Frank Lloyd, 74-75
Written communications skills, 175, 204
  assessment of, 220

About the Authors

PHILIP A. PERRONE completed his graduate work in human development, individual assessment, and career guidance at Syracuse University in 1962. Dr. Perrone joined the faculty at the University of Wisconsin the same year. His research, writing, and teaching focused on career development and career guidance until 1975 when he became Director of the Guidance Institute for Talented Students (GIFTS). Since then his interest in talent development has broadened from primarily a career perspective into an attempt to better understand the nature and needs of young people who evidence exceptional potential.

ROBERT A. MALE is a faculty member in the Counselor Education Department at Portland State University, Portland, Oregon. He serves as a consultant in and around Portland, specializing in guidance programming and the education of gifted and talented children.

Dr. Male has had extensive experience in many phases and levels of public education: teaching physical education in grades K–12, teaching junior high school science, coaching five different varsity sports, and serving as school counselor for both elementary and secondary school pupils. He was a research assistant in GIFTS, which involved him in extensive research and developmental studies of gifted and talented youngsters. In 1980 he served as Acting Director of GIFTS.

Both Drs. Perrone and Male have published numerous articles and materials relating to the identification, education, and development of talented persons.